1200
Lch

◁ **W9-BUW-852**

WITHDRAWN

PS
221   The forties   69-6510
F6

JUL   2009

Date Due			
		JUN	
		JUL 09	
		JUL X X 2015	

The Forties:
Fiction,
Poetry,
Drama

Edited by
Warren French

CUMBERLAND COUNTY COLLEGE
LIBRARY P.O. BOX 517 VINELAND N.J.

EVERETT / EDWARDS, inc.

133 SOUTH PECAN AVENUE
DELAND, FLORIDA 32720

PS
221
.F6

69-6510

Copyright © 1969
by
WARREN FRENCH
All Rights Reserved
LCCCN: 69-10440

First Printing

"An Island Galaxy"
appears with the permission of the author, John Ciardi.

Manufactured in the United States of America
E. O. Painter Printing Company, DeLand, Florida

To
the memory of
FREDERICK JOHN HOFFMAN
(1909-1967),
who was to have been
a contributor,
this book is affectionately
and sorrowfully
dedicated.
It is unlikely that his
contributions to the understanding
of American literature
will soon be equalled.

About the Editor:

WARREN FRENCH *is Chairman of the
Department of English at the University of
Missouri/Kansas City and Chairman of
the University of Missouri Press Committee.
A graduate of the University of Pennsylvania,
he received his Ph.D. in American literature
from the University of Texas in 1954.
He taught in Kentucky, Florida, and Kansas,
before settling in Kansas City in 1965.
He has written three books for the
Twayne United States Authors Series:* JOHN
STEINBECK *(1961),* FRANK NORRIS *(1962),*
J. D. SALINGER *(1963), and he has edited*
A COMPANION TO "THE GRAPES OF WRATH"
(1963). His major work is THE SOCIAL NOVEL
AT THE END OF AN ERA *(1966), an intensive
study of American fiction at the end of the 30s.
He has also written* SEASON OF PROMISE:
SPRING FICTION, *1967 for the University of Missouri
Press "Literary Frontiers" series. He edited*
THE THIRTIES, *a companion volume to this one,
and co-edited with Walter Kidd* AMERICAN
WINNERS OF THE NOBEL LITERARY PRIZE *(1968).
He is at work on a final volume in this series,*
THE FIFTIES, *and a critical study of
Thornton Wilder.
He served for eight years as editor of
"Current Bibliography" in* TWENTIETH CENTURY
LITERATURE, *and he is at present a director of
the Midwest Modern Language Association.
In addition to contributing articles and reviews to
scholarly journals, he regularly reviews books for
the* KANSAS CITY STAR. *He also teaches courses in
film and is a member of the Film Advisory
Committee to the Missouri Council
on the Arts.*

v

Contents

iii		Dedication
v		About the Editor
1	WARREN FRENCH	GENERAL INTRODUCTION: Remembering the Forties
5		PART I: THE LITERATURE OF WORLD WAR II
7	WARREN FRENCH	Fiction: A Handful of Survivors
33	DAN JAFFE	Poets in the Inferno: Civilians, C.O.'s and Combatants
63	JORDAN Y. MILLER	Drama: The War Play Comes of Age
83		PART II: HIGHLIGHTS OF A DECADE
87	A. S. KNOWLES, JR.	Six Bronze Petals and Two Red: Carson McCullers in the Forties
101	ROBERT J. GRIFFIN	Eudora Welty's *A Curtain of Green*
113	GERALD RABKIN	*The Skin of Our Teeth* and the Theatre of Thornton Wilder
123	JACKSON R. BRYER	"A Nightly Miracle": The Early Musical Dramas of Rodgers and Hammerstein
141	KINGSLEY WIDMER	American Apocalypse: Notes on the Bomb and the Failure of Imagination

155 JONAS SPATZ — Dreiser's *Bulwark*: An Archaic Masterpiece

165 DONALD SHEEHAN — The Ultimate Plato: A Reading of Wallace Stevens' "Notes Toward a Supreme Fiction"

181 DAVID G. PUGH — Reading an Old Best-Seller: The Obvious and the Unobtrusive

191 JAMES H. JUSTUS — All the Burdens of Warren's *All the Kings Men*

205 SY KAHN — O'Neill's Legion of Losers in *The Iceman Cometh*

217 ELEANOR WIDMER — The Drunken Wheel: Malcolm Lowry and *Under the Volcano*

229 KENNETH JOHNSON — The View from Lord Weary's Castle

239 WILLIAM FREEDMAN — *The Middle of the Journey*: Lionel Trilling and the Novel of Ideas

251 C. W. E. BIGSBY — Tennessee Williams: Streetcar to Glory

261 GENE W. RUOFF — Truman Capote: The Novelist as Commodity

273 LOIS GORDON — *Death of a Salesman*: An Appreciation

287 ROBERT A. CORRIGAN — Ezra Pound and the Bollingen Prize Controversy

299 SHELDON NORMAN GREBSTEIN — Nelson Algren and the Whole Truth

311 Bibliography

319 About the Contributors

324 Appendix

327 Index

The Forties:
Fiction,
Poetry,
Drama

General Introduction:
Remembering The Forties

The Forties constituted one of the longest, unloveliest and most ominously significant decades in human history. Like the most dread kind of visitor, they arrived early, stayed late, and made an awful mess of the place.

Strict chronology won't do in dealing with the 40s; yet the decade can be demarcated with the same neat precision as the 30s. An era began on September 1, 1939, when Adolph Hitler decided that it was time to take back from Poland the land "stolen" from Germany by the Versailles treaty and World War II broke out; it did not really end until June 25, 1950, when one part — which still is not determined to everyone's satisfaction — of the remote and backward nation of Korea — which had been artificially divided into North and South after being taken over from Japan at the conclusion of World War II — invaded the other, shattering the uneasy peace that had existed since Japan's surrender on August 14, 1945. The true mid-point of the decade, however, and one of the greatest turning points in human history was not this anti-climactic day of capitulation, but August 6, 1945, on which a single American plane appeared in the sky high above the embattled island and dropped a single atomic bomb on the city of Hiroshima.

This novel act divided the decade with deadly accuracy into two eras of "hot" and "cold" war that are reflected by even the

1

structure of this survey of the American literary highlights of the period. The plan of this book varies greatly from that of the companion volume on the 30s, in which it was possible to compartmentalize neatly American achievements in fiction, poetry, and drama. The first section of this book is a kind of continuation of the earlier volume, in which three long essays treat the fiction, poetry, and drama of any lasting significance directly engendered by World War II. A different plan seemed necessary, however, for dealing with the literature of the decade that was not directly concerned by the War—although almost all was in some ways influenced by it — because, especially after V-J Day, one becomes less conscious of literary genres, more conscious of a series of "events" that highlighted the development of our literature. The "island-hopping" mentality of the Pacific War seems to have altered the whole American consciousness, and even literary people began to think in terms of "great moments" rather than mass movements.

Accordingly, the second part of this book is chronologically organized around a series of "highlights," around particular dates on which events of literary consequence occurred. This "literary decade" is shorter than the political one. It began really in June, 1940, when the first novel of a brilliant young writer, Carson McCullers, whose significant achievements were to be limited to this decade, appeared; it ended in February, 1949, when the award to Ezra Pound of the Bollingen Prize divided the literary world as the Korean contretemps would the political world more than a year later.

As far as American literature was concerned, the decade was a less distinguished one than the 30s, though probably a more distinguished one than the 50s. Poetry continued to lose ground with the public, which delighted in sentimental productions like Alice Duer Miller's *The White Cliffs of Dover* that critics scorned. If there are relatively few poetic "happenings" among the highlights of the decade, the doleful truth is that except for the first publications of Robert Lowell and the fuss over Ezra Pound, poetry made little impact outside of professional circles.

The situation in the theatre was better. Although many of the men who had dominated Broadway in the 30s — Robert Sherwood, Maxwell Anderson, S. N. Behrman, Kaufman and Hart — failed to add much to their reputations during the 40s, Eugene O'Neill reasserted himself and two men who continue twenty years later to dominate commercial theatre in this country and abroad—Tennessee Williams and Arthur Miller — made their spectacular debuts.

It is possible, however, to do justice to the highlights of the theatre during the decade in this book. Except for the work of the three playwrights mentioned and Thornton Wilder's monumental *The Skin of Our Teeth*, America produced few memorable plays in the 40s; even the best of the others — Mary Chase's *Harvey* and Sidney Kingsley's *Detective Story* — have little impact today.

It is not possible, however, to do justice to the fiction of the decade. The novel became, even more than it had been in the 30s, the dominant American literary form. Almost half of the essays in this book deal with fiction, and still some important figures have been neglected. Fortunately, Chester E. Eisinger's *Fiction of the Forties* provides a comprehensive guide to the most important work of the period; still I regret the omission from this account of the "highlights" of J. P. Marquand (especially *H. M. Pulham, Esq.*, 1941), Walter Van Tilburg Clark (*The Ox-Bow Incident*, 1940), Mary McCarthy (*The Company She Keeps*, 1942), Jean Stafford (*Boston Adventure*, 1944), Willard Motley (*Knock on Any Door*, 1947), and John Hawkes (*The Cannibal*, 1949). An essay on Paul Bowles, whose *The Sheltering Sky* was one of the literary sensations of 1949, was to have been contributed to this collection by the late Frederick J. Hoffman. The major novelists of the 30s also produced important work during this period — Faulkner, *Go Down, Moses* and *Intruder in the Dust*, and Steinbeck, *Cannery Row*. Whatever one may think of it as literature, one of the most influential novels of the decade was Ayn Rand's *The Fountainhead* (1943), and I regret that none of the company preparing this book could be tempted to make a dispassionate analysis of this best-seller and its effects.

The company of which I speak is again — as in the preparation of *The Thirties* — a group of friends, or at least friends of friends. The authors of the other two major essays on the literature of World War II have been valued colleagues; the other contributors' work I have known and valued, for sometimes as long as two decades. As in *The Thirties*, no effort has been made to achieve any homogeneity of tone or approach; yet I think that the collection is marked by a certain consistency of tone because of the contributors' sympathetic views on literature and life.

And once more — as in the 30s volume — all the essays have been especially prepared for this book and have not previously appeared elsewhere, although Robert Corrigan's account of the furore over the award of the Bollingen Prize to Ezra Pound represents a different approach to material that he used also in "Ezra Pound and the Bollingen Prize Controversy" (*Midcontinent American Studies Journal,* Fall, 1967), a longer article with an exhaustive bibliography of materials relevant to the controversy, which we were not able to include in this volume.

While the contributors were free to say what they pleased, the responsibility for selecting the subjects and the contributors is exclusively mine. If there is an unusually heavy concentration on material published in 1946 and 1947, it is because these were the bright years of the decade. Before 1946 the war diverted energies that might have gone into literary creation elsewhere and paper shortage precluded experimentation; after 1947, the hope that accompanied military victory began to evaporate and television began its insidious job of reducing to sub-literacy the audiences that might have helped a new literature to flourish. It was nearly another decade before — largely under the prodding of the much-deprecated Beatniks — young people tore themselves away from the tube and began to rediscover the joys of literary experimentation.

—Warren French

PART I:
The Literature
of World War II

Fiction:
A Handful of Survivors

by WARREN FRENCH

Although the United States has been involved in six major declared wars, as well as innumerable skirmishes with Indians, border incidents, police actions, and fiilibusters—as the activities in Viet Nam would have been described in the nineteenth century, it has produced surprisingly few "war novels" of enduring artistic merit.

The entire nineteenth century produced only Stephen Crane's *The Red Badge of Courage*—the work of a man who had not been involved in a war himself. Of the fourteen other "best Civil War novels" that Robert A. Lively lists in his study of five-hundred-odd works in *Fiction Fights the Civil War* (1957), only two—George W. Cable's *Dr. Sevier* and John W. DeForest's *Miss Ravenel's Conversion*—were published during the nineteenth century. The outstanding nineteenth-century novelists were conspicuously unsuccessful in treating war. Cooper's "Leatherstocking Tales" have outlived his romances of the Revolution, and *Israel Potter* is surely Melville's least noted novel. Although Crane and Norris witnessed the Spanish-American War, neither did more than write reports about it, and the Mexican War figured largely only in the subliterary predecessors to the dime novel.

The situation is not much different in the twentieth century, despite the enormous increase in the production of fiction. Stanley

Cooperman has provided in *World War I and the American Novel* (1967) what he probably prove to be the definitive history of this subgenre. He finds only a dozen books worthy of extended examination, and of these probably only E. E. Cummings' *The Enormous Room*, Dos Passos' *One Man's Initiation, Soldiers Three* and *1919* and Hemingway's *A Farewell to Arms* can be considered actually living parts of our literature. Neither the Korean conflict nor the Viet-Namese adventure has produced a novel of any artistic stature. What of World War II ? How many of the hundreds of American novels it provoked deserve continuing attention and a permanent place in our literature ?

Before we can cope with this question, we must ask what a war novel is. If any story written about a period when a nation is at war is a "war novel," the list becomes monstrously long and the term loses utility. If by "war novel," we mean any whose action is substantially influenced by developments occurring during military action, then we must include Fitzgerald's *The Great Gatsby* and Faulkner's *The Mansion*.

Lively dodges the problem of definition by confining his efforts to those novels "published about the War" collected by Richard H. Wilmer, Jr., and contributed to the University of North Carolina library. (Wilmer's criteria are not specified, either.) Cooperman perhaps wisely also avoids a specific definition. I feel compelled to explain, however, that these remarks are limited to novels that deal with men and women in military service during the period of active military hostilities and depict the direct impact of these activities. Novels about life on the "home-front" or veterans' problems are ignored (except for possibly Saul Bellow's *Dangling Man*, the loss is small). By further restricting myself to the decade of the war itself, I am obliged to rule out extended discussion of James Jones' *From Here to Eternity* and Joseph Heller's *Catch-22*, which view the war from the perspective of another period in history.

Only a handful of novels written about World War II while it was still in progress or fresh in men's thoughts and feelings leap to mind—Cozzens' *Guard of Honor*, Mailer's *The Naked and the Dead*, Irwin Shaw's *The Young Lions*, Steinbeck's *The Moon Is Down*, Michener's *Tales of the South Pacific*, Thomas Heggen's *Mister Roberts*, John Horne Burns' *The Gallery*. It is frequently theorized that there are few good war novels, because war is too vast, complicated and traumatic a subject for a writer to cope with.

This objection, however, is frivolous, for it assumes that the purpose of a "war novel" is to report what happened during the war. This is the task of the historian. When the novelist attempts it as Irwin Shaw did in *The Young Lions,* his work is likely no more than a decade later to be unreadable as either history or fiction. (Two decades later, Shaw's is indeed unreadable, and I shall make no further references to it. It can be regarded today only as one of many warnings to would-be writers with too solemn a sense of mission.)

The best "war novels" have reported very little about military engagements or even the politics of catastrophe. The battle that plays an important role in *The Red Badge of Courage* is never identified. An important retreat is described in *A Farewell to Arms,* but someone seeking a historical reconstruction would be ill-advised to consult Hemingway. *Guard of Honor* deals with three days' evasions and confrontations in a stateside Air Force training camp. A "war novel" clearly need not be panoramic, nor need it deal with causes and consequences in geo-political terms.

Novels are not chronicles; they are records of feelings. The great novels from *Pamela* to *Herzog* have enabled us to share the emotional responses of sensitive individuals to personal crises of general significance. The great "war novels" have precisely this capability. *The Red Badge of Courage* is only incidentally about the Civil War and primarily about one neophyte soldier's reaction to a brush with death. *A Farewell to Arms* is only incidentally about the Italian front in World War I; it primarily depicts Frederic Henry's disillusionment in his search for a force that will bring his life into meaningful focus. The few great novels of World War II are similarly concerned with an individual's initiation into a less provincial concept of reality.

The reason that great war novels are even less common than great novels in general (and these never abound) is probably—as Hemingway (whose works remain the greatest of the lot) has suggested—that the qualities demanded for successful soldiering and the qualities demanded for greatness in writing fiction are almost totally incompatible. Great fiction demands of its creator an extreme sensitivity to life that makes it almost impossible for him to endure gross physical shock or painfully boring passages of inaction—the two things of which World War II was compounded. Military success demands not the kind of gallantry that occasionally wins medals, but an indifference to violence and suffering (perhaps even a sadistic relish for it) and a capacity for accepting monotonous chores without rebellion. Many who might have been able to fictionalize war-time experience most sensitively probably spent the war in disciplinary barracks, conscientious objector camps, or in civilian life with a 4-F classification. Ominously those who wrote the best American fiction about World War II died tragically at early ages and the best publicized—Norman Mailer—has often been in trouble because of his impetuosity.

The Army demands the kind of man who can be successful also in the bull-ring or on the auto race-track; but such men rarely have the temperament for creating fictions. Great writing demands intensive introspection, but military men cannot be meditative. Great writers must treat language as a discipline and a mode of discovery, but military men must view it as a tool for quick communication and superficial propaganda. The good writer and the good military man do alike need to have a strong internal passion and a coolly controlled style, but one man is rarely able to blend these as Hemingway did during his best years, until the passion ran away with the style. Most writers succumb much sooner than he did; most soldiers are not moved by an altruistic enough passion to allow them to write without some partisan narrowness. And some men who command the style lack the passion.

The most striking example of this last-mentioned type is James Gould Cozzens, whose *Guard of Honor* has often been praised by conservative critics as the best American novel of World War II. Cozzens—like his Pulitzer-Prize winning work—occupies an unfixed place in American literature. He is ranked among our major writers by some critics, ignored by others. What one thinks of Cozzens depends upon what one expects from the novel. Those who think of it as a kind of panoramic report of what happened admire Cozzens; by the criteria I have set up in this essay—which demand that the writer give us the "feel" of experience—Cozzens is a pedestrian author. I agree with W. J. Stuckey's analysis in *The Pulitzer Prize Novels* that "the relative complexity of Cozzens' style and his philosophic balance somewhat hide a certain moral and psychological superficiality. . . . Cozzens' style, especially when it becomes most highly involved, merely glosses over and makes attractive the surface of things and events."

I also agree with Richard A. Long's observation ("The Image of Man in Contemporary American Fiction," *CLA Journal,* 1967) that Cozzens, "who spares himself both hope and pity, in that same act exempts himself from the circle of those who truly speak to men. He is at best an accomplished reporter in self-imposed exile from the house of art." Cozzens, in short, writes novels for people who don't really like—or trust—novels. It is small wonder that Granville Hicks is able to praise the writer at the same time that he observes in his University of Minnesota pamphlet that few of Cozzens' characters "are capable of strong emotions," acknowledging that the author "does not approve of strong emotions." Scarcely the man to deal with war, which could not flourish without such emotions.

Cozzens' avoidance of emotion results in his novels lacking both color and depth, and it is unlikely that *Guard of Honor* survives as an evocation of the psychological atmosphere during the war. Cozzens has often been branded a conservative (even Long uses the term), but Stuckey is correct when he maintains that "to label Cozzens a conservative is merely to beg the question. . . . The basic difference between Cozzens and the serious novelists who have dominated American fiction over the past forty-five years is that whereas these writers are critical of the social, political, and moral drift of American life, Cozzens is more or less satisfied with the way things are." Even this somewhat oversimplified explanation misses, however, the reasons for the lack of passion in Cozzens' work, for one can become a passionate defender of the status quo. As his manipulation of the characters in *Guard of Honor* indicates, Cozzens is not so much satisfied with the way things are as unconvinced that they could be any different. His acquiescence is a sophisticated form of despair.

The man treated with most respect in the novel is Colonel Ross, who has been pulled out of a civilian judgeship to function as Air Inspector at Ocanara Base in Florida, where he becomes principal advisor and confidante to the youngest general in the Air Force. At the end of the book he quotes a Latin phrase that he translates as meaning, "Who's going to pick up after me?" The commanding general replies, "I'll do the best I can, Judge; and you do the best you can; and who's going to do it better?"

In Cozzens' novel, nobody. Colonel Ross's point of view is revealed in one of the key passages. Another influential general offers to confide to Ross some of the results of a high-level conference in Quebec, but Ross doesn't want to hear "the inside story— what momentous plans had been agreed upon, what grand decisions reached." Rather he encourages the general to rattle on because "General Nichols might tell Colonel Ross a good deal about General Nichols." What he learns is that

> General Nichols might be coming late to the realiza-
> tion of the important truism that men are men, whether
> public or private. A public man had a front, a face; and
> then, perforce, he had a back, a backside, and in the nature
> of things it was so ordered that the one was associated with
> high professions and pronouncements and the other with
> that euphemistically denoted end-product. . . . If you let
> yourself imagine that the one (no matter which) invali-
> dated or made nugatory the other, this was the measure of
> your simplicity.

The inevitable conclusion of this inert resignation is Ross's reflection upon the people with whom Nichols must deal as those who

> . . . carried over, gave a grown-up handling to, the boy's
> complicated world of imaginary characters; the boy's long,
> long, illogical thoughts; the boy's unwarranted entertain-
> ment and unfounded terror in a state of things systemati-
> cally misunderstood. . . . Their make-believe was really
> serious to them. You found it funny or called it silly at your
> peril. Credulity had been renamed faith. Each childish
> adult determinedly bet his life and staked his sacred pride
> on, say, the Marxist's ludicrous substance of things only
> hoped for, or the Christian casuist's wishful evidence of
> things not so much as seen. Faiths like these were facts.
> They must be taken into account; you must do the best
> you could with them, or in spite of them.

At first glance this presentation of a purely rationalistic position seems seductively sensible, stripped of all infantile self-seeking; but it becomes clear that there must be an unstated premise when one asks why Ross feels "you must do the best you could with them." If hope of progress is delusive, why continue to grub out more than a merely ant-like existence? Why fight Nazis? And how can a novelist write derisively of "a complicated world of imaginary characters," when the phrase precisely describes a novel? Cozzens is motivated by some kind of faith himself in the necessity of maintaining some kind of "life-force," but he is reluctant

to commit himself. His lack of forthrightness deprives his novel of vitality.

Guard of Honor has often been described as "about" the awkward handling of a racial incident that occurs when a group of transient Negro officers at the Florida base demand to use the White Officers' Club. But Cozzens is not concerned with integration or segregation; there is no reason to suppose that he does not feel, like the Washington official that General Nichols quotes, that the facts are "that Southern Whites feel that Negroes cannot be allowed social or political equality" and that "Negroes don't enjoy being treated like animals." "The whole situation is a nuisance to us," he continues, "and we wish it didn't exist." But he doesn't expect the Commanding General to find a solution, and neither does Cozzens.

The problem is simply one of those things that come up to disrupt the working day, like the drowning of some parachutists during an unnecessary ceremonial. If it weren't these things, Judge Ross reflects, "It would be something else." "Every day," he concludes, the "white man's greed and folly proved that his claimed superiority was a lie. He was not clever; he was not strong; he was not good; he was nobody's born master. All he was, was, to a black man's sorrow and his shame, a little too much for most black men." This is not conservatism, but simply misanthropy. Colonel Ross also has thoughts about ordinary men:

> Though the level of intelligence in the average man might be justly considered low, in a very few of them would it be so low that they accepted notions that they fought, an embattled band of brothers, for noble "principles." They would howl at the idea; just as, in general, they despised and detested all their officers; hated the rules and regulations and disobeyed as many as they could; and from morning to night never stopped cursing the Army, scheming to get out of it, and hotly bitching about the slightest inconvenience, let alone hardship.

Again, however, the question arises why should man endure these hardships? If Cozzens does not view Ross sympathetically, why is he not presented as disdainfully as the others? Why does the book find its title in Ross's comment on a ceremonial for the men killed in the parachuting accident, "Ceremony is for us. The guard, or as I think we now prefer to call it, escort of honor is a

suitable mark of our regret for mortality and our respect for service
—we hope, good; but if bad or indifferent, at least, long."

From this speech, we see that Cozzens can be a man of passions,
but negative passions. His hidden faith is that of the old Puritans
with the hope of heaven that gave it its fervor gone. As for the
role of the writer, his own view seems similar to that expressed
by one of his officer-characters, formerly the editor of an influential
magazine, who explains to a fellow officer who has been offended by
a third's depiction of the second in a short story, "Edsell doesn't
mean anything personal. . . . He just sees a situation he thinks
he can write a story about. Then he dresses it up and twists it
around to make a story. That's what they pay him for." "Anyone
who lets himself stay around a writer," the former editor observes
on another occasion, "may expect to be wounded by what he will
consider malicious misrepresentations."

Unlike Celine or Dahlberg, Cozzens has learned to veil his
distaste for the rest of mankind beneath a mask of sophisticated
rationalism, but in so doing he drains his work of the venom
that makes the writings of the great haters interesting. He writes
for people who feel that it would be unrefined to let the world
know the contempt they feel for it. Thus his novels suffer from
a thinness that results from his expressing attitudes like Swift's
without Swift's vigor. He is not even much concerned about
World War II. If it weren't that, to borrow Colonel Ross's phrase,
it would just be something else. Another key passage in the novel
suggests that nothing matters in any struggle but superior force.
Praising Benny Carricker, a young pilot, the commander observes
that the United States is going to win the war, because it has
men like Benny; but Colonel Ross reflects,

> It seemed more probable . . . that they were going to
> win the war, not because they had a few more Bennys, but
> because they had thousands and thousands of run-of-the-mill
> pilots; and thousands and thousands of planes; and hills of
> bombs; and dumps of supplies as large as small cities, which
> could not be neutralized, as Benny had so nearly been, by
> one burst from one automatic rifle in one ditch.

The one quality Cozzens admires is honesty. "He did not have the
nerve to be honest," he says of a character he treats satirically.

Yet dogged honesty and a reconciliation to the power of brute
force are not enough to make a good novel, for the latter does not

rule out pity and the former seems useless unless coupled with hope. Cozzens' novel articulates his distaste for the human condition. The distaste may be understandable, but one who finds his consolation in statistics is not likely to become more than what Richard Long calls "an accomplished reporter."

Cozzens, nevertheless, merits respect as a serious writer if scarcely an effective creative artist because of his own dogged refusal to use "gimmicks" to whip up fictional fantasies that will please the crowd as Herman Wouk's *The Caine Mutiny* did. Inspired by his discovery of an article in the Naval Regulations about relieving a Commanding Officer, Wouk whipped up a fantasy that delighted every under-officer and enlisted man who had dreamed of getting rid of his commander during the war. In the end, however, it turns out it was all really a joke, because even though the commander is incompetent, we owe him a debt of gratitude for serving in the Navy during peace-time. Kiddie may dream of destroying pappa, but we must really respect his authority—and presumably that of every time-serving bureaucrat in City Hall.

Even today it is hard to believe that this obsequious tripe headed best-seller lists for two years. Most people's recollection of the work, in fact, are based on the suspenseful stage play and motion-picture versions. The book itself is loosely constructed and unbelievably tedious reading. It can be regarded only as a shockingly meretricious effort to play upon people's hostile fantasies in order to lure them into lapping up a little Establishment propaganda, which the Pulitzer Prize committee not surprisingly seized upon as a fit candidate for "best novel of the year."

The two other writings about the war that carried off the Pulitzer novel prize are not really bad novels, but non-novels. John Hersey's *A Bell for Adano* (1944) is a competently concocted confection about an Italian-American school drop-out from a tough New York neighborhood who emerges as a kind of modern saint when he is put in charge of the military government of a small Italian town. His personality is adequately suggested by this description:

> Major Joppolo's desire for popularity in Adano stuck out all over him. It was not just that he wanted to do a good job, and felt that popularity was one sign that he had. It was not much tied up with wanting the Americans to be

well received, though he did want that. It was mainly that
he himself wanted to be liked.

His technique for winning friends and influencing people is
illustrated by his treatment of some roughneck soldiers who have
destroyed some art treasures in a private home, "The Major said:
'I'm going to make this your punishment: to have this man's unhappiness on your conscience, and from now on to keep his house
as clean as if everything in it belongs to your own mother.'"

Hersey, who was later to achieve his greatest renown for his
report on the first atomic bombing, *Hiroshima* (first printed in
its entirety as the sole contents of one issue of the *New Yorker*),
is another able reporter. His account of the operation of the black
market, for example, provides valuable information about "what
it was like," but when he tries to create characters, this novel—
like his subsequent ones—degenerates into timely soap opera.
Hersey never tells us, for example, how Joppolo—in view of his
background—develops his remarkable tact and insight; Hersey
just thinks it would be nice if such a man existed, so he invents
him. The novel is useful today only as pathetic evidence of what
war-time Americans—uncomfortable in their role of world conquerors—could be prevailed upon to accept as serious literature.

Not many people probably really regard the other Pulitzer-
Prize winner, James Michener's *Tales of the South Pacific* (1947)
as serious literature, although it has probably been the most
popular work of American fiction about World War II (I am con-
sulting the twenty-seventh edition)—and deservedly so. It is a
far better book than Hersey's, once one understands the kind of
book it is. One just must remember that *Tales*—like Michener's
subsequent works—must take its place not in the history of literature, but in the perhaps far more interesting history of gossip.

The limitations and strengths of Michener's collection of mis-
cellaneous anecdotes are apparent from the ingenuous opening
section, in which the narrator observes, "But whenever I try to
talk about the South Pacific, people intervene. I try to tell somebody what the steaming Hebrides were like and first thing you
know I'm telling about the old Tonkinese woman who used to
sell human heads. As souvenirs. For fifty dollars!" The statement
suggests a person with two characteristics: no real purpose in con-
versing except entertaining and delighting and titillating a bit and
an imagination that functions in terms of anecdotes—the archetypal

gossip. It doesn't matter that the tales may be fabrications; those of the great gossips usually are, I suspect.

The difference between a Hersey and a Michener is that the Hersey is incurably deluded that his fables are FRAUGHT WITH SIGNIFICANCE—he is the descendant of the revivalist preacher seeking through print a larger congregation; Michener does not take himself that seriously. He may garnish his tale with a banal little moral about the way of the wicked world, but his real relish is in the telling. He cannot conceive a grand design; rather he specializes in details. Imagine inserting a dissertation on cacao-growing ("at first the miniature pods are light purple. Then as they grow to be full size, they become a weird greenish purple, like the paintings of George Bracque[sic]") right into the middle of the suspenseful account of the development of a romance be-tween a Navy nurse from Arkansas and a mysterious Frenchman! Yet Michener does, because he has not the artist's interest in rigor-ous selection, but the gossip's interest in overlooking nothing.

Michener's popularity is, however, well deserved. The regret-table thing about American writing today is that there are few men around with his talents as a raconteur and too many around waiting like Hersey to pound a moral into our heads. If Michener's diverting works are recognized for what they are, they might be used to lure back to reading some of the people scared off by the pomposities of the Herseys.

We must concede that the Pulitzer-Prize winning novels about World War II have, however, little to recommend them as works of art. Perhaps, however, the judges — in their relentless pursuit of arresting superficial journalism—overlooked some worthy con-tenders.

There were war novels almost as soon as there was a war. The race into print was won by William Bradford Huie's *Mud on the Stars,* which reached bookstores in May, 1942, only six months after Pearl Harbor. Its author has since—like John Hersey—gained a considerable reputation for his controversial non-fiction (*Three Lives for Mississippi,* for example). He had already published *The Fight for Air Power,* an early plea for the development of our sky fighters, before writing his first novel, which shows "how one young American has reacted to the national experience since 1929." The novel consists mostly of 28-year-old Peter Garth Le-Falcon's punchy explanations of his childhood traumas, education at the University of Alabama, and reactions to the problems of the world. He sounds off on page three, "War is a filthy, brutal business to me. There is nothing about it that thrills me. I have only one reaction to it. It was inevitable. We are in it. So let's go on with the goddam thing and get it over." He is still going strong on page 360, "I believe that Hitler is an effect and not a cause, and I believe that the causes of Hitler can be found within ourselves. . . . When Hitler and Japan have been defeated, the fighting will only have begun. For this is a war, not only to defeat the immediate enemy, who is an effect, but to defeat the causes which lie within our own nation and within our own powers."

These echoes of the inter-chapters of Steinbeck's *Grapes of Wrath* reflect a relatively common state of mind as the United States was reluctantly, but determinedly driven at last into war in 1941. They exemplify also the failure of not just this novel, but most of the others written while the war was in progress, to come to life. While people did harbor such sentiments, nobody ever talked —and talked and talked—the way Peter G. LaFalcon does except in canned propaganda speeches. The novel is the author's hurried representations of what people should have been saying if they had phonograph records for tongues. It is artful rather than artistic; but the surprising thing is that—in view of the speed with which it was produced—it was as good as most of what followed. If we consider only its superiors, we narrow the field to a few contenders.

Not much later, the first of the major novelists to meditate on the war—Steinbeck himself, then at the height of his reputation— was ready with an allegorical novel-play on the self-destructiveness of tyranny, *The Moon is Down*. The novel has had a curious history. It greatly disappointed American critics, but it was received with enthusiasm in Europe, especially by the underground Resistance forces. Steinbeck unquestionably came closer to catching the desperate but not yet resigned feelings of the Europeans than the determined but still annoyed feelings of the Americans, who—as Huie's monologue suggests—never really came to view the war as more than a necessary nuisance. European intellectuals, too, have always been more hospitable to the kind of two-dimensional allegory that Steinbeck produced than have American readers, who are suspicious of worthy sentiments unsupported by fictional characters with whom they can firmly identify.

The Moon is Down suffers from an artistic malady that might best be called "premature universality." In an effort to maintain the kind of oracular objectivity that he must have supposed demanded of a man in his position, Steinback refused to call his Norwegians and Germans by those names, but laid the action of the novel out of place and out of time. The world—at that moment in the grip of partisan feelings—was not ready for such detachment; nor really was the author himself, who in a unique moment of self-sabotage, has one character argue that the invading power is "in all the world . . . the only government and people with a record of defeat after defeat for centuries." If Steinbeck had followed up the implications of this statement, he might have produced a powerful tract, for one can hardly disagree with a book that argues the thesis that "the one impossible job in the world" is "to break man's spirit permanently"; but the very trouble is that the book demands agreement rather than insight. Steinbeck's pretentious confusion of propaganda with art has been the weakness of almost all of his books since *The Grapes of Wrath,* in which he created his impact by calling California California.

Steinbeck was probably pretentious, too, in supposing that it's possible to write anything but propaganda while war rages without dehumanizing one's self. The outstanding novelist of World War I, Ernest Hemingway, however, did not benefit from waiting until after the war had ended and the passions it engendered had cooled down; for his *Across the River and Into the Trees* (1950) was even less successful than Steinbeck's novel. Although Hemingway's book really lies just beyond the scope of this survey, it is impossible—because of his eminence as a war novelist—not to observe in passing that after two decades it can be seen that the fault with *Across the River and Into the Trees* is basically that though it seems to be about the aftermath of World War II, it isn't. As one looks back upon it now, with the added perspective of *The Old Man and the Sea,* one can see that it is really about Hemingway and his struggle with the critics. Colonel Cantwell, like Old Santiago, is Hemingway himself, embattled and nearing death, fighting off the sharks.

Actually symptoms of this preoccupation were apparent even in the irrelevant attacks upon some Loyalist generals in *For Whom the Bell Tolls;* Robert Jordan was also Hemingway — alone, brave, betrayed, virile — sacrificing his talents to an insensitive world. *For Whom the Bell Tolls* remains a great work, however, because Hemingway's involvement with Spain and his fascination with man's capacity for violence provided objective correlatives strong enough to maintain his artistic vision. But World War II provided no parallel involvement and a victory achieved through mechanical might rather than direct confrontations of men with "cojones" failed to fascinate him. The world had passed by Hemingway, as it had Colonel Cantwell, and both were peeved. *Across the River and Into the Trees* is the kind of tirade that King Canute directed against the encroaching sea. The novel degenerates into a series of irate editorials against other writers, President Truman ("The place has not even been swept out yet and they have an amateur pianist beating on the box.) and General Eisenhower as an example of the impersonality of modern warfare (". . . no one has ever commanded from that far back in history").

If the established writers could not do much with the wealth of material that World War II had provided, neither could the newcomers, for the most part. Symptomatic of the failings of the large number of "first novels" about the war is Peter Bowman's *Beach Red,* Book-of-the-Month Club selection for December, 1945, which, like *The Naked and the Dead,* dramatizes the invasion of a Japanese-held atoll in the Pacific.

The first thing that makes one uneasy about the book is the typesetting. It looks like a poem of "The White Cliffs of Dover" school; yet the dust-jacket advises that "the typographical arrangement of lines and sections was devised by the author to represent the rigid timing by which each step of such an action is governed" and that "it is written in prose and should be read as such." (Since this information is not repeated in the book, I don't know what readers of copies that have lost their dust-jackets would make of the arrangement.)

The greater problem is that the content is as emptily pretentious as the form. Bowman is not content simply to describe an action, as Harry Brown does in the modest but still readable *A Walk in the Sun* (a tale of an Italian beachhead published in 1944), he must also moralize over it. Since the descriptions are overblown and the moralizing is fuzzy, the book strikes one as nothing more than noisy confusion.

The approach to an island under fire is described thus:

You can see the island now—a weird, looming blotch
shaking with violent epilepsy in the tremulous haze of
dawn.
There is sickeningly green water beating itself in frothy
desperation,

trying to escape the restraining ministrations of reef and
    sandbar,
And lurching in giddy drunkenness and vomiting on its
    clothes.

The moralizing comes near the end:

When there was only one man in the world there
were problems, and when there were two men in the
world there were twice as many problems, and when another
man came along the problems were multiplied by three.
    But
now there are many more men and there are many
more problems and they've reproduced and spread them-
    selves all over
the earth in a great crawling germ. Wherever you go
you find men and their problems. . . .

This is followed by a remarkable metaphor—"living is an empty
pot and thinking is a can-opener." The novel attempts to conceal
beneath a façade of typographical eccentricity a staggering banality
of both thought and image. While it is unfair to linger long over
yesterday's mishaps, even a brief dip into *Beach Red* makes it
glaringly clear that the United States—granting that its young men
had to be subjected to the horrors of war at all—was not producing
a generation with the sensitivity and insight to make artistic capital
of their experiences.

Norman Mailer's *The Naked and the Dead* has generally been
hailed as the striking exception to this doleful generalization.

How does it read two decades after it was greeted with widespread acclaim? I was disappointed to discover that time has not
mellowed, but soured the novel.

Once I had a chance to ask John Dos Passos about the younger
generation of novelists, and he singled out for praise those chapters
in *The Naked and the Dead* that describe the activities of the recon-
naissance platoon headed by Sergeant Croft. These do indeed contain some of the best reporting to come out of the war. Yet if there
had been nothing more to the novel than them, it would probably
have made no more impression than *A Walk in the Sun*. The great
excitement over Mailer and his novel stemmed, I believe, from
his being the only new, young writer to come up with a provocative ideological explanation of the dehumanizing effects of young
Americans' wartime experiences.

Chester E. Eisinger in *The Fiction of the Forties* describes *The Naked and the Dead* as "one of the few successful novels of ideas written during the entire decade," and there is no disputing the assertion, although the shocking condemnation of our creative writers' intellectual achievement embodied in the statement grows greater the longer the perspective from which we contemplate it. The intellectual strategy of the novel is fairly simple. On one side are the authoritarian figures, Sergeant Croft and General Cummings, representative of an incipient national fascism that perhaps came to a head only twenty years later in the George Wallace/Curtis LeMay presidential ticket. The general represents a kind of slick, genteel, *Wall Street Journal* fascism; the sergeant, the folksy, Southern, intuitive brand. (Significantly, the "folk fascist" who finally destroys his opposition in the novel also heads the presidential ticket; whatever the United States is ready for, it's not elitism.) Ranged against them we have Lieutenant Hearn and typologically assorted members of the platoon, who stand for all that is decent in man. As a result of a series of blundering military operations, the "good guys" are either demoralized or destroyed and the fascists come out ahead, though really accidentally. The better a man is, the more gruesome his fate; and the more awful, the greater his triumph.

Mailer's construct is neat, and it has some relationship to the truth. Things have not worked out quite so badly as Mailer predicted they would in his vision of an untempered fascist triumph; but in judging *The Naked and the Dead* as a war novel, one is not primarily concerned with Mailer's virtues as prophet. Whatever we may think of the novel as prophecy—and we may still have to wait a while to judge the accuracy of the vision — it is just not very good as a novel. At the time of its appearance nearly everyone was so excited about its political significance that they overlooked its artistic weaknesses. Since then people have been asking wonderingly why Mailer has failed to live up to his early promise. The answer is, I think, that the promise was an illusion. All the weakneses of his later novels are apparent in his first, but we overlooked them in 1948, because we responded with such enthusiasm to the recollections that the book invoked of the war we had so recently endured. Since Mailer—though he has tried to exploit Hollywood, violence, and even Viet Nam—has never been able to find another subject with as widespread appeal as military injustice during World War II, his later works have not enjoyed the success of his first. And now that the emotions responsible for the first excited response to *The Naked and the Dead* have cooled down, we can begin to see why the dissenting critics have been more right about the later novels than the first.

What's wrong with *The Naked and the Dead*? Three related things. First, Sergeant Croft is not just a conniving bastard; he is insane. But there is no evidence in the novel that the author recognizes that he has created a madman. In the climactic scene of the ideological struggle between Croft and Lieutenant Hearn, the sergeant cold-bloodedly arranges that his superior walk into an ambush and be gunned down so that Croft may retain the power he has usurped over the platoon. The killing is pre-meditated and Croft has no qualms about it. No personal or ideological grievances are involved; yet Croft betrays the military discipline on which his whole personal concept of order depends. He thus shows that he cannot recognize any checks upon his behavior, but has confused universal order with his own private gratification.

At the time the novel appeared, many readers—including me—frustrated by our own war-time experiences with incompetent non-commissioned officers (mostly Southern) were willing and eager to sublimate our private revenge fantasies by accepting Croft's actions as the perfectly normal outcome of the patterns of behavior responsible for our own real or fancied harrassment. Looking back without anger, however, but with a tough eye for those qualities of objectivity that artistic endurance demands, we must admit that Mailer appealed with enormous skill to our own sentimental self-indulgence. He was as successful a spokesman for the party of love and disorder as all the Sergeant Crofts and General Cummingses we had known were for the parties of hate and order; but he had pushed beyond the bounds of reason in portraying Croft, who was an amoral killer who should have been gunned down himself if any balance were to be maintained in the fictional world that Mailer was fabricating.

Objecting at such length to the treatment of a single character may seem quibbling; but the acceptance of Mailer's whole ideological construct rests upon our acquiescence in Croft's triumph through insane violence. If the fascists are, after all, simply mad, the struggle against them lacks the complexity that would justify a novel of this scope. While I am reluctant to look outside of a work of fiction itself in judging it, I think that we must acknowledge that Mailer's weakness as an artist has consistently been his infatuation with violence. To reflect reality, an artist must be prepared to recognize violence and its far-reaching effects; but if he becomes a propagandist for it, he ceases to be an artist, and his works become the same kind of special pleadings as temperance tracts. The praise of violence is perhaps a necessary outlet for anti-social feelings in a world that increasingly smothers the individual, but works primarily motivated by it can hardly lead man to the understanding of himself that serious art must.

The second weakness of *The Naked and the Dead* is that really none of the characters, with the possible exception of the religious fundamentalist Ridges, develops or changes during the work. When we meet them on the isle of Anopopei, they are the inexorably fixed products of the forces that are sketchily suggested in "the time machine" passages of the novel. The novel thus becomes a battle between a group of stereotypes—the farm boy, the New York Jew, the bum, the shanty Irishman, the prep school boy, etc. Mailer does a shrewd job of choosing the most familiar American stereotypes and dramatizing the grievances that arise between them; but his achievement is repertorial rather than artistic. There is no evidence that any of these characters is in any way altered by his war-time experience; yet American life distinctly underwent a change of tone and texture following World War II.

This observation brings us to the third and most important objection to *The Naked and the Dead* as a "war novel." It just does not tell us anything about the unique effects of World War II upon American character. The war simply provides a convenient and interesting backdrop for the struggle that Mailer dramatizes. This struggle between power-mad authoritarians and decent human beings has gone on at all times in all societies. Mailer's novel does not especially concern World War II, nor is it even peculiarly American. The failing of the novel is precisely the opposite of that of *The Moon is Down*. Steinbeck attempted to endow a struggle peculiar to a particular time and place with a spurious universality; Mailer attempted to suggest that a universal struggle was peculiar to a particular society at a particular moment of its development. The very excellence of the passages about the reconniassance platoon works against the tenor of Mailer's argument. Steinbeck tried to write a novel-play that turned out to be too nearly an essay: Mailer attempts to turn into a novel-play (there are even fully dramatized passages) what should have been an essay. Mailer is a gifted spellbinder; but the less immediately we are moved by the scenes he creates, the more superficial his technique appears. His work gives us not the true feeling of a period, but a sense of the obsessions of one of the most eloquently outspoken opponents of the status quo.

But if *The Naked and the Dead* is finally to take its place with *Uncle Tom's Cabin* and *The Jungle* (and think how pitifully few of even such great tracts there are!), does that mean that the horrors of World War II so overwhelmed Americans that none could maintain his aesthetic discipline? Very nearly. But not quite —for two modest books should remain as artistic monuments.

Thomas Heggen's *Mister Roberts* has been such an enormous success as a stage play and film that people rarely take it any more seriously than Michener's *Tales of the South Pacific.* Having reserved it for rereading after the novels that I have already discussed or dismissed, I admit that I approached it with great trepidation. Surely it, too, would prove just another slick, superficial comedy that had originally gratified my service-bred resentments.

I found, however, that as I began once again the slow, sullen voyage on the *Reluctant,* Heggen's ironic, economical language brought remote days vividly back to life:

> Now, in the waning days of the second World War, this ship lies at anchor in the glassy bay of one of the back islands of the Pacific. It is a Navy cargo ship. You know it is a cargo ship by the five yawning hatches, by the house amidships, by the booms that bristle from the masts like mechanical arms. You know it as a Navy ship by the color. . . .

We might dwell at length on the achievement of the third sentence quoted. Heggen is using two perilous techniques: the "you" that had undone Peter Bowman in *Beach Red,* and the present tense that makes the events seem to be happening as we read about them. He succeeds with both, however, because in the prepositional phrases he unobtrusively provides the details that make the reader see for himself the ship as not some vision from the past but a present reality. He succeeds in involving the reader, too, because—as in the fourth paragraph of the novel, he magnificently plays off the empty rhetoric of the patriotic poster against the realities experienced by the millions who spent the war not in the combat zone but in the service areas that stretched for half a world behind them:

Surely, then, this is One World, the tranquil ship is only an appearance, this somnolence an illusion. Surely an artillery shell fired at Hanover ripples the air here. Surely a bomb dropped on Okinawa trembles these bulkheads. This is an American Man o' War, manned by American Fighting Men: who would know better than they that this is One World ? Who indeed ? Of course, then, this indolence is only seeming, this lethargy a façade; in actuality this ship must be throbbing with grim purposefulness, intense activity, and a high awareness of its destiny. Of course.

Readers who did not live through World War II may miss the references to Wendell Willkie and Franklin D. Roosevelt; like all war novels, *Mister Roberts* has become to some extent a period piece. But if anyone is interested in learning what ordinary men's feelings were during that time, one who recalls the period can assert confidently that Heggen is telling it like it was.

Like *Tales of the South Pacific, Mister Roberts* is composed of a series of sketches that are seemingly related only by the reappearance of the officers and men of the *Reluctant*; but these sketches are not simply casually related anecdotes. They are linked by the author's concern with the same matters that troubled Norman Mailer in *The Naked and the Dead. Mister Roberts* is an understated, seemingly joking account of the conflict between authoritarianism (as embodied in the commander of the *Reluctant*) and human decency (as embodied in the much admired Lieutenant Roberts). Roberts, like Mailer's Hearn, is also destroyed at the end, though through an ironic accident not as a result of deliberate malice. Roberts' death is not wasted, however, because it inspires in the seemingly hopelessly frivolous Ensign Pulver some of the bravado that may be essential in continuing the struggle against the authoritarians.

Compared to the action in Mailer's novel, of course, the action in *Mister Robers* is trivial; but most Americans, after all, lead relatively trivial lives. The very lack in *Mister Roberts* of the violence that abounds in *The Naked and the Dead* makes Heggen's novel truer, I think, to the typical American's war-time experience. Most Americans did not spend the war invading Pacific islands; they spent their time performing the stultifyingly boring background tasks essential to the success of such dramatic operations.

They spent the war trying to assume some small measure of responsibility for their individual destinies despite the mindless and faceless machinations of an impenetrable system that sought to reduce them to ciphers. They fought the kind of war that Hemingway hated because the contributions of the individual man were imperceptible.

The problem with a novel like *Mister Roberts* is not that it is farcical or superficial, but that it is such a fragile work that it demands the same kind of careful attention as a collection of miniature paintings. It has rarely found the sensitive response that it demands; yet without such a response the whole point of the novel is missed, for what Heggen is fundamentally concerned with is not even the struggle between authority and decency, but the subtler and perhaps more significant struggle between sensitivity and insensitivity. The individual in the modern world may not be able to control his political destiny, but he could still control his power to respond. The thing that was unique about World War II was its deadening assault upon man's sensitivities. The increasing noise that it is necessary to use—the increasing violence that it is necessary to employ to penetrate people's resistance and command their attention in the post-war world is dramatized in miniature by the increasingly strident measures Mister Roberts and his followers must take to penetrate the self-seeking indifference of the man in charge. Heggen looked at the war and saw what was distinctive about the conditions that it produced instead of simply drawing upon it for examples to illustrate a pre-conceived philosophy as Cozzens and Mailer did.

If World War II had produced no hardier monument, however, than this delicate and deceptively difficult book, the feeling of the period might be inaccessible to future readers. But there remains John Horne Burns' *The Gallery*.

Gore Vidal, whose own first novel *Williwaw*—a slick account of an Army transport ship in a storm—is far superior to the run of first novels about the War, has said that "of all the well known books of the war, I have always thought that only Burns's was authentic" (*New York Times Book Review*, May 30, 1965). The others he considers the results of ambition or literature, but Burns' grew out of the author's falling in love with the idea of life as the result of his experiences in Naples during the American military occupation of the city. Burns' book, Vidal is arguing, is a sensitive man's genuine effort to come to terms with his own feelings. Because Burns succeeded better than any other of our young servicemen-authors in discovering what his own feelings were and in finding a form to communicate them, *The Gallery* succeeds better than any similar work in conveying the impact of the war on a sensitive American transported into an alien world.

The structure of the novel has puzzled some readers. There are two kinds of material. The continuity is provided by ten short recollections of a corporal named John of his experiences in Casablanca, Oran, and Naples. Set into this stream of reminiscence are nine much longer "portraits," none of which involve either the same characters or any of the characters from the "promenades," as most of the corporal's reminiscences are called. Because of this unusual construction, the novel has sometimes been regarded as only a collection of short stories, like Hemingway's similarly organized *In Our Time.* Burns did not, however, borrow or devise a peculiar form—as Peter Bowman did——to disguise the banality of his reflections. The form is essential to the communication of the author's vision.

Burns wishes to convey the feeling that the United States has become a "hermetic" country and that its people are emotionally dead because of an obsessive narcissism. Through the series of "promenades," he describes one sensitive American's breaking out of his antiseptic shell and participating fully for the first time in the joys and miseries of human life. "In the nineteen days of crossing the Atlantic," the corporal reports, "I remember that something happened to me inside. I didn't know what adjustment to make for where I was going, but I think I died as an American." When he realizes that he may have come overseas to die, he comments, "I was put for the first time in my life against a wall which I couldn't explain away by the logic of Main Street or the Weltanschauung of Samuel Goldwyn." Later he explains that "I remember that this was the first time I'd come upon the European idea of being *sympathetic,* an idea which doesn't exist in the American language," because Americans are "leery of abstracts."

Ultimately through his experiences abroad, the corporal discovers the "realities" that Americans have all but forgotten—"tears, art, and love." Americans, he argues, "assume that tears are wet and that life should be dry" and live mostly in the vacuum that "laughs or smiles." Italian artists, he discovers, are different from American ones, because "the Americans always announced that they're artists" and were "glib about their techniques and their souls," whereas the Italians never told anybody they were artists or talked about the problems of artists, so that one only learned about their work when one got to know them. Finally, because in America, "there is felt to be something shameful in two human beings taking their pleasure together," love is "often divided into the classifications of Having Sex and Getting Married," neither of which "has much to do with love." These discoveries lead the corporal named John to the conclusion that "perhaps we must soon all come to the point where we're proud only to say: I am a human being, a citizen of the world."

The profound change that occurs in this one American when he moves for the first time outside of his stulitifyingly protective environment has special significance because it mirrors a widespread change in Americans as a result of World War II. While no such change affects everyone, many Americans—especially the alert and influential—did shift as a result of war-time experiences from rigid isolationists to "citizens of the world." Perhaps, as our embarrassing involvement in Viet Nam suggests, we have swung too far in this direction and must attempt to recover a balance, but anything like our involvement in Viet Nam would have been inconceivable in 1939. The alteration in Burns' corporal is reflective and prophetic of the most striking general change that American character has undergone in the mid-twentieth century.

Even had Mailer sensed this change, he could not have depicted it in a novel conceived around a situation like that dramatized in *The Naked and the Dead*. Mailer's soldiers never really are exposed to an alien reality. The "enemy" they meet are simply puppets to be annihilated; and though the platoon roams the remote island of Anopopei, it has really intellectually and spiritually never left home.

Thus the really important passages in shaping *The Gallery* are not the striking "portraits," but the much more understated "promenades" in which the character that unifies the book records his "death as an American" and his rebirth with a new identity as a citizen of the world. What then are the "portraits" doing there? The answer in Burns' own words is found in the "fifth promenade," in which the corporal comments, "I began to ponder on variety and difference. I lost something, because I became other people by thinking about them. For better or for worse I think I annihilated myself at this time." The "portraits" are thus not to be read as a string of isolated, objective short stories, but as the corporal's subjective projection of himself into other people. His vision centers upon Naples' Galleria Umberto Primo because "most of the modern world could be seen in ruins there in August, 1944." The novel is thus unified because, despite a seeming diversity of characters, all the characters are merged into one and the novel is a communication of the corporal's vision.

The "portraits" do more, however, than simply re-inforce the message of the "promenades." As one studies them in relationship to each other, one is struck by the darker side of the author's vision. In one of the portraits, the spirit of a dead officer speaks with what can now be seen as horrifying accuracy of the unfortunate results of America's new international consciousness:

> "The rest of the world hates Americans because they're so crude and stupid and unimaginative. . . . They will win this war. They'll reduce Europe to a state of fifteen hundred years ago. Then their businessmen and their alphabetical bureaucracies will go into the shambles of Milan, Berlin, and Tokyo and open up new plants. . . . International carpetbaggers. . . . Millions of human beings will be dead, and most of human feelings will be dead forever. . . . Hurray for our side. . . . We're destroying all the new ideas and all the little men of the world to make way for our mass production and our mass thinking and our mass entertainment." (Ellipses in text)

The "portraits" are of two clearly distinguishable types of people. Michael Patrick, Hal, Father Donovan and Chaplain Bascom, the sergeant in "Queen Penicillin" and Lt. Moses Shulman are all kind, thoughtful, decent people—men of good will; and they are all destroyed, either literally or spiritually. Louella, Momma, Major Motes, and Giulia, in contrast, are all greedy, self-seeking opportunists (Giulia is described as "mad, but in a precise and scheming way"), and they all survive and flourish. The animus in the sexual differentiation of the groups is notable; not even Major Motes is a true exception, for he is really neuter and, though not homosexual, as receptive to other men's attentions as the women in the other "portraits." The division is ironic in that women are generally stereotyped in the thinking of the characters in the book as creative, protective forces and men as arrogant and destructive; Burns, however, sees women as ruthless predators and men as the doomed bearers of concepts of beauty and justice.

The contrast between the fates of the selfish females and the selfless males is especially ironic in view of the corporal's speculation in the seventh "promenade": "I wondered if perhaps the world must eventually be governed by individuality consecrated and unselfish, rather than by any collectivism of the propagandists, the students, and the politicians." The whole structure of Burns' novel suggests both his agreement in theory with this vision and his despair that it can ever become a reality.

Mister Roberts and *The Gallery* stand out above the other American novels about World War II because they are accounts of an individual's discovery of his capacity for feeling that are artistically enough realized so that they can stimulate a similar discovery of his own feelings on the part of a reader attentive and sensitive enough to be able to hear the authors' voices. The novels are alike in that both present the author's vision not through an old-fashioned "plot," but through a series of impressionistic sketches and in that both depict the destruction of those upon whom the hopes for a better world might rest, not by the machinations of the vicious but by the chance operations of an indifferent fate.

Curiously, both authors were to die under mysterious circumstances at early ages. At 29 Thomas Heggen drowned in his apartment bathtub after possibly taking an overdose of sleeping pills. At 36, after returning to Italy, Burns died of sunstroke, although Gore Vidal suggests that he was drinking himself to death. Heggen never finished another work after *Mister Roberts*; Burns published two novels after *The Gallery*, but neither was an artistic nor commercial success. Without delving deeply into the circumstances behind these unhappy deaths, one seems able to conclude that the only two men who made an adequate artistic response to American involvement in World War II were too sensitively organized to sustain the stresses of ordinary life. If the novel is indeed dying—as some continue to argue—and surely it has not flourished since 1945 as in the preceding two centuries, it is largely, I would argue, because men's sensitivities have failed to develop at the speed of his technology. In every one of the portraits in *The Gallery* in which the potentially decent are destroyed, technology is somewhere at fault—the hysterical pace of American life destroys Michael Patrick and Hal, a truck cuts down the chaplains, Moses Shulman is gunned down, a new "miracle" drug which saves many lives destroys the sergeant's vision of love in "Queen Penicillin." On the other hand, the coldly efficient automatons triumph by adjusting themselves to the realities of a mechanical age—Louella to her "airplane drivers," Momma to her cash register, Major Motes to his production-line system of censoring other men's stumbling efforts to articulate their feelings, Giulia to the necessity of burying the past and accomodating herself to those whose superior mechanical power has overwhelmed her people.

At bottom, a survey of the novels of World War II reveals a staggering failure of American education, which has made men efficient and enabled them to triumph physically, but which has failed to detect and cultivate those rare sensitivities that might make something more than a nightmarish mockery of those triumphs. As a lieutenant from Yale tells the corporal in the forth "promenade" in *The Gallery*, "If the murder gets over, everything will then be geared to the lowest common denominator, as it is in the American public schools. The queer, the beautiful, the gentle, and the wondering will all go down before a race of healthy baboons with football letters on their sweaters."

The shocking thing is that Americans are not—as their foes look into the mirror and see them—embodiments of evil, which can be comprehended and even possibly destroyed. They are simply an unfeeling people who are willing to sit back and see those who embody the race's finest potential capriciously destroyed because they have not developed the capacity, as Burns puts it, "to distinguish between talent and ballyhoo." They are a people epitomized by the callous medic's remark to the heartsick sergeant in "Queen Penicillin," "We ain't interested in making these shots painless." Small wonder that the little noteworthy American fiction to come out of World War II was a cry of pain—largely unheeded.

Poets in the Inferno: Civilians, C. O.'s and Combatants

By DAN JAFFE

On the stretchers of coarse linen
they are carrying away the young men
with red bellies and grey skin. They
are carrying away the young men. But
who knows what good it will do.   —Louis Aragon

The poets of the forties wrote in the face of terror and barbarity. Perhaps more than any earlier generation of poets they
shared a common, pervasive experience. For although the history
of man is the history of his wars, World War II had far greater
global impact than any previous blood letting. This was true not
only because of the geopolitics of the struggle, not only because
of the simultaneous threats in the east and west, but because air
power made those who would have been safe in earlier times
vulnerable. For the first time even oceans provided scant protec-
tion. While those outside the war zones wondered if they would
eventually be bombarded, they listened to regular radio reports,
reports that by the standards of the 1960's would probably seem
vague and unsophisticated but which at the time were enormously

33

graphic and immediate, perhaps more intimidating than television because they left more to the imagination.

Perhaps it is a mistake to think of war poets as only those who picked up foxhole fungus or waded onto hostile beaches. Some of our best poets were combatants, but at the same time some of the best poems written about World War II and about the meaning of war in general were written by non-combatants. The war was in the atmosphere; and the real poets, nourished as they already were on Siegfried Sassoon, Wilfred Owen, and Stephen Crane, breathed it in even if they were miles from the battlefields.

Crane had already provided us with the clearest example of how the poetic sensibility operates. His research, his insights, and his ability to project known human capacities for feeling into imagined situations provided us with one of the great novels about war, a novel he wrote before he had ever observed combat first-hand.

The real test of any poet is how he deals with his material, a literary rather than a biographical test. When we judge war poets we must examine their poems rather than their lives. To be sure, some of the poets of the forties performed gallantly as military men as well as writers. But some far from the scene smelled the suffering of war as intensely as those who felt the actual wounds. It is after all the writer's job to empathize, to feel himself into situations he has not experienced, to write more than his own autobiography. And it is this capacity that is our only hope. For if we have to experience war directly to realize its dangers, we are doomed to repeat our unfortunate history. All poetry, war poetry included, would have dubious value except as classroom exercise.

Generalizations about poetry of a particular time always mislead. How much balderdash has been spouted about "modern" poetry, as if T. S. Eliot and Dylan Thomas were twins—not exact duplicates but too much alike for differences to matter. And one can hear nonsense about "modern" poetry where you would least expect it, on the campus, from professors as well as students. All of which goes to show that too often people pay more attention to period introductions in anthologies than they do to the substance that follows. It is the character of a real poem to be unique; the generalizations forget that. But nevertheless, we can talk about thematic differences, differences in emphasis and direction meaningfully if we remember that we're talking about matters that may contribute to the reality of particular poems but really do not define that reality.

The poets of World War II learned from Isaac Rosenberg, Wilfred Owen and Siegfried Sassoon. Of course, they had far fewer illusions about war than their World War I counterparts. The "war to end all wars" had been fought but never ended. John Ciardi, Karl Shapiro, Winfield Townley Scott, Richard Eberhart, and Randall Jarrell, to name only a few, knew what had happened to the "Great Adventure." The abiding illusion of the forties, except perhaps for recruitment posters, was not that war is glorious and creative. The fascists played that tune and the Allies generally recognized it as another noxious totalitarian notion.

The poets of World War II did not have to undermine a home-front myth to show, as Wilfred Owen had done so powerfully, that to die for one's country was not sweet and altogether fitting. To be sure some of the brute stuff of war got into their poems, but the introduction of the apparatus and the ache of war was not the central necessity as it so often was with Owen. He had done it; they had to go on from there. They took on a larger task. And it was the acceptance of that larger task, the attempt to confront the problems of guilt and cause as well as pain, that gave their poetry is direction. One senses time after time the probing of the self for answers to questions outside the self, a curious reticence to blame even the Nazis for the ills of the world. What has commonly come to be called existential guilt permeates many of the poems by both combatants and non-combatants.

Almost without exception, American poets of the forties asked repeatedly how man had lost his innocence? how even those who had not consciously contributed to genocide allowed the world to be so victimized? Time after time one notices the psychological and philosophical tone of conjecture and self-doubt.

During the past couple of years we have heard a great deal about poetry readings against the Viet Nam War. Almost to a man contemporary American poets bitterly assail U. S. policy and tactics in the Far East. Poets as different as Robert Bly, Lewis Simpson, Allen Ginsberg, and Bill Stafford view the war as a debasement of the American Dream, a signal of moral malaise. And the poets have organized, cooperated, and petitioned. And, of course, they have written. Curiously, their public gestures and pronouncements, i.e., Robert Lowell's refusal to appear at the White House, have had more impact than their poems, perhaps because, with certain exceptions, most of the poems have direct political, propagandistic intentions. The poets mean them, as did the Marxist writers of the thirties, to produce results; and it would seem the results matter more than the poems. This may be one of the few times in which poets contribute to a successful revision of national policy. If so, they should certainly be honored. It may be that the gradual realization of American intellectuals that those supposed to be most sensitive to the national climate, those whose purpose is to see beyond illusion, viewed the war as disastrous, made possible some of the reexaminations of the war now taking place in the American mind. If so, the poets' efforts have been enormously rewarding and successful. Nevertheless, most of the Viet Nam War poems will probably date; they seek to embarrass the administration rather than to provide the sort of experience that will still be humanly valid when American foreign policy has changed. These poems are often just metaphorical editorials, tight innuendos, literary embodiments of much needed political activism. It may very well be that as a group these poems may emerge importantly even after the current political situation changes, but that still seems uncertain.

It was a human dilemma rather than a political one that concerned the poets of World War II. They did not generally seek to justify or attack the war itself. They meant to show how war stripped man of his manhood, reflected his absurdity and capacity for evil, forced him to take stock or fade into the stripes of the tiger.

There is a sense in which all poets are war poets, for all poets do battle, at least while they write, against the forces that produce war. Poetry is a battle against chaos and disintegration, an attempt to make and maintain wholeness. The poem is a gauntlet in the teeth of death. The war poet deals explicitly with this subject, but all poets deal with it implicitly in the very practice of the art, in the attempt to form and hold together.

Probably the poem most often and most immediately mentioned as the great poem of World War II is 'In Distrust of Merits" by Marianne Moore. Miss Moore's poem is graceful, philosophical, and didactic. She attempts to give meaning to the conflict, but she does not simply maintain that evil has been identified and must be destroyed. This is a poem sutured by paradox. The fighting is against the blind, against the enslaved. For, says Miss Moore, ". . . the enslaver is enslaved; the hater, harmed." The real war goes deeper than any slivers of shrapnel. It is a moral conflict, a conflict within self. Hate is death, and unless anger is stilled, the breathing victor is only an iron wolf, the maker of new disasters and self-doomed.

> Hate-hardened heart, O heart of iron,
>   iron is iron till it is rust.
> There never was a war that was
>   not inward; I must
> fight till I have conquered in myself what
> causes war, but I would not believe it.
>   I inwardly did nothing.

It is the refusal of man to recognize his own culpability, the way in which he lies to himself, that is the real enemy. But the recognition is not enough because "We are/not competent to/make our vows." There is only the hope that "they're fighting that I/may yet recover from the disease, *my/self*."

In a time of national crisis, Miss Moore refuses to write the nationalistic poem. The national crisis is insignificant compared to the human crisis. This is a theme that World War II poets refer to repeatedly. Faced by a global conflict they assume a global perspective.

Winfield Townley Scott also refuses to assume the easy nationalistic posture in his poem "The U. S. Sailor with the Japanese Skull," a poem about which one hears more and more as each year goes by. It may very well be the best poem written during and about World War II by an American, if such comparisons are not invidious. Curiously, it is the one World War II poem which has been repeatedly reprinted in order to put the Viet Nam War into perspective. It has not dated. If anything it has become even more menacing and significant with the passage of time.

Scott's view is remarkable considering the tone of U. S. homefront propaganda during World War II. On innumerable posters Japanese pilots who looked like monster dwarfs peered from tiny planes. Each had an enormous set of teeth which pointed out and down, each tooth like the barrel of a field piece. Americans were regularly encouraged to view the enemy as subhuman. We were fighting a tribe of malignant insects or worse. That view now seems ludicrous. But unfortunately one fears that it will only take another time when it is advantageous to excite the folks at home to set rolling the mechanisms that produce such sickness.

Scott, of course, did not succumb. His poem undercuts the

mindless hatred of the enemy that dehumanizes the hater. He does not speak directly about this dehumanizing process as Marianne Moore does. He dramatizes it; we watch the American sailor sabotage himself as he callously makes an ornament of a human skull; we come to recognize that he is the real enemy, his inability to feel compassion or to imagine that lives other and different than his own have value. He is the warmaker personified, but he is "our sailorboy."

Scott's technique is to show in grisly detail the decapitation and the curing of the skull, to move his reader to near disgust and fear and then to redirect these emotions to the souvenir hunter and what he stands for. At the same time, the poem becomes a kind of elegy for the unnamed Japanese soldier and all those who are stripped of the memories and credentials of manhood by the unfeeling.

What happens in "The U. S. Sailor with the Japanese Skull" happens in a war setting, but Scott's focus is not on the war but on what produces war, man's capacity for self debasement.

"The U. S. Sailor with the Japanese Skull" is one of those poems that weathers even such a thematic oversimplification. Because the incidents of the poem are so graphically rendered, because the rhythms always appropriately intensify the meaning, and because word plays against word with great precision, the reader comes to feel horror, guilt, and compassion, all. This is hardly just an immaculately packaged theme.

Richard Eberhart's "The Fury of Aerial Bombardment" combines the explicit questioning of "In Distrust of Merits" and the unexplained graphic detail of "The U. S. Sailor with the Japanese Skull." It begins with three highly rhetorical quatrains, formal, insistent, and metaphysical. Taking an almost Mosaic stance, Eberhart figuratively breaks the tablets of faith.

> You would think the fury of aerial bombardment
> Would rouse God to relent; the infinite spaces
> Are still silent. He looks on shock-pried faces.
> History, even, does not know what is meant.
>
> You would feel that after so many centuries
> God would give man to repent; yet he can kill
> As Cain could, but with multitudinous will,
> No farther advanced than in his ancient furies.

> Was man made stupid to see his own stupidity?
> Is God by definition indifferent, beyond us all?
> Is the eternal truth man's fighting soul
> Wherein the Beast ravens in its own avidity?

Only the reference to "aerial bombardment" suggests World War II thus far. The poet's purpose is more Miltonic than Mauldinesque. The nature of man and God are questioned rather than the justice or injustice of the war.

The final stanza of the poem abruptly changes the tone. What might have, if continued, become righteous rant is sharply transfigured. The rhetorical questions are answered. The reader is not merely left to assume the questions are just statements in disguise. The poem becomes much more than an impressive way of putting a philosophical dilemma; it becomes a drama in which two different textures pull against each other, the cosmological versus the ordinary, the ageless versus the contemporary, the abstract versus the specific. Each in its own way is part of the other and it is this relationship that gives the poem its meaning as it moves from the infinite spaces of Pascal to the parts of an M1.

> Of Van Wettering I speak, and Averill,
> Names on a list, whose faces I do not recall
> But they are gone to early death, who late in school
> Distinguished the belt feed lever from the belt holding pawl.

One hopes that these three poems by Miss Moore, Mr. Scott, and Mr. Eberhart will represent their considerable achievements. Despite differences in tone and treatment, these poems in a sense define the position of most of the poets of World War II. Each of the poets has clearly been stunned by what the war has revealed about man. The problem is not merely to squash the enemy, the Nazi or totalitarian, but to change the nature of the animal that calls himself a man. This is the poetry of the disenchanted who nevertheless remain idealists.

Their disenchantment is not the disenchantment of the defeated but of the sophisticated. Perhaps there is no more difficult poetry to write than the poetry written in the face of uncertainty, the poetry that attempts to order chaos when the belief in order itself has been threatened.

The temptation when speaking of decades of literature is to emphasize the main currents and trends of each decade without paying enough attention to writers whose work reflects the chief concerns of an earlier decade and foreshadow those of a later one. We tend, therefore, to think of the thirties as the era of depression writers and the forties as the era of war writers. It is merely truism to reflect that condition of the thirties gave rise to the occurrences of the forties, and that there were writers aware of what was coming, war poets before the war. At the same time even after the war had struck there were those writers who continued to put what was happening in the perspective of the depression that had precipitated the crisis.

Muriel Rukeyser exemplifies those who graduated from the depression to the war. She carried the baggage of thirties into the forties; the weight of that baggage intensified her feelings of despair. She fought back, searching for some justification for the way of things, some reason for being, chasing love as if it were the hound of heaven. She sought a reconciliation of horror and hope, trying to "make a way for peace," both personal and social.

> Years of betrayal, million death breeding its weaknesses
> and hope, buried more deep more black than dream.
> Every elegy is the present: freedom eating our hearts,
> death and explosion, and the world unbegun.
> Now burning and unbegun, I sing earth with its war,
> and God the future, and the wish of man.

Often as in these lines from her "Tenth Elegy. Elegy in Joy" she settles it seems for a too easy affirmation, but it is an affirmation come to only after feeling and appraising the worst the world has to offer.

In U. S. 1 (1938) Miss Rukeyser attacked the injustices of industrial society. The poems in this volume are marked by a doctrinaire liberalism much like that of Erskine Caldwell. She asserts the destructiveness of the moneyed interests, and she maintains that change is inevitable. She seems to be suffering from the Wall Street syndrome, noting almost everywhere the factories that "bellow mutilation." These poems of social consciousness are weighted with the images of the ashcan school, of job hunting, neon, young men fleeing from the city.

Instead of the depression leading to the new social order, as she had dreamed, it led to the new global war, to new wounds and greater hurt. And so in "Democritus Laughed" Miss Rukeyser presents the ancient philosopher laughing as he sees his world destroyed. This is a tight, bitter, and ironical poem that seeks to magically destroy the "ghostly vengeance dark at the source." Out of the ashes something better must rise.

Few poets have piled up as many symbols of the world's agony as Muriel Rukeyser. In "Correspondences," spokes of black emanate apocalyptically from Hitler's head, children's games turn into sacrifices, the cities are "high in a boneyard," the sky turns over and the wind turns the stars. In "Black Blood" she says,

> As I ran I heard
> A black voice beating among all that blood:
> Try to live as if there were a God.

Here, as elsewhere, is the embodiment of the fear of the world, a world where there is no peace, but a world which somehow must be transcended, if not by easy faith, at least by courage, love, and poetry. There is, after all, as she points out in "Who In Our Lifetime," always the possibility of courage in the face of desolation, the possibility of a classical dignity in the face of tragedy. And so in "First Elegy . Rotten Lake" she lists love's vulnerable: those lined up at the employment bureau, students taking exams, hungry men and exhausted lovers, all of whom go down to Rotten Lake "hoping for wonders." The lake gives back the reflection of need and weakness. Nevertheless the poem ends with a "private rising," a "ride to survival" . . . "up from dead lakes," as even the weakness that makes war is somehow shed by the phoenix that is man.

For Muriel Rukeyser war presents graphically and concretely those symptoms of the disease man must cure himself of. But most important the poet's response is to insist on the necessity for man to strengthen and remake himself. He must somehow overcome the essential ambiguity of his being, an ambiguity defined in "Second Elegy . Age of Magicians." Images of death and destruction besiege the mind in this poem: "the table of diplomats,/the newsreel of ministers, the paycut slip,/the crushed child's head,/clean steel, factories. . . ." Technology and bureaucracy are the means by which man in the early twentieth century has degraded himself and the world, the means by which the magicians try to lift themselves higher than the world. The consequence of all of this, according to Miss Rukeyser, is that even the avenger must act brutally, that cause and avenger become one. Man is a tree, "half green and half burning."

In many ways, Muriel Rukeyser anticipates poets like Allen Ginsberg, despite the fact that so much of her imagery is plucked from the bag of the thirties. The rush of her language, her refusal to settle for neat symbolistic patterns, the great individual cry against the artificial structures and strictures of civilization, the violence she willingly does to grammar and clear literal sense for the sake of giving vent to emotion, all make her in a sense mother of the Beats. What comes clear in reading her poetry is the way in which World War II provoked her to such overpowering emotions that she was forced to break free from the coercive structures of the symbolist tradition. A symbolist she is in the sense that all poets are, but she undoubtedly felt that the tradition T. S. Eliot had made so academically acceptable, if not popular, could not cope with the feeling she had with absolute chaos so close.

Where does an era begin and end? Only the neatness of numbers determines that we discuss the poetry of the forties or the poetry of the thirties. By the late thirties the possibility of a widespread war had already overshadowed the actuality of widespread depression. And so Josephine Johnson's *Year's End* though it appeared in 1937 probably ought to be thought of as a World War II book rather than as belonging to the pre-war period. *Year's End* reveals how clear the imminence of terror was, how necessary some sort of purification. In "Apostrophe to Truth," the opening poem of the book, Miss Johnson asks for the arrival of Justice. Man, she indicates, must be crucified on the cross of his own achievement. Violence may be the only way in which justice may manifest itself.

Once again one realizes the enormous dilemma faced by the poet. She faces the corruption of man and society and must opt for violence as a source of renewal in the absence of any other reasonable alternative. But the only option is a corruption. A hard choice, but one that must be faced. And so in "But for Ourselves," the references to death are linked to the suggestion that the democracies are unwilling to accept the reality that threatens them.

This is a theme that she returns to often. In "Black Ballad" Satan mixes a "brew of pain." Miss Johnson comments in metaphorical terms on the conditions of man as a heartbreaking decade draws to a disastrous conclusion.

In the 1960's one cannot help but read Miss Johnson's poems in historical and political terms. When she says in "On a Decision" that it is cowardice for civilized man to turn away from all that "justifies his rich inheritance of mind," Chamberlain inevitably comes to mind. When in "The White Spring" she says, "You cannot serve God and the Government simultaneously" not only the New Testament but the destruction of individuality by the totalitarian state immediately suggests itself.

It is of the diminishment of man, the diminishment of the possibilities of civilization, the disminishment of the values and lessons of the past, that Miss Johnson writes. At her best she is not explicit; therefore the poetry that may be viewed from a historical perspective in the sixties continues also to seem surprisingly modern in the sixties:

> The small island is shrunken,
> Year after year the loud sea encroaching,
> Killing the inland grasses, salting the clover.
> Wind warps the pines. The sea storms come inland.
> There is no hollow nor fruit grove from which the high
>   dunes are now hidden.
> The sea storms have wrenched both the corn and wild lilies.
> There is salt in the hill springs; the hill rain is bitter.
> All night you hear the sound of these breakers,
> The black sea, the shark waters moving,
> Poured in, retreating, pounding the beach sand.
> Sound that is suffering and warning. Threat. Lamentation
> Go Inland. Go inland back to the peace groves.
> Go down; through the hill caves.
> Hide. Shut your ears. Shout and sing loudly.
> —The sound is still there.
>
>   (From "The Island")

The excitement of this passage is that it updates Matthew Arnold, even as it echoes him. It may be read in terms of the late thirties and early forties. It also may be read in terms of the new terrors and threats; as a metaphor for the threat of Fascism and the refusal to see the actualities of the Third Reich; as a metaphor for the threat of atomic radiation and the rush to comfortable, padded backyard shelters; or as a metaphor for the threat of internal idiocy that refuses to glance in the rear view mirror for the signs of urban decay just off the throughway that the blindly air conditioned ride in on vinyl hypocrisy until the windshield shatters.

Some readers may complain that such a reading is an unwarranted extension. Josephine Johnson asks for such a reading. She notes the "grease thumbed menus of the world." She weeps for the denial of hope and love. She characterizes those who resist change as blind shepherds, the traditions that merely harness men as ponds of slimy water. She sees the necessity of change, fears the loss of that which gives man reason and dignity. "War is the poverty, and poverty of greed, and greed is of the undisciplined heart. . . ."

It is curious that Josephine Johnson's poetry is hardly mentioned any more, that she is remembered first as a Pulitzer-Prize winning novelist. The tone of her language, the pertinence of her subject matter commend themselves to us still. As a poet she took on the demanding task of facing philosophical, political and physical chaos; and if many of her poems appeared in magazines today one would not be aware that they were written two decades ago.

It is curious, if not really surprising how many women poets of the forties figuratively drafted themselves, feeling perhaps that the sources of life itself were being threatened. In the first section of *Take Them, Stranger*, (1944), Babette Deutsch deals with many of the same themes as her contemporaries. To be sure her voice is different. It is a quiet controlled voice, as a consequence full of an almost terrifying pathos.

Miss Deutsch sees the war as an awful inheritance, "We are haunted by the Roman/Face, ominous and tired. . . ." In the mirror of the past ("Reflection") she sees the causes of violence, authority and the "evasion of the burden of choice." She wonders "if a sandstorm will rise, if the/mirror will crack or the/image break."

But nature, too, is culpable. In "The Gift" she defines the present as a time

> . . . when the mad are free
> To rage, deceive, and rule:
> Sly pupils in the school
> Of nature's treachery.

War is a return to the primeval slime, to a condition that negates the mind and the heart. It is incomprehensible in terms of intellect or feeling. And so in "Flight" she says, after picturing roads "streaming with fugitives," "trains fleeing," and the enemy parachuting into "cities that cannot escape," that the mind and heart, too, attempt to flee from the "meaning/Nobody can guess."

The problem for Babette Deutsch was the problem of how to endure being "whacked over the head" by the past, how to outlive the growth that gnawed Europe like the cancer that had killed Napoleon only literally.

The heart and mind face annihilation. How may they be protected ? In "Carapace" she rejects total defense and isolation. In a poem studded with war images the heart is defended against barbed wire, drowning, the hot ashes of shriveling cities, wounds, and even the chill of fear. But asks the dramatic voice, . . . "who would hear/If once this heart should cry?"

This same pessimistic note is echoed in "The Sick," a poem bereft of solace, in which history lies "in the odor of fresh amputations. . . ." Once again the theme of man's essential illness, so often found in the work of this generation, is reiterated.

This is not to say that Babette Deutsch surrenders. Her advice is clear. Like Marianne Moore she demands that the walls of the world and the spirit be broken down, that man stop seeking to take on "a stature taller than/His simple flesh and bone. . . ." At the same time he must, supported by a fate she maintains has given man "the heart to suffer and endure" despite all, kill the Napoleon "deep in the private breast."

Nevertheless only the mind can preserve man in such circumstances. In "Counsel" Miss Deutsch's advice is direct. In time of war she says, "look hard at joy;" take her image home to the mind's solitude. To be sure there is danger in such advice, the danger of ignoring what cannot be ignored. As she points out in "Dawn in Wartime," one seeing the sunrise "tumbling in like a surf of flowers" may forget the "sore scabby face/Of poverty and war. . . ." The spirt wanders into a brightness of flowered sea images—the poem reemphasizes that there is still a sustaining field of joy that man may draw upon for sustenance.

Marianne Moore, Muriel Rukeyser, Babette Deutch, and Josephine Johnson became participants in the war by acts of the imagination. William Stafford resisted active duty; his resistance was an act of conscience.

Undoubtedly Stafford's feeling that any contribution to war, even to a war as clearly defined as World War II, contributed to the destruction and dehumanization of man led him to serve as a conscientious objector. While Archibald MacLeish was rallying the anti-totalitarian forces in the name of humanity, Stafford was fighting the same fight in the Pacific Northwest, on the forest-fire line.

Stafford has rarely been thought of as a poet of the forties. It was not until late in the 1950's that his first volume of poems appeared. And even then the uniqueness of his voice made him seem young and almost *avant garde*. But it was as a result of his experiences as a conscientious objector, as a result of his arduous contemplation of World War II, that he first came to print. *Down in My Heart*, his master's thesis at the University of Kansas, was released by the Brethren Publishing House in Elgin, Illinois in 1947. The content of the book and the circumstances of its publication make it evident that Stafford's intention was not to seek literary attention but to maintain a position important for the good of the entire society.

Today *Down in My Heart* would be labeled a non-fiction novel. As Stafford says in his acknowledgments, "All incidents are based on fact. . . . I have, however, changed chronology and names, because experience in our program would be considered prejudicial. . . ."

This account has particular relevance today. Stafford's musings, his idealism, his lingering sense of disillusionment with the self-destructive ways of man, his sense of the subtle ironies the larger society ignores, all make *Down in My Heart* as much a book about the circumstances of the 60's as of the forties. Nor have the attitudes Stafford documented changed much.

Down in My Heart is clear, unpretentious, graphic, and rhythmic. It suggests both Robert Frost and Ernest Hemingway. Each chapter of the book begins with a short italic section. Some of these sections are set up as poems. Those that are not might well be considered prose poems. They deal directly and indirectly with violence and the threat of violence, as well as the destruction of innocence.

One of these prose poems is composed of three paragraphs, each equivalent to a stanza. Each stanza characterizes a different C.O. as he contemplates how to react to the threat of a violent mob. Each acts as a foil for the others. George suggests they meet the mob with coffee and cookies, attempt to surprise with friendliness. Larry imagines himself knocking heads with stove wood. Dick thinks of hiding in the brush. He says, "I don't want my death on any man's conscience." The economy and colloquiality of this piece mark all of Stafford's pieces. They are the mark of his later work as well.

The free verse poem that opens the chapter "A Story From the

Social Antennae" again suggests the omnipresence of violence. It does so less directly than the first piece, through the connotations of its images. A man, "casual denim-tiger," walks to supper below wheeling buzzards. He will eat a "casual" supper, maybe the "body of a soft rabbit."

Perhaps the most ironical of poetic vignettes in *Down in My Heart* is the one which describes three forest-fire fighters huddled over a campfire on a ridge above the fire line. Because of the seriousness of the current fire, C.O.'s, state prisoners, and servicemen (not yet shipped out or awaiting discharge) fight it together. Of the three men huddled over the campfire one is a purple heart winner who had killed 53 Japanese in combat. One is a Filipino prisoner who says, "I killed a Jap, too, but I guess it was out of season." The third is "up because he refused to kill the Japs."

Stafford does not comment. The ironic juxtaposition says enough about the ambiguity of violence in the world and the inability of civilized man to deal with it. This is a theme Stafford returns to in the concluding poem in the book, "The End of the War":

> All lost by dusty roads, all fled with love,
> all hid along with play:
> All hurt by what we lost who conquered in the war—
>   so violent, so lost, so far away.

Down in My Heart deserves reprinting not only because it provides us a still relevant view of how war looks to a C.O. but also because it announces an authentic poet whose work continues to be marked by concerns that began during World War II. Stafford continues to hear "the end of things." He continues to examine the world with an unsentimental nostalgia for the possibilities man deprives himself of.

> "Nostalgia," they said, "nostalgia,
> a feeling men have; you will know it, later,
> all your life . . . at dawn, at dusk, in mist . . .
> you and all men, lost, even in sun's brightness."

So he wrote in *Down in My Heart* and so it is in our time.

Robert Lowell's service as a conscientious objector during World War II has become fairly common knowledge. Karl Shapiro, after all, used Lowell as subject matter for a poem that stands as startling evidence of the poet's ability to view circumstances from more than one point of view, standing as it does against the Shapiro poems that grew out of the mud holes of New Guinea. Throughout his now long literary career Lowell has written about war, calling it, in a poem after Rimbaud, "the furnace of affliction." Nor has his conversion from Baroque to Confessional altered the intensity of Lowell's concern. That concern has recently reflected itself in his public and political acts. One of the most internal poets of our time has repeatedly dramatized his opposition to the Viet Nam conflict. One suspects that for Lowell this is really not a contradiction at all; that for him war is a kind of objective correlative, ironical as that term may seem, for the inner dissolution he has so often dealt with.

Perhaps because Lowell himself has been so beset by conflict, struggling to free himself from the name of his past and to resolve his desire to fight fascism (he tried to enlist twice) and his realization of the barbarity of "total war," that the rhythms and overtone themes of so many of his war poems give one an almost physical feel of that exterior conflict he never experienced.

> Now you dive for the global crust.
> How can frail wings and clay
> Beat down the biting dust
> When Christ gives up the Ghost ?
> (from "The Bomber") .

In this early Lowell poem, the bomber is the mechanism that kills God, the sting of war kills Christian principle. The piling up of harsh consonant sounds, the image of the dive (the fall), the suggestion of the shattering of earth (the source of growth) produce terror and tension particularly because of the ambiguity of the last line, a line repeated at the end of each of the poem's three stanzas. Lowell is implying that Christ is dying, that Christ has separated himself from the source of his Godliness, and that Man, made bomber, despite his frailty, destroys the essential and makes the "noonday night."

In other poems, too, such as "On the Eve of the Feast of the Immaculate Conception: 1942" and "The Dead in Europe" Lowell views man devouring himself and his principles; war becomes the embodiment of Satan, a black mass reversing the meaning of the sacraments. "Our sacred earth in our day is our curse." Like Richard Eberhart, Winfield Townley Scott, and Marianne Moore, Lowell locates guilt in the depths unmarked by insignia.

No American Negro has had to experience war in order to understand the nature of suffering. No matter what his economic circumstances or the quality of his achievements he has been blessed by the culture with at least a psychological understanding of the nature of human violence.

It is disconcerting to look at the poems Melvin Tolson wrote during the early forties. One has the sense that fate is a white ironist. The Viet Namese War has often and logically been seen as one of the great hindrances to the improvement of the situation of black Americans. But Tolson views World War II as a fight against the same injustices that threaten the Negro at home.

Of all the American poets who wrote well during the early forties, Tolson is the most explicit and doctrinaire about the war.

> The Nazi knave paraded the Quisling clown
> As quicksands sucked eons of freedoms down.
> Man sits like Rodin's Thinker in the ruins,
> But still he wears the fool's rag-tattered crown.

Although Karl Shapiro celebrated him as one of the really important American poets in a lead article in the Sunday *New York Times*, Tolson has yet to acquire a reputation to match his poetic achievements. His poetry is an odd blend of the erudite and the folk, drawing upon sources as widely disparate as the *Cantos* of Ezra Pound and the voices of Harlem.

Tolson labels man as a "cosmic blunderhead" because he bellies downward only "to glut," because he "diademed the blond Neanderthal" forgetting that all are raked into "the mute democracy of death." But Tolson still believes that the will to live will necessarily doom tyranny.

In *Rendezvous With America* (1944), Tolson relates the war abroad and the war at home. "The Furlough" dramatizes the dilemma of a soldier who returns home and imagines that the worst has happened while he was gone. He describes his woman, probably the symbol of America, as ". . . a passion flower of joy and pain/on the golden bed I came back to possess."

The view in "The Unknown Soldier" differs considerably. The dramatic voice of the poem identifies with American heroes at Concord, Lake Erie, Stony Ridge and Corregidor. The Unknown Soldier insists almost naïvely that he opens "doors to the rights of man" and promises to haunt the world until "the global war becomes a global peace."

The poems that don't try to make the future but respond angrily to the past, seem to me more successful. He attacks the vanity of the Nordic in "The Braggart." After a pious declaration that racism and its consequences are part of "Nature's plan," a big game hunter responds, "I saw a horde/of ants unflesh a lion as he roared." This satisfactorily stills the rhetorical flourish that preceded it.

Although these poems may seem at times simplistic and untutored despite Tolson's wide range of reading, Tolson comes through as a man of range and power, a writer whose dreams and passions are clear, who can be didactic and iconoclastic, sophisticated and terribly idealistic, angry and sentimental.

> He dumped the debris of customs on the refuse heap,
> He tore down fences propped with a great Amen,
> He set apart the huddling goats and sheep,
> He let the oxygen of the freedoms in
>
> (from "The Gallows")

Stanley Kunitz, John Frederick Nims, and Richard Wilbur are all well known as virtuoso technicians, poets who play the game of poetry with remarkable skill and dedication. One ordinarily thinks of them in this regard rather than as poets obsessed by a single subject or point of view. All three, however, were influenced and write about World War II. It is hard to think of any of them as primarily "War" poets, but it is important to recognize that they did respond to the impact of the most important events of the forties, that their technical concerns did not, as too many superficial critics would like us to suppose in the case of subtle craftsmen, force them into a sack of aesthetic irrelevance. There is always an intense sense of order in their poems, even when they deal with the despair and calamity of the disordered world or the disoriented mind.

One respects and admires the skill of a poem like Kunitz's "Careless Love" (with its overtones of the popular music of the period), but at the same time one cannot shed the feeling that Wilfred Owen's "Arms and the Boy" may have had as much influence on the poem as Kunitz's (observation) of the war:

> Who have been lonely once
> Are comforted by their guns.
> Affectionately they speak

To the dark beauty, whose cheek
Beside their own cheek glows.
They are calmed by such repose,
Such power held in hand;
Their young bones understand
The shudder in that frame.
Without nation, without name,
They give the load of love,
And it's returned, to prove
How much the husband heart
Can hold of it; for what
This nymphomaniac enjoys
Inexhaustibly is boys.

Despite the literary influence, "Careless Love" evokes a feeling of illness, of basic forces out of control, of healthy possibilities turned into cancerous realities.

This is a theme that Kunitz often develops in *Passport to the War* (1944). In the opening poem, "Reflections by a Mailbox," he remembers his immigrant parents and the ancient terrors, thinks that the past is only two days away and that the "hunters of man-skins" are at large. The soul, he senses, has "been given to petroleum." He waits for his "passport to the war" and thinks of Pavlov and "sequence, consequence, and again consequence."

The poetry of Stanley Kunitz yokes past and present; the technical pressures he so admirably maintains become a way of hanging on to the fragments of a splintering world. So here we find the history of the melting pot, the ravages of Nazism and history in general, the new and somehow dehumanizing science, Communism and dialectical materialism, as well as the personal dilemma in the face of pressures and trends that seem so many times understandable but uncontrollable.

Kunitz is often ambivalent. In "The Last Picnic" the point of view is one of unalterable pessimism ,". . . we once could say,/ Yesterday we had a world to lose." But in "The Old Clothes Man" "poor blind wounds" are mobilized and the dramatic voice warns proudly, "Let/The enemies of life beware/When these old clothes go forth to war." Although his poems are full of anger and self accusation, he regularly rejuvenates hope in the midst of desolation. And so, although in "The Guilty Man" he says, "None may forgive us for the ancient ways," and in "My Surgeons" portrays the surgeons of his own disillusionment squeezing "the bright liquor of sympathy" from his veins, still he can conclude "My Surgeons," "Yes, I believe in love."

For John Frederick Nims, World War II was another reason for doubting the ability of man to comprehend man. In his introduction to the selection of his poems in *Five Young American Poets* (New Directions, 1944) he said, "I don't understand . . . mankind . . ., The Chartres-erecting, Negro-slugging, pup-caressing monster." Like Kunitz, Nims is an intellectual caught between his hopes and admiration for man, his fears and disdain. Often he seems to mock his own swings of attitude. So in "Apocalypse,"

> But some in the bland spectacle of learning
> With holywater sponge the blood away,
> See pie in the sky and chortle hallalujah,
> Yoo-hoo the silver lining, the new day.

Ordinarily Nims deals with the war only indirectly, drawing upon it for images and metaphors to illuminate other subjects. This is the kind of thing he does in "Madrigal" in which an image of the war dead is thrown up to sharpen the parting of lovers whose love has been cheapened by haste and fear. And so, too, in "Wreck" the dramatic voice lies in a hotel surrounded by the "submarine dark" of the Wyoming night and thinks of his hospitalized "darling." His blood seems to cry, "Like fugitives rocked in a raided town by night."

The more explicit war poems often operate in the opposite way. They introduce images of peace as foils for the subject. In "Shot Down at Night," Nims elegizes a young pilot, a former student who wrote neat themes. Most of the poem recounts the innocent days, the images carefully ordered to suggest only by the most delicate nuances the boy's fate over the desert.

The images of the pleasures of peace add pathos to the death of the pilot in "Shot Down at Night." But in "Singapore" images drawn from the same sources come to suggest an arrogant naïvete'. An "elegant captain of colonials" assumes a god-like posture, certain of the invulnerability of his defenses:

> In linen leisure he invented pingpong
> And fussed to birth concoction in tall glasses;
> Discovered tennis wile and chukker ruses
> But not the way to keep a city safe.

At the end of the poem the captain is wreathed by "The silver gut of boys, by bayonet culled;/The blood-bright hair of maidens in the dust."

The war seemed to shock Nims to a recognition of startling opposites. As he says in "Colt Automatic,"

> My heart (the lover of song and girls once)
> Having surveyed the season, takes a new friend,
> Sees at the belt a rare and terrible angel.

Later poems by John Nims and Stanley Kunitz, of course, reflected the war, too, both directly and indirectly. No poet survived the holocaust only to forget; necessarily one unearths, reflects, reconsiders. The war's total poetic impact is, therefore, impossible to ascertain especially because of the way in which the poetic imagination operates, transfiguring and transmuting the stuff of experience, often disguising it, often unaware of its sources.

Of the many poets whose reputations were made after the war, Richard Wilbur may be the best. His first book, *The Beautiful Changes,* appeared in 1947. Because Wilbur is one of the best poets of the decade and because some of these post war poems remind us that no war ever really ends, it may be worthwhile to mention Wilbur here. One suspects that the immaculate handling of violence in Wilbur's ballad "Tywater" may well be his attempt to deal with those disconcerting memories I mentioned. The poem deftly plays the theme of violence against the theme of repose. The figure may be literary but the violence theme (*charred, clotted, knife, punch, gritted, hit, clumsy*) might well do justice to a more explicit rendering of the early forties. As if to make that point clear, the next poem in the book is "Mined Country." In it Wilbur says, ". . . it's going to be long before/Their war's gone for good." He goes on to remind us that "Danger is sunk in the pastures, the woods are sly,/Ingenuity's covered with flowers!"

In "On the Eyes of an SS Officer" Wilbur identifies his horror less delicately: "I ask my makeshift God of this/My opulent bric-a-brac earth to damn his eyes." In "Place Pigalle" the dramatic voice speaks out of the confusion of the war as he embraces a prostitute:

> "Girl, if I love thee not, then let me die;
> Do I not scorn to change my state with kings?
> Your much touched flesh, incalculable, which wrings

> Me so, now shall I gently seize in my
> Desperate soldier's hands which kill all thing."

In "The Peace of Cities" the Luftwaffe wafts "what let the sunshine in." Repeatedly Wilbur mixes peace and war, love and hate, the innocent and the destructive. Each alters and intensifies our view of the other, giving us the sense of the world's irony and the difficulty of coming to easy meaning.

Three poets encountered the war more directly and write about it more vividly in the literal sense than any of those mentioned so far. Other poets dealt with here served in the armed forces, but these three served up front. A great deal has been written about the war poems of John Ciardi, Randall Jarrell and Karl Shapiro. Only synecdoche is possible here. They were the combat poets; they looked at the actual possibility of death, wondered between missions or patrols if the poem forming in the mind would ever be completed. The war didn't make them poets, but it rushed them into maturity.

Karl Shapiro's *Person, Place and Thing* (1942) thrust him on the literary scene and made him famous. It was followed by "V-Letter" (1944). In his introduction to the "V-Letter" poems,—almost all written in Australia or New Guinea—he says, "I have tried to be a guard against becoming a 'war poet'. . . . There is no need to discuss the private psychological tragedy of a soldier. It is not the commonplace of suffering or the platitudinous comparison with the peace, or the focus on the future that should occupy us; but the spiritual progress or retrogression of the man in war, the increase or decrease in his knowledge of beauty, government and religion. . . . We learn finally that if war can teach anything it can teach humility; if it can test anything it can test externality against the soul."

That old commonplace about poets always lying about their own work might well be unearthed here. What Shapiro says in his introduction is only half so. The tragedy of the soldier (but not only) is dramatized in poems like "Aside," "Troop Train," "Full Moon: New Guinea," "The Leg," "V-Letter," "Elegy for a Dead Soldier," "Nostalgia," and "A Cut Flower." In "Elegy for a Dead Soldier," for example, he writes:

> By chance I saw him die, stretched on the ground,
> A tattooed arm lifted to take the blood
> Of someone else sealed in a tin. I stood

During the last delirium that stays
The intelligence a tiny moment more,
And then the strangulation, the last sound.
The end was sudden, like a foolish play,
A stupid fool slamming a foolish door,
The absurd catastrophe, half-prearranged,
And all the decisive things still left to say.
So we disbanded, angrier and unchanged,
Sick with the utter silence of dispraise.

No reader I know would insist that the tragedy of the soldier, psychological and otherwise, is not dealt with here. No reader would make light of the suffering so intensely underlined by the series of pauses as the soldier dies. Nor is this stanza just one isolated example of a Shapiro passage that contradicts his introduction.

Nevertheless, this is more than just a war poem in the sense that term so often signifies. It does more than identify the absurdity of the glorification of war. It brings into question the logic of life and man; it refuses to honor mindlessly, even while it feels intensely. "Elegy for a Dead Soldier" puts this dramatized moment in a larger context, but at the same time demands its individual importance. Much of the poem discusses the social, political, and psychological forces that lead to individual tragedy. Shapiro comes to no doctrinaire conclusion but to a hope:

> . . . if you can lift your eyes
> Upon a peace kept by a human creed,
> Know that one soldier has not died in vain.

Unfortunately the triteness of the phrasing in this epitaph leads one to believe that Shapiro felt the inadequacy of such a resolution. Today the only satisfactory reading may well be an ironical one. Nevertheless, the real force of the poem remains undiminished and the insights into the workings of American society, into the system we have so often become victims instead of masters of, are apparent. Like many other Shapiro poems "Elegy for a Dead Soldier" speaks to us in our current circumstances with a clarity few of the poems written today can match.

Despite the fact that Karl Shapiro has revolted from the tight forms he worked in during the forties, maintaining it seems that they silence the eloquence of the personality wandering through the substrata, the style of *V-Letter* and *Person, Place, and Thing* immediately identified Shapiro the man. But style turns Shapiro into more than a single soldier at war, into man confronting history, madness, and a contradictory universe.

> Laughter and grief join hands. Always the heart
> Clumps in the breast with heavy stride;
> The face grows lined and wrinkled like a chart,
> The eyes bloodshot with tears and tide.
> Let the wind blow, for many a man shall die.

The development and changes in the poetry of Karl Shapiro's poetry, the influence of his aesthetics on his techniques, the way in which single poems register, certainly merits a number of volumes, not just a few paragraphs of approval.

Evidence of a poet's stature comes really not from critics, however, but from the gestures and responses of the listening but untutored audience. Shapiro's poems still reach that audience. The first poem the public encountered in *Person, Place, and Thing* was "Scyros," a poem that undoubtedly would be labeled "psychedelic" today, an unpunctuated group of highly symbolic and disorienting images revealing the nature of modern war while implying many of the causes, a poem in which images of innocence and barbarity are mixed on a global scale. Recently I read this to a group of the draft-eligible. Here's the first stanza:

> The doctor punched my vein
> The captain called me Cain
> Upon my belly sat the sow of fear
> With coins on either eye
> The President came by
> And whispered to the braid what none could hear

They were startled. Someone knew what it was all about. They asked who the poet was, certain he was one of their generation.

Between missions as a gunner, John Ciardi played poker and wrote poems. He learned the game of survival, reminded himself of the joys of the ordinary. His poems and his career attest to both his pragmatism and his feeling. Unlike Karl Shapiro he makes no protestations that reporting the responses of the individual in combat has little significance. *Other Skies* (1947), his first book after the war documents many of those responses. But these are not poems of self-pity or cool analysis. They share the pressures of

dislocation, the loss of what one loves, the constant possibility of
the extinction of self. So in "Suddenly Where Squadrons Turn"
he notes,

> Here across the iron sky
> Iron squadrons simplify:
> We must stay alive.

Guilt is one of the inheritances of that struggle to stay alive. "The
Innocent keep other skies," says Ciardi. In "Take-Off Over Kansas"
he dramatizes a moment of such realization.

> What shall the guns think when a shadow spans
> The digits of a sight, and triggers move ?
> Was any human part in the machine
> That left its smoke to show which way it dove ?
> You only see the first plume and first fall.
> You think, "It was not human after all."
> Once past the sight of faces, where they fade
> Immeasurably back to field and seed,
> Only arithmetic and scattered cloud
> Stay whole above the thundering of speed.
> And someone's voice crackling the interphone,
> That later you remember was your own.

These two stanzas clearly foreshadow those profound comments of
today's sociologists and political commentators. How long it has
taken public spokesman to learn that the technology that makes
possible murder at a distance increases the chances of man's extinction. It does so because it encourages the elimination of human
feeling. How long it has taken for us to learn that men become
their weapons more and more as they retreat from the sight of
each other's blood.

John Ciardi does not denigrate the personal view, but he provides insights that have more than personal significance, insights
come to earlier and more meaningfully than by logic or research.

The ways of survival are many, physical, psychological, moral.
To experience any of these is to enhance one's own chances. Ciardi
offers his readers such opportunities, often in odd ways, in the
ambiguity of a "drawn-out bedroom joke" at the end of "Death of
a Bomber" or in the irony of the blind hope at the end of "Port
of Aerial Embarkation." Recognition of the ways of survival

58

matters, but Ciardi does not forget to remind us of the consequences:

> Now, our intentions bloodied late by need,
> We sit our jungles hemispheres apart; . . .
> And death run loose like shadows in a wind
> On all the reasoned motions of the mind.
> (from "Poem for my Twenty-Ninth Birthday")

Perhaps the best known of Ciardi's war poems is "Elegy Just in Case," in which he contemplates his own death, at first almost mockingly, and moves to the mystery behind all personal loss, a mystery really always present in the insistent sombreness of a trochaic drumbeat.

When the mystery is removed and man becomes mere instrument, danger is most imminent. In *Live Another Day* (1949) the civilian professor views his student reservists:

> I know that boy. Six friendly days in tweed
> He carries books and answers from his desk
> Whatever meaningless questions I might ask,
> But this one day is uniforms and speed
> In the reserve of death, whose metal voice
> Answers no questions, whose command
> Is wired by reflex to his hand
> Where only earphones name a moral choice.
> (from "Sunday Afternoon Near the Naval Air Base")

Ciardi has written too many war poems to recount here. But almost always the intention is the same, to provide as completely and immediately as possible a sense of responding to and dealing with the many pressures of war, sometimes successfully, sometimes not so. Success may come in many ways; failure, too. This is what we see in "The Pilot in the Jungle," "Letter from a Rubber Raft," and "On a Photo of Sgt. Ciardi a Year Later." Read in these terms the celebration of "V-J Day" is not extravagant; it combines the sadness of memory and the wisecrack of reality with the joy of release.

As much as any of the other poets dealt with here, John Ciardi has remembered the lessons of World War II and continued to explicate them. He has taken the trip back often, in poems like "A Box Comes Home," and "At a Concert of Music, Remembering the Dead in Korea." But he has done more than sport the poetic medals of a veteran. He has looked directly at himself and his past, contemplated the personal man and the personal imagination. In "Island Galaxy" (*In the Stoneworks*, 1961) he leads us back to what may seem at first an insignficant observation of his war years, then turns this observation into the apprehension of incomprehensible and universal forces he can only survive by shaping them to a poem.

AN ISLAND GALAXY

Once on Saipan at the end of the rains
I came on a flooded tire rut in a field
and found it boiling with a galaxy
of pollywogs, each millionth micro-dot
avid and home in an original swarm.

For twenty yards between the sodden tents
and a coral cliff, a universe ran on
in a forgotten dent of someone's passing.
Clusters and nebulae of whirligigs
whorled and maddened, a burst gas of life

from the night hop of unholdable energy.
Did one frog squatting heavy at the full
of its dark let out this light, these black rapids
inside the heart of light in the light-struck dent
of the accidental and awakened waters ?

There on the island of our burning, in man's place
in the fire-swarm of war, and in a sunburst
lens, I stood asking—what ? Nothing.
Universes happen. Happen and are come upon.
I stood in the happening of an imagination.

Ten days later, having crossed two seas,
I passed that rut again. The sun had burned
the waters back to order. The rut lay baked.
Twenty upthrust shoreline yards of time
slept in the noon of a finished imagination.

And the bed and the raised faces of the world
lay stippled with the dry seals of the dead,
black wafers with black ribbons, as if affixed
to a last writ, but with such waste of law,
I could not read its reasons for its proofs.

"The Death of the Ball Turret Gunner" by Randell Jarrell is probably the most often quoted poem to come out of the war:

> From my mother's sleep I fell into the State,
> And I hunched in its belly till my wet fur froze.
> Six miles from earth, loosed from its dream of life,
> I woke to black flak and the nightmare fighters.
> When I died they washed me out of the turret with
> a hose.

There are a number of reasons for the power of the poem: the indirection of the last line which only magnifies one's feelings of revulsion, the onomatopoetic internal rhyme of the fourth line, the telescoping of symbolic metaphors with which the poem begins, and the shift from diptic lines to a single, flat, final fact. This poem suggests the loss of love and security, the victimization of the individual by the society, and the drowning of feeling in mechanics.

Jarrell's best poems generally are loaded with the concrete stuff of war. The details have a force of their own; they undoubtedly bring back graphically memories of a generation of servicemen: "In bombers named for girls, we burned/The cities we had learned about in school —" So he writes in "Losses," a poem full of ironic juxtapositions which make us feel the distraughtness of the dramatic voice at the end of the poem:

> But the night I died I dreamed that I was dead,
> And the cities said to me: "Why are you dying?
> We are satisfied, if you are; but why did I die?"

In "Eighth Air Force," too, Jarrell does more than revitalize the ordinary detail whose meaningfulness may have been overlooked. He moves from images of a puppy lapping water, a sergeant shaving, and "murderers" yawning between missions, to the crucifixion as the dramatic voice alludes to Pilate.

> This a war. . . . But since these play, before they die,
> Like puppies with their puppy; since, a man,
> I did as these have done, but did not die—
> I will content the people as I can
> And give up these to them: Behold the man!

What we are left with is more than a scene but a sense of guilt and the attempt to resolve that guilt. The allusion transposes the question across time. In "Second Air Force" ("The years meant

this?), "Mail Call" ("The letters always just evade the hand."),
'Siegfried" ("*—What will you do now? I don't know—*"), and
numerous other poems, Jarrell leads us to the overwhelming
question, "Why?" If it is not stated overtly, it is implied. If it is
not implied, we are often left in a silence that forces us to ask it.
So at the end of "A Camp in the Prussian Forest" as an American
soldier laughs hysterically over the new graves of concentration
camp Jews:

> I laugh aloud
> Again and again;
> The star laughs from its rotting shroud
> Of flesh. O star of men!

The same question is come to far less reverently in "Gunner."
The poem concludes:

> And the world ends here, in the sand of a grave,
> All my wars over? . . . It was easy as that!
> Has my wife a pension of so many mice?
> Did the medals go home to my cat?

To be sure Jarrell deals with many other themes, but returns
always to ask why of war and man. He does so, it seems to me,
more often, more insistently, with greater feelings of guilt and
doubt, than any of the other poets of his generation. He may not
be the best of these poets, but he sounded the keynote of all their
concerns most emphatically.

Wilfred Owen made it insufficient for the poets of World War
II only to dramatize in a more modern way the truth of General
Sherman's crisp summation, "War is hell." Many, of course, provided new evidence to substantiate that cliché. They recounted
the new kinds of punishment man had devised for himself and the
altered form of the inferno. But they took on a much heavier load.
It is only rarely that they dealt with the political-historical causes
of the conflict. There was no need for them to compete with what
was so widely broadcast. They took in effect a Danteesque journey,
a journey through the battlefields of the world and the battle-
grounds of self. They sought to finally achieve at least Purgatory
if not Paradise, stung by the notion that only by showing man
at his worst could he be led to some sort of fulfillment. It seems
not strange but appropriate that one of them, John Ciardi, should
have become his time's foremost translator of Dante.

Drama:
The War Play Comes of Age

by Jordan Y. Miller

The very heart of tragedy is the *agon,* or argument, and all the textbooks constantly remind us that conflict is the fundamental basis of drama. What better source of argument, of conflict, than war, surely the subject to offer the best in dramatic potential. Moreover, the possibilities of high theatricality would seem endless.

However, most of what we see on stage concerning warfare from the ancient classics to the beginnings of contemporary realism is hardly about war, as such, at all. Gods and heroes, sometimes performing their alarums and excursions, sometimes not, are the subjects of most plays. Little concern is paid to the fighting except for certain spectacular displays of theatrical techniques which more often than not are ends in themselves. The effects of war upon the ordinary men who do the fighting are generally of little importance to the writer. Warfare is conveyed as something with formal, even dignified rules. Those best qualified to conduct war are, of course, the properly commissioned gentlemen, the officers, whose skill and gallantry must remain unquestioned. Wars are won, to be sure, on the playing fields of Eton, or at least Sandhurst, St. Cyr, or West Point. Until the unimaginable carnage of the First World War shocked playwrights out of their timeless romanticizing of combat, the drama in English made little effort to do other than it always had, remaining constantly detached, almost aloof, from the real meaning of war's pointless horrors and fundamental inhumanity.

Plays on the subject of war have existed on the American stage since before the Revolution, although very few from any era have been noted for significant dramatic or literary value. As a type, the American war play has passed through three phases which I choose to call, however artlessly, childhood, adolescence, and maturity. Oversimplified and unoriginal as these labels may seem, they accurately reflect the development of the war play from a certain naive and artificial innocence into a highly sophisticated exploration of war's effects on the men who fight it.

André, William Dunlap's 1798 discussion of the Benedict Arnold treason, is difficult to read today with any sense of objectivity, so patently ridiculous does it seem by current standards. The war itself seldom intrudes, acknowledged, when the characters do discuss it, as a fine and noble struggle. Platitudes roll from the mouths of all, especially The General, a noble officer indeed, who must stand on principle and hang the spying Major André while through several acts the hysterical, near mutinous Capt. Bland pleads desperately that his heroic British enemy be given a gentleman's death before a firing squad. Instead of a war play, *André* is almost a homily on how good men should behave in war, practicing the rules of decorum while demonstrating a certain gracious concern for the enemy. The real meaning of war to the large numbers of men involved in it remains ignored.

The two best representatives of Civil War drama are Bronson Howard's *Shenandoah* of 1888 and William Gillette's *Secret Service* of 1895. The child is growing up; the petulant displays of Dunlap's posturing characters have disappeared. The war now reflected is a devastating full-scale national ordeal, fought by tremendous citizen armies. Casualties are on a scale never before experienced anywhere, and the conclusion brings annihilation to the losing side. Yet neither playwright can escape the ancient assumption that it is only the officers who count and only their gallantry which matters.

Howard places his war in a grandstand. It becomes a circus of trained men and beasts, witnessed and commented upon by ladies of both allegiances spending a social visit together at a country home in the Shenandoah valley. The war goes on around them; their men meet, wound, and capture each other upon the battlefield; and the Army of the Potomac moves back and forth across the stage in retreat and victory. After the conflict has ended and enmities are forgotten, only a profligate son who has redeemed himself in heroic deeds and a rascally turncoat spy have died. Nobody who matters has suffered much of anything. Gillette, however, provides quite another story, and his play can still be acted with good effect if one will admit to certain of its arbitrary conventions. Practically every melodramatic situation known to nineteenth-century drama is encountered before the final curtain. There are secret messages, fugitives hiding behind curtains, desperate hand-to-hand encounters, a spy who shoots himself to avoid detection, and an impossible last minute reprieve. The scene most difficult to take seriously requires the spy-hero, Capt. Dumont/Thorne, to inform the sergeant of the guard charged with his execution that his loving lady friend has removed the charges from the firing squad's guns. Such is the behavior of an officer and a gentleman.

But the war is much closer in *Secret Service* than in its predecessors. We are in the midst of besieged Richmond, where the action is tense and convincingly foreboding. Men are actually fighting, getting shot, and risking their lives in desperate attempts to save themselves and their armies. Though Capt. Dumont/Thorne's description of his job as a spy in the Secret Service becomes too lyrically romantic, we know that what he does is dirty work and that war is a very special hell. This is the first time in an American war play wherein we can find some recognition, however slight, that glory and noble deeds are not everything.

The first soldier in American literature to suggest the genuine article appears not in a play but in a book. He is Henry Fleming of Stephen Crane's *The Red Badge of Courage*. As he loses all of his illusions, he learns that war is a frightening, filthy, nauseous business that kills and disfigures, with very little nobility involved. Heroism, yes, but heroism of a sort that Henry discovers can never be imagined, only experienced. By telling us that soldiers do not really want to die, and that the glories of combat are a slanderous fiction, Crane opens new paths in the literature of war that lead to a rapid "growing up" into that period of adolescence where the innocence of childhood is abandoned and the more sophisticated outlook of adulthood is in sight.

In 1924 the shouting, cursing, blood-and-filth smeared shocker, *What Price Glory?* by Laurence Stallings and Maxwell Anderson blasted off the American stage once and for all every previous concept of stage warfare. The inconceivable frightfulness of a conflict that bogged down millions of men who machine-gunned millions more over a square mile of mud held little room for gallant "gentlemen." The Capt. Flaggs and the Sgt. Quirts curse and fight and fornicate along with their men, share their slimy infested dugouts and curse the high brass who wouldn't know a war if they saw it. It is a hideous, blasphemous, obscene world that *What Price Glory?* shows its audience.

What Price Glory? has its flaws, of course, displaying as it does a certain romantic attitude toward the heroic doughboy. He uses dirty language, and he has some brute instincts, but there will always be the wounded Quirts stumbling out into the street to follow their outfits back to the front, shouting "Hey, Flagg, wait for baby!" *What Price Glory?* was also badly needed, the first play to come close to achieving Crane's accomplishment in the novel: the serious exploration of what happens in the minds and souls of men who must perform the most appalling deeds and live the most violent, painful lives so abhorrent to their essential nature because they have no choice. *What Price Glory?* gives us a prolonged look at what occurs when all the appeals to patriotism, flag, home, and mother become irrelevant.

The better war plays of the 1940's, though disappointingly few in total number, follow the lead of *What Price Glory?* as they turn for their primary dramatic source to the individual human being who is forced to exist under war's inhuman tensions. Realizing, however, that the scope of the conflict is global, with soldier and noncombatant alike facing a violent death under conditions incapable of being transcribed onstage, the writers of the few excellent war dramas make no effort to create a product resembling the impressive but somehow overdone *What Price Glory?* War has become everybody's immediate business, instead of something "Over There," where democracy is being saved and Lafayette repaid. A viable stage product must now be more honest, more serious, and more mature.

On November 3, 1939, when Clare Boothe's *Margin for Error* opened in New York, the Second World War was hardly three months old. It was in its stalemated "phony" stage, and America stood firm behind neutrality, confident that the old allies of Britain and France would take the measure of the man with the funny mustache. Miss Boothe's play, called the first "genuine" play about the war, is subtitled "a satirical melodrama," purporting, if one is to believe the eulogistic foreword written by her husband, Henry Luce, to go all out in taking care of the monstrous Thousand Year Reich by laughing it to death. The trouble with *Margin for Error* is that the melodrama takes over and the satire is reduced to a one-man show involving the amusing Jewish policeman whose sleuthing procedures are straight out of the Agatha Christie or *Thin Man* tradition. The last act, with all suspects gathered on-stage, seems almost a parody, closely reminiscent of the methods of Fred Allen's old time radio detective, One Long Pan, who was constantly forced to "le-enact clime" in order to get to the bottom of things. Sure enough, after a complex series of guesses and assumptions, the truth is out, but with a twist. Nobody did it; the victim, the detested German consul, did himself in by virtue of accidental suicide.

Miss Boothe has little need for, and does very little to create, a single noteworthy characterization. Baumer, the arrogant shaven-headed Nazi consul, is the stereotyped Eric von Stroheim man we love to hate. He deserves to die, and he does. The American Nazi, Horst, is an ignorant fool, marked for death by the men who direct the very system he so enthusiastically embraces. Max von Alvenstor, Baumer's aide, doomed because of his Jewish grand-mother, is a "good" Nazi and little more. Dr. Jennings is a pitiful dime-a-dozen refugee out of any Grade B movie. Sophie, Baumer's wife, who hates her husband and all he stands for, and Denny, the American she loves, have little to offer. The "first genuine war play" is nothing but a routine meller wherein the bad guys wear swastikas instead of black hats, and the good guys are everybody else.

On April 29, 1940, Robert E. Sherwood offered the first play to involve the fighting itself, and we can say that the "mature" treatment of the theme of war has begun. We are still not directly involved with the central struggle on the continent, but instead with Finland's brief but fierce sideline war with Russia. Nonetheless, Sherwood's dramatic view of war has begun to outgrow the adolescence of Stallings and Anderson's approach.

The contrast between *Margin for Error* and *There Shall Be No Night* is the difference between a stagey invention for melodramatic effect and a stageworthy investigation into the thoughts and actions of a people grossly underequipped for the unequal war they must fight. There is no question but that it must be fought, with the final catastrophe a foregone conclusion, but Sherwood skillfully avoids the routine melodramatics and sentimentalities which the situation could easily entertain. Instead, he shows with compassionate effect the terrible ironies of a peaceful nation driven to defend itself as a matter of honor against its giant of a neighbor. One might accuse Sherwood of making his Valkonen family too good, or his Nazi Ziemssen too frightfully chilling. His strongest point is, however, that he refuses to surrender to hysteria or mere sensation. He is able to draw an effective picture of a group of decent human beings compelled to act against nature, but unable to do anything else and still call themselves men. The adaptability and universality of Sherwood's theme are shown by the easy transfer of the play's setting to Greece, once the Finnish war was over, without significant alteration or loss of impact. In its Greek form it was successfully toured by the Lunts, who had originated it, through wartime England after the close of the New York run.

By the end of 1940 Hitler had stunned the world by slipping Norway and Denmark into his pocket, polishing off France, and stripping England down to a preposterously outnumbered air force and Winston Churchill's rhetoric. America looked on with awe, still hid behind the shield of neutrality, and tried to act as though everything would somehow come out all right. Only a handful of American plays pertinent to the war were produced between December 1940 and October 1942, although a few imports from England of the chin-up, carry-on variety represented by *The Wookey* in September 1941, and *Heart of a City* the following February came, failed dismally, and vanished.

The first American effort of the period, Elmer Rice's *Flight to the West,* appeared on December 30, 1940. It was hailed as one of the season's most important and timely plays. It had a highly realistic setting by Jo Mielziner, representing the interior of a Pan American Clipper (how pleasant, luxurious, and quaintly leisurely it appears today!), and it starred the talented Betty Field. But *Flight to the West* is no more a war play than *Margin for Error.* Again relying on overt melodramatics, it is too reminiscent of the old thriller, *Subway Express,* with its murder in a simulated subway car. The striking illusionistic set is half the show. The war is present in the sinister background of Europe succumbing to the Nazis, and so provides all the proper motivations, but within the narrow limits of the Clipper's cabin the thirteen passengers and three crew members enact a familiar story of good and evil that might as well have taken place inside a careening stagecoach as in this lumbering flying boat.

As soon as the *dramatis personae* are introduced the action and its outcome are easily predictable. Count Vronoff, the German spy headed for the U. S. mainland to wreak havoc among the shipyards of San Francisco, will certainly be exposed. He is. Hermann Walther, spouting all the Nazi clichés, and Frau Rosenthal, the Jewish refugee, will undoubtedly clash in violent debate on matters of racial superiority. They do. Marie Dickensen, fleeing the Germans with blinded husband and lovely little daughter, will do something drastic, like shooting somebody. She does. The tall Texan, Col. Gage, bumbling and loud mouthed, will be the embarrassingly unfunny funny man. He is. The charming newlyweds, Charles and Hope Nathan, on their way to home and safety, will probably get hurt by becoming involved in something dangerous. It happens. And finally, Howard Ingraham, the economic idealist with all the answers, who knows everything wrong about democracy and everything right about "orderly" systems such as National Socialism, will eventually suffer some kind of trauma and discover that the German way is wrong after all. And that's precisely what occurs.

Rice's most effective point comes at the end as the shocked Ingraham, facing the cold rationality of the German mind, discovers why he is wrong. The occasion for his change is the climactic facedown which sees Charles Nathan take the bullet fired at Walther by the enraged Marie Dickensen. The idea that Nathan's deed in leaping in front of the gun was a naturally humane act is incomprehensible to Walther's Nazi rationale. When asked if he has no sense of gratitude at being saved, even by a Jew, Walther can only spout nonsense about Nathan's irrationality in terms of mental debilitation from overexposure to liberalism and democracy, a form of "biological retrogression." Had Nathan been trained "to function logically, instead of being warped by the corrosive philosophy of liberalism and the insidious poisons of Jewish mysticism," says Walther, he would have permitted his enemy to die. That is about all that Rice has to say. Suspenseful theatre, not particularly original drama, and not much of a "war" play.

The following April 1, 1941, Lillian Hellman's *Watch on the Rhine* met three times the success of Rice's play if length of run is significant. But more than that, Miss Hellman's thematic development compares favorably with Sherwood's in its quiet revelation of the horrors of Naziism through a demonstration of what it can do to individuals of honesty and integrity who choose to engage in warfare against it, while remaining far from the battlefield itself. The underground nature of that particularly nasty kind of war makes the complacent isolation of America's myopic view of the conflict all the more shameful. Miss Hellman's refugee family are decent peaceful people, themselves repelled by violence, but coldly determined to wage their part of the battle vigorously, inviting death, and worse, all along the way. At the end of *Watch on the Rhine,* unlike *Flight to the West,* things do not "come out all right" with villains arrested and heroes sure to survive. Nothing can possibly "come out" in Miss Hellman's play, so long as Hitler's Germany, though thousands of miles away, can enter the comparative safety of an American home and leave its inhabitants so profoundly shaken.

Miss Hellman chooses in most instances to underplay, rather than overplay, and she makes good use of her fine sense of dramatic construction. Fanny Farrelly, the dowager Washingtonian in whose house all action takes place, is perhaps too much of a stereotype, and perhaps the learning of her lesson is too pat. She is often painfully close to the archetypal stage mother-in-law, spoiled, rich, and always in the way, but fortunately the playwright knows enough to keep her more or less on the sidelines. One might also accuse the refugee villain Tech de Brancovis of being too obviously sinister, but within the framework of the plot, he fits acceptably.

It is the Müller family, conceived in Miss Hellman's best style, who force the realization that this is a war play. She has created a charming family unit of amusing, if somewhat wondrous wise children, and attractive three-dimensional adults. It would have been an easy task to turn the plight of these attractive intelligent people into a sentimental tear-stained exposé of the horror of their situation, but the playwright refuses to become entrapped. These five, parents and children alike, are the combatants, and their battlefield is wherever they are, even in America. Their fight is constant and deadly, with quarter neither given nor asked. The more the shock, then, when this group, apparently secure at last, are again torn apart by the warring forces which have hounded them; the stoic calm of the family under these horrendous pressures makes fine drama. The impact of the audience's realization that the tolerant, honest, and respectable father is, when necessary, a coolly efficient killer who acts in order that his kind of honesty and respectability can endure, is devastating. Like Sherwood's Finns, these representatives of humane decencies who must function as savages in a world gone wildly awry are superb creations. War's ultimate meaning is stronger here than in any amount of noise of battle or slime of simulated trenches. Compared to the contrivances of *Flight to the West, Watch on the Rhine* is a superior work of art.

In 1941 Maxwell Anderson, who would write one of the best and one of the worst of the decade's war plays, composed a romantic love story with the war as a background called *Candle in the Wind,* starring Helen Hayes, which opened on October 22. This distinguished actress was forced to appear in a slow and talky play concerning the desperate attempts of the heroine, Madeleine, to free her French naval officer sweetheart from the Gestapo. The audience quickly learns that she will fail and fail and fail and be betrayed and betrayed and betrayed. It is all hardly worth the saying, even though Raoul, the lover, does eventually escape and flee, we assume, to fight another day. If only the characterizations could amount to what Lillian Hellman accomplishes in *Watch on the Rhine,* or what Anderson himself is capable of doing. Madeleine and Raoul, when compared to Anderson's Miriamne and Mio of *Winterset,* for instance, are sadly inferior creations. The intrusion of two touring American old maid schoolteachers is, moreover, simply ludicrous. The war brings suffering, but somehow these cardboard lovers bring very little of the realization of its meaning in the way that Hellman earlier had done and Anderson later was to do.

By the second week of January 1942 *Candle in the Wind* had closed. Not until John Steinbeck's adaptation of his own novel, *The Moon Is Down,* opened on April 7 was the war a subject of any play worthy of attention. For less than a month during the Christmas season something called *Letters to Lucerne* by a Viennese named Fritz Rotter introduced the opening days of the war into a Swiss girls' school peopled by young female European nationals who suddenly see old friends as new enemies. In *The Man with the Blond Hair* Norman Krasna told of the "democratization" of two escaped German aviators in the home of a New York Jewish girl. It quickly faded away.

In terms of dramatic values, *The Moon Is Down* is in a class with *There Shall Be No Night* or *Watch on the Rhine,* but surprisingly enough it met with less public acceptance than Anderson's *Candle in the Wind.* Perhaps, only four months after Pearl Harbor, the plight of a small village in Scandinavia was too remote. Perhaps, had it presented a less sympathetic attitude toward the enemy (which, for some strange reason, is never specified as German), it would have done better. Still, Steinbeck's picture of the totalitarian mind is much more convincing than Anderson's Gestapo officer from *Candle in the Wind* or Miss Boothe's Prussian consul of *Margin for Error*. We are probably closer, instead, to the icy rationale of Rice's Walther in *Flight to the West,* for Steinbeck's Col. Lauser cannot overcome his inability to understand why a free spirit will not be subdued by executing hostage after hostage, even unto the mayor himself. What makes Steinbeck's Germans more sympathetic than audiences might prefer is his picture of their fight to maintain their own personal identity and self-respect in the midst of the town's refusal to recognize their existence as human beings. The quiet, determined Mayor Orden, his wife, and his fellow townspeople succeed in doing more damage to the conquerors' spirit in this manner than they could possibly inflict through a shooting confrontation. The episode of the young Lt. Tonder best shows the pitifully lonely state of any occupying soldier as he desperately seeks out the companionship of Molly Mordon, unaware that her husband has been summarily executed. Without compunction and as unfeeling as Herr Müller, she kills him with her sewing scissors. Steinbeck's revelation of the brutalizing effects of this form of guerrilla warfare on both sides should, one thinks, have done much better with the public.

With the undistinguished war romance of *Candle in the Wind* out of his system, Maxwell Anderson created in one-half of *The Eve of St. Mark,* which opened on October 7, 1942, the first of what I wish to call the completely "adult," or "mature" war plays. In its study of the men who do the fighting he wrote one of the best plays of any type to come out of the decade of the 1940's. It had a rewarding run before New York audiences, as well as a highly successful appearance of some two months in London beginning July 4, 1943, performed before soldier audiences by a soldier cast.

Anderson divides his play into two distinct parts, alternating regularly between scenes in the rural New York home of the young draftee, Quizz West, and the army. It is best, however, to ignore the back-home sequences, for they become at times excessively maudlin. They can, in fact, be entirely eliminated, as they were from time to time during the play's London run. The intimate and fumbling "can't we be together" scene between the virginal Quizz and Janet, his girl next door fiancée, was so painful to the

London soldier audiences that it was greeted nightly with guffaws. The rest of the play, on the other hand, encountered no trouble.

In *What Price Glory?* the fighting men are Marines, led by a tough professional officer and his equally tough professional top sergeant. In *The Eve of St. Mark* Anderson has caught the spirit of the conscriptee, the reluctant citizen soldier, without once intruding with a single officer or old line fighting man except the comic but believable Sgt. Ruby. Furthermore, the entire soldier portion of the play avoids any of the sensational histrionics of *What Price Glory?* Considering its subject matter, *The Eve of St. Mark* is a surprisingly low-key, even-tempered play with a thoroughly authentic and compassionate portrait of the Second World War G.I. Through some superb characterizations and some exceedingly funny scenes, Anderson displays a form of maturity of approach to the whole unnatural situation of men at war that well underlines the shortcomings of the style of *What Price Glory ?*

In the first encounter with these doomed young men the audience enters a barracks where an enthusiastic group are indulging in the most popular forms of army amusement: crap games, ridiculing the non-coms, and discussing the pursuit of drinks and women. There are types, but no stereotypes, even though there is the inevitable boy from Brooklyn, the Southerner, and the chaste nice guy from down the street, the central figure Quizz. The hulking topkick, Ruby, familiar as he is, does not descend into a trite portrayal. By the time the play is over, we have become rather intimately acquainted with several of these young people, and, what is more, every one of them, top sergeant to private, is healthy and emotionally stable, and they each and every one remain so for the entire evening, succumbing only to the ravages of jungle malaria. Nobody is shown to be a coward, and nobody comes out a hero. There are no fights, no murders, no perversions. No sadistic officers enforce brutal orders, and no girls are raped. Instead, we are introduced into the rowdy, profane and very real world of the barracks, and thence to the besieged Pacific outpost where these men fight a war that is a monstrosity they cannot explain, but something they must endure and perish in, while struggling to retain their essential human decencies.

The best single character that Anderson ever created is probably Francis Marion, the softspoken, heavy drinking, dreaming idealist from the South, hopelessly indebted to every friend he has while he waits for his inheritance from the family that won't die, pines for The Wraith, his dancer sweetheart, and quotes T. S. Eliot. He is not the tall Texan; he is not the racist backwoods redneck. He is certainly not the noisy and obnoxious unreconstructed rebel. He is a gentleman, literate and well-mannered, thrown into the army against his will, who, discovering his world literally shot to hell, finds solace in *cuba libres* and his own thoughts. He is the finest comic character in all of Anderson and one of the finest comic conceptions to emerge from all the better plays of the decade, war or otherwise. His explanation of his love for Iseult, his poetry quoting approach to the awed, slightly tarnished Lil and Sal at the Moonbow Cafe, his hallucinations during malaria, and his groggy banter with Mulveroy the Brooklynite are superb scenes.

Most important, it is to Marion that Anderson assigns the final speech by which the survivors on the island outpost are persuaded to remain, virtually without hope, to take the heaviest toll they can from the onrushing enemy. Marion's appeal, typical of his character and of the play's subdued tone, is an exceptional statement of why men fight and why they can die. His reason for staying, even after a slim chance of escape seems possible: "Because," he says, "man is not a reasonable creature. Because I'm essentially a fool like those rutting ancestors of mine, those oratorical ancestors who preferred death rather than slavery." Romanticized. Sentimental. No doubt. But persuasive and acceptable. Indeed, man is not a reasonable creature. Only the mind of the trained Nazi as Rice portrays him in Walther acts with rationale and reason. And he is hardly human at all.

Between *The Eve of St. Mark* and *Storm Operation,* Anderson's next war play of January 1944, appeared James Gow and Arnaud d'Usseau's little chiller, *Tomorrow the World* on April 14, 1943. Its 500 performances reflected more success than almost any other play with a war theme, distant from the conflict as it is. The theme itself prevents our bypassing the play, because its picture of what might happen when an orphaned German boy, thoroughly indoctrinated in the ideas of the Master Race, appears as a ward in an American home is clearly pertinent. The idea has some very sound dramatic potential, even though the ending is readily forecast. The treacherous Emil, deceitful and cruel, is eventually shown the futility and meanness of his ways by the forgiving American girl cousin whom he all but kills, and everything ends far better than one has a right to anticipate.

Maxwell Anderson was back with another try, *Storm Operation,* on January 11. It was total disaster. The original director, summoned from England where he had done so well with the G.I. production of *The Eve of St. Mark,* did not even stay with the show long enough to see it open. Within twenty-three performances it was gone. And good enough. Everything that Anderson did so well with both *What Price Glory?* and *The Eve of St. Mark* is totally undone here. The picture of a small corner of the North African campaign may be more or less authentic, but where *Glory* succeeded with its theatricality and St. Mark with its sensitive insight, *Storm Operation* lets us down with absurd situations and totally unconvincing characters.

The main interest of *Storm Operation* centers around the conflict over tactics between American First Sergeant Peter Moldau, senior in command, and Capt. Sutton, attached from the British army, who finds taking orders from non-coms somewhat of a bloody bore. Furthermore, things are complicated by the presence in the midst of the sand and heat of a beautiful Arab slave girl "owned" by one of the Americans, and two equally beautiful and talented American army nurses. Nothing rings true. The love triangle of Moldau, Sutton, and one of the nurses intrudes unforgiveably, culminating, of all things, in a battlefield wedding performed by Sutton for his rival. Moreover, all the characters talk and philosophize too much. The whole situation is completely contrived, including the sacrificial death of the loyal slave girl defending her "master," and the military campaign itself. Even the dialogue fails. The euphemistic approximation of "ruttin" in *St. Mark* becomes "mucking," but the foolish coverup collapses when SNAFU is explained as Situation Normal, All Mucked Up. So goes the entire play. There is fighting, and dying, and suffering from wounds and desert sores, and there is comedy, but we lack the keen humor and honesty of *The Eve of St. Mark.* Even a raging Flagg or Quirt would be welcome.

Through 1944 as the Atlantic Wall was breached and the war raced on toward its inevitable conclusion, only the late December production of Paul Osborn's *A Bell for Adano* seems worth a pause. Three other plays appeared during the war's last full year, but none deserves much more than a passing glance. Lillian Hellman returned in April with *The Searching Wind,* a play more about national morality and individual responsibility, particularly foreign American embassies which did not oppose the coming of Mussolini or the growing anti-Semitism of Germany, than about the war itself. In October 1944 Rose Franken, whose *Claudia* of 1940-41 had been so well received, tried her hand at speculating on what might occur when soldier-husbands return to civilian life in a moderately attractive romance called *Soldier's Wife*. Laurence Stallings attempted to regain some of the prestige he once shared with Anderson in *The Streets Are Guarded* in November. Like *Soldier's Wife*, this mystic bit about a Marine, three sailors, and a Dutch nurse on a desert island remains unread and forgotten.

For the first time since *What Price Glory?* and almost as far back as *Secret Service*, the playwright of *A Bell for Adano* (adapted from John Hersey's novel) centers his actions on the commissioned officer. The situation has changed considerably. Major Joppolo is not the dashing spy Dumont/Thorne. He is anything but the cursing fighter of Capt. Flagg. He is merely a hard working field-grade officer, constantly frustrated by the impossible restrictions imposed by invisible rank-conscious generals. As a member of Allied Military Government forces, charged with a tiny portion of winning the peace, Maj. Joppolo is first humane and then authoritative, or, in another way, first a man and then a soldier.

It is fortunate, I think, that in his final version Osborn chooses to place the shouting heartless general offstage. The audience can, in this fashion, better concentrate upon the important central figure. Shocked and enraged by the general's gross display of incredible military stupidity and crass ignorance, Joppolo can only fume, but he is then given the opportunity to prove that, in spite of the general's heartless arrogance, Americans are not just another gang of militaristic sadists. Joppolo succeeds, first by countermanding the general's orders which would have destroyed the town's economy, and then by replacing the singularly important symbol of the town's identity, the church bell.

A Bell for Adano is a good example of the kind of play that I like to call the "comedy of sensibility." Although basically serious, it is a play of much charm and sensitivity, moderately sentimental, appealing to our fundamental human decencies. The major's downright humaneness and courage, and the pathetic appreciation shown him by the little town, are well contrasted to the narrow mind of the general and the literalness of the military policeman, Capt. Purvis. Joppolo himself learns a valuable military lesson in how to take some risks, face the consequences, and retire defeated yet unbeaten in the face of superior forces.

A war play without fighting, but about combat soldiers in an active war zone; without suffering or pain, but laid in a military hospital; and without violence of any kind, but with a leading character dying, would seem to be a strange war play indeed. Perhaps John Patrick's *The Hasty Heart* of January 3, 1945, is not precisely a "war" play. Yet only warfare could have produced this specific atmosphere and the situation which Patrick explores in a warmly humorous study of human nature.

The patients in this southeast Asian base hospital are a grab bag of nationalities. There is the inevitable Yank (though he comes from Georgia and stammers), Tommy with a cockney accent, Kiwi from New Zealand, Digger from Down Under, a huge black Basuto who can speak only his name, Blossom, and Lachie, the moody lonely Scot. They talk of all the things soldiers talk of anywhere, and the stage would seem to be set for the usual uninspired collection of trite situations, particularly when the attractive nurse, Sister Margaret, is placed among them. Compounding the situation is the fact that Lachie is going to die and that he is the only one who does not know it. The skill, however, with which Patrick is able to guide his hulking soldiers through everything from their clumsy paces of therapeutic needlework to their eventual success in winning the confidence of the untrusting Lachie, is excellent dramaturgy. He has created a comedy of considerable humanity in the midst of a jungle war theatre, appealing, as does Osborn, to our finer sensibilities. He can permit Lachie and Margaret to fall in love without resorting to worn banalities; and he can break the stubborn will of the haughty Scot without rancor. Furthermore, at the conclusion, faced with separating old friends by having them rejoin their fighting units and by Lachie's anticipated return home to die a hero, Patrick makes hilarious use of the age-old question of what a Scot wears under his kilt, a mystery that has been carried as a running gag throughout the play. As the group gathers for its final photograph, Tommy at last completes the often frustrated mission. To Lachlin's consternation, Tommy shouts with glee, "I found out! I peeked! I found out!" But the audience never knows.

Arthur Laurents' psychological study of the soldier in battle called *Home of the Brave,* which opened December 27, 1945, is the second of a trio of the best of the mature war plays of the 1940's, standing with the soldier portions of *The Eve of St. Mark* and with William Wester Haines' *Command Decision* yet to come. Encountering only the briefest contact with the enemy, Laurents' characters say more about what goes on in the souls of men in combat than a dozen Flaggs or Quirts. With not a single female around nor a single back with the home-folk sequence, Laurents gives us the hopes and fears that everybody experiences under these conditions, and, more important, the terror, fright, and ultimate joyful relief in watching others die while you yourself survive.

No other play of this war or any other have accomplished exactly what Laurents is able to do in *Home of the Brave.* For the first time on stage he shows his audience the profoundly shocking effect that the matter of killing or being killed under the conditions of war can have on the basic functioning of the human mechanism. Plays have admitted, as in *What Price Glory?* and *The Eve of St. Mark,* that most men do not want to fight and that they dread the experience. But more than that, *Home of the Brave* shows the sometimes incapacitating psychological conflict within the normal human being who must admit to himself that he is often terribly afraid, and who discovers a delight in his own survival which can drive him into psychosis.

Laurents chooses to make his point on a small but dangerous mission to a hostile Pacific island. Most of the action takes place in a tiny clearing; the total number of men is five. The mission has nearly succeeded; return to safety is very close. Then, a mishap. One man, Finch, is hit, and must be left behind, still alive, while the others rush ahead. Offstage, the wounded man has been captured and is being tortured. Finally he crawls into the clearing, and his closest friend, Coney, watches him die. When Coney attempts to flee, he cannot move, though obviously he is not wounded. Through a long process of recall, the doctor at the base hospital brings out the reasons. A Jew, subject of unwarranted baiting by one T.J., a member of the fatal mission, Coney has none the less found a strong friend in Finch. But in the heat of things, Finch almost says what T.J. has said, that Coney is a "yellow Jew bastard." He doesn't, quite, but enough is enough. When Finch dies, Coney is subconsciously glad, and that is sufficient to give him powerful enough guilt feelings to cripple him through psychosomatic suggestion.

By means of the simplest of "battle" scenes Laurents has created a grimly frightening play. Using narrow human prejudices in combination with the sinister terrors of jungle warfare, he explores the guilt complexes of a man who does not realize how much he shares with every other fighting man. The experience in the theatre is profound, as well as a very exciting one.

William Wister Haines in *Command Decision* of October 1, 1947, completes the "three best" of the 1940's. Far from any combat zone or direct confrontation with the enemy, Haines places all his action in the headquarters of a heavy bombardment division in England, actively engaged in daylight precision bombing over Germany. Assuming that war is conducted by competent command officers, and assuming that his audience, having already experienced the most extensive war in history, need not be told the fact by any graphic depiction of bloody reality, Haines proceeds to write an emotionally controlled, serious study of the almost unbearable pressures and frightful loneliness of a capable and conscientious general officer faced with performing the savage business of war while abhorring every order he must give despite his West Point professionalism.

We are once more witnessing the affairs of the Army officer. In the case of *Command Decision,* he is the most privileged officer on active combat duty, high in rank, living comfortably at a base far from where the shooting is, and where the food, drink, and women are all plentiful, satisfying, and clean. Comparatively safe and secure as an officer's life is, however, the audience soon learns of the devastating trials of command responsibilities. From behind all the day-to-day functions with wall charts, routine reports and the toting up of the last mission emerges a realization that the figures so casually discussed represent the lives of hundreds of highly trained young men and their fabulously costly equipment. More important, behind the off-handed coolness of the discussions of Operation Stitch with its 20% loss of men and planes, we find a truth that may be surprising to those who view the top echelon officer as one who plays at war, using lives like pawns in a game of chess. We come to realize that, suffering as they must the enraged accusations of "butcher" thrown by those who assume to know how to fight a war from an armchair, every major, colonel, and general involved in this entire operation is feeling many times the revulsion of their worst critics, of such intensity that it can become, as it did upon the occasion of General Dennis' predecessor, fatal.

Probably the best aspect of *Command Decision* is the manner in which Haines develops his excellent dramatic irony. General Dennis, the kind of man whom we must trust without question if we mean to win, finds himself hemmed in by the very men whom he is doing his best to protect. The total lack of comprehension by the dignitaries who descend upon Dennis' command post and who try their best to suspend the war while their little inquisition proceeds, is appalling and infuriating. Their narrow perception of the war from behind a Washington desk labels Dennis a vicious murderer and demands his removal, all but stopping him from completing the mission that, were it to fail, could mean the eventual destruction of every one of these self-righteous visiting firemen. To compound the insults of their shortsighted outlook, Dennis is to receive the Legion of Merit and be sent home. The final scene with its vindication of Dennis as a general completes the well-developed irony. Given the intelligence which Haines has assigned to his responsible commander, there is only one thing that the affable ambitious Garnett can do, even though it could mean the quick end of his own career, and that is to follow through with Operation Stitch while there is still time. Thereupon, the weary Dennis, resigned to his fate as a chairborne trooper in Washington, receives news of his transfer to the Pacific for an even more important command, demonstrating that even the bigger wheels at the top know one of their best men when they see him.

Haines' success with *Command Decision* can also be attributed to his excellent character creations. He makes use of but a single enlisted man, Sgt. Evans, who is almost the gag-quoting G.I. but not quite. As a seasoned combat veteran he has a healthy disrespect for inflated rank, and, in turn, he is respected by the general he serves. Malcolm, the Southern congressman, borders on caricature, but he is no ignorant Claghorn. Kane, nearest of all to the familiar bumbling officer, remains thoroughly recognizable to any who have served under his kind. And the prize scene of all goes to Capt. George Washington Culpepper Lee and his comic, pathetically heart-searing Easter celebration. *Command Decision* produces an admirable total effect of human dignity in the midst of the worst of human depravity.

When discussing *Mister Roberts* with his graduate class in modern drama at Columbia while the play was still running, Joseph Wood Krutch strongly condemned its schoolboy antics and its Mr. Chips atmosphere. As one experienced in the ways of the service echelons, I would debate the point, for the officers and men alike ring very, very true. *Mister Roberts,* opening on February 18, 1948, went on to become one of the longest run plays in New York theatrical history, and, as the last war play of the 1940's, it is a happy note on which to close the decade.

Is one shocked that the men on this tub are not a very disciplined lot? He should not be. Men so isolated and so used by bigoted superior officers such as this Captain will demonstrate their independence of spirit in any way they can, and when they are held in contempt, as by this same officer, they will react predictably. Mister Roberts himself is no Mr. Chips, nor anything closely resembling it. He is merely an understanding human being who appreciates the fact that the men under him eat, breath, and sleep the same as he. The antics of Ensign Pulver are fine comedy, but Pulver is not silly; he is merely very funny. His laundry room firecracker, while fairly elementary farce, is not inconsistent with the rest of the play, and when he tosses the Captain's palms overboard and demands to know what's happened to the movies, he is thoroughly admirable. One could, perhaps, accuse the authors of turning their sailors into wild unruly animals as they view the showering nurses or explode in violent shore leave. Whoever makes such accusation, however, must admit to complete ignorance of service life. Exaggerated as they may be, the antics of these caged men make sense.

Thus ends the decade of the 1940's. The greatest war in history had occupied a good portion of it. Unlike its counterpart of a quarter century earlier, America had played a leading role. Stunned by the suddenness of the beginning, the nation had turned in fury and had utterly destroyed its antagonists. Surely the source material for great drama lay everywhere.

The conflict, however, defied the artist. No catch songs nor slogans, and no sense of glorious mission as before. Oh, yes, there was of course Irving Berlin's latter day *Yip, Yip, Yaphank,* known as *This Is the Army* of midsummer 1942, Lindsay and Crouse's semi-burlesque *Strip for Action* in the fall, and Moss Hart's episodic saga of how to become an airman in *Winged Victory* of November the following year. There was even a thing called *At War with the Army* by James Allardyce in 1949. These were not war plays, but soldier shows, and to read them, or to read about them now, indicates only how thin and surfacy was their content. Somehow, even with "This Is the Army, Mr. Jones," or "Praise the Lord and Pass the Ammunition," there was nothing to sing, because there was very little to sing about. Survival of the nation and the extinction of totally evil forces in East and West alike were the absolute essentials. The "real" war plays, then, were few and far between. Most of what passed for "war" plays were not very good. Only a scant handful are worthy of evaluation as pieces of lasting dramatic literature, and the three, or perhaps as many as five if one wishes to count *There Shall Be No Night* or *Watch on the Rhine* succeed the most when the war itself is least emphasized.

There were more to come in the next decade. Bevan and Trzcinski's *Stalag 17* in 1951; Patrick's *The Teahouse of the August Moon* in 1953, and in 1954 probably the best war play of all, *The Caine Mutiny Court-Martial*, which gets no closer to battle than a San Francisco military courtroom. But even then, in numbers, there isn't much. Maybe it is better that way. For all its seeming dramatic potential, the cataclysmic horror of man's greatest self-torture is better left well enough alone. Best to leave to the motion picture its portrayal of *The Thin Red Line, The Battle of the Bulge,* or *The Longest Day.* No stage could ever hope to compete with the near epic proportions of *The Bridge on the River Kwai.* Ironically, as the cinema itself becomes more and more capable of an almost literal transcription of battle, the television camera, sending around the globe the pictures of men surviving in jungle bunkers and dying in front of your eyes, denies every possibility of artistic "realism" as reality itself explodes, live and in color, from the parlor screen at the flick of a switch.

The stage can do its best by continuing where it has left off, in a sense returning full circle from where it began. The mode of *The Red Badge of Courage* or *What Price Glory?* now seems out of the question. The talky banalities of an *André* cannot suffice, either, but the dramatic impact of an *Eve of St. Mark* or a *Command Decision,* compromising between the extremes, must be the style of any future successful "war" play.

PART II:
Highlights of a Decade

June 16, 1940

Spring and summer are the big seasons in the book trade. It is evident, therefore, that the publishers, although they had awarded Carson McCullers a generous fellowship, did not have great confidence in the appeal of *The Heart Is a Lonely Hunter,* the first novel by this young woman from Georgia.

The critics, however, were generally enthusiastic, especially Richard Wright, who had just himself scored a sensational success with *Native Son.* Mrs. McCullers' first novel was quickly followed by *Reflections in a Golden Eye* and *The Member of the Wedding.* This third novel, later converted into a play, especially won its fragile author an enthusiastic following.

Yet few people during the violent 40s could have recognized that Carson McCullers, whose work of distinction was confined to this decade, was producing the works that best reflected the underlying problems of the period—the difficulty of love, the frustration of the individual seeking to affirm his identity. During the 40s, she was often viewed as merely another "Southern writer," a Gothic cousin of Faulkner's. Today she has achieved in her own right a legendary status for her cryptically understated works, the two earliest of which have only recently—as the film-going public has matured—been turned into haunting movies.

Since publication dates of novels are rarely meaningful—because of premature releases—the date given here is that of the appearance of the review in the *New York Times* that introduced the young writer to the American public. A similar date will be used for the other novels discussed in this section.

WF

85

Six Bronze Petals and Two Red: Carson McCullers in the Forties

by A. S. KNOWLES, JR.

We are dogged by coincidence. As this essay is written, Carson McCullers has succumbed to a long illness, bringing to earth all the rumors of her decline. At the same time, in theatres across the country a controversial motion picture version of *Reflections in a Golden Eye* has stirred new interest in this curious imagination that first captured our attention nearly thirty years ago. The writer perishes, the reputation is nourished: not the exchange we would have wanted, but more acceptable than complete oblivion. Nineteen sixty-seven has, ironically, managed to be another "McCullers year," although more than a decade has passed since her last novel, and in retrospect her active career as a writer seems a very small one. Conscious of these ironies, we now look back upon her work and ask, How did it seem then, and How does it seem now?

Perhaps these questions are best approached by beginning at the beginning: *The Heart Is a Lonely Hunter.* Her first full-length novel, it still seems to capture Carson McCullers' total sensibility more completely than her other works. It might even be said that whatever else she wrote was a more particularized investigation of some theme, or some mood, that first appeared here. But, granting the novel's pre-eminence, if we go on to ask how the novel struck

87

us in the decade with which this book is concerned, we must also say a word about the mood of the early Forties and about some other writers who may have shaped our first reaction to Carson McCullers.

The Heart Is a Lonely Hunter was issued in 1940. The war had started in Europe. Here "preparedness" was ending the long economic depression of the thirties. But certain feelings that had been kindled by the depression remained; the war would take them over, transforming some of them slightly, amplifying others. One of these was a feeling for the "little" people, for the once-buried lives of the lower middle class and the poor, unearthed in the national self-consciousness produced by our economic collapse. To speak of this as "a feeling" oversimplifies the matter considerably, for our involvement ranged from simple pity to fervent assertions that new instruments of social justice, perhaps revolution, must be created to permit these meek to inherit their due portion of the earth. However mild or violent such expressions may have been, however, behind them lay a sense that it was here, among the little people, that one would find whatever was left of honesty, courage, decency, true gentleness and love. Powerless they might be, and incapable of either the grand tragedy or high comedy of the prosperous, but they were real, in touch with the fundamental rhythms of life, and their survival seemed important far out of proportion to their influence over those events of which they were, in fact, often the victims.

Such sentiments as these—rooted so deeply in the depression, the approaching war, and our instinct that only the simplest, most fundamental forms of life might possess the virtues that would enable them to survive complex events—were given sentimental encouragement in the literature of the period. John Steinbeck and William Saroyan, to mention only two, had achieved enormous popularity on the strength of their ability to distill the comedy and the pathos out of little lives. Standing not far behind *The Heart Is a Lonely Hunter* are Steinbeck's *Tortilla Flat* and *Of Mice and Men*; Saroyan's *My Name is Aram* was published in the same year as the McCullers' novel, and *The Human Comedy* was shortly to follow. Whatever their dissmiliarities, all of these works focused their attention upon the American lower classes, finding among them virtues of humor, courage, and sympathy that elevated them, as human beings, far above the politicians and statemen who had led the world to the edge of chaos.

It would have been easy enough, certainly, in the early 40s to have placed *The Heart Is a Lonely Hunter* in this same broad tradition. All the characters are little people, their lives rescued from oblivion only by the author's concern. There are no great events in the novel, only events that mark, almost silently, a few obscure lives. The locale is a Southern mill town, by its very nature isolated not only from the rest of the world but from the rest of America. News of the growing European crisis (the last section of the novel occurs on August 21, 1939) filters in through the radio, but is scarcely understood. It is a silent, stagnant town. In such an environment, Mrs. McCullers locates her people, moving the focus of our attention from one to the other while carefully weaving the threads of their lives together: Singer, a deaf mute; Mick, a girl growing into adolescence; Biff, a cafe owner; Jake, a transient revolutionary; Dr. Copeland, a Negro physician, and others whose lives are tied to theirs.

While things happen to these people, there is no sharply delineated narrative structure. Mick grows up, encountering along the way her first sexual experience; the saintly Singer loses his deaf mute companion, Antonopoulos, to an insane asylum, becomes for a while a kind of confessor to the others, then commits suicide upon being told of Antonopoulos' death; Biff's wife dies, and he undergoes strange alterations of personality; Jake leaves town, frustrated in his attempts to organize the downtrodden against injustice; Dr. Copeland retires to a country farm after his attempts to arouse his people into effective action have failed. At the end of the novel, nothing is different and everything is different: all plans have failed, but no one of the characters is the same. Each has been marked by some event on the quest for love, companionship, justice, or brotherhood, but the marks, while deep, hardly show.

When the novel appeared, Richard Wright in the *New Republic* praised Carson McCullers' ability to "embrace white and black humanity in one sweep of apprehension and tenderness." This is, in truth, what the novel does: not tell a story but make a testament to its author's impartial understanding and concern. The Negro characters are drawn superbly, with little of the sentimentality that undetermined the good intentions of other authors of the period. But Carson McCullers also felt distress at injustice, and so a major factor in her examination of the little people is a depiction of the economic and social oppression of the white worker and, especially, of the Negro. What sets her apart is her realization of the degree to which the white worker was a victim of his own apathy, and the "Negro problem" a function of the Negro's inability to develop a consistent idea of himself and his goals. Her Dr. Copeland sees the future of the race in terms of dignified amelioration through education, but his own sons and daughter fail him by slipping back into stereotyped, "ignorant Southern Negro" behaviour. It is to Mrs. McCullers' credit that she sees both sides of this situation; her portrait of Copeland's daughter, Portia, is full of sympathy and an understanding of the essential goodness that lies behind Portia's unmilitant nature; Portia is, in fact, a heroine of the novel.

In her portrait of the Negro community Carson McCullers, only twenty-two when *The Heart Is a Lonely Hunter* was published, brings off a remarkable bit of prophecy. She saw, in 1940, the precise nature of the present Negro movement, what would cause it to arise, where it would try to go, and the agony it would produce. Exasperated because dignity and silent suffering have gotten him nowhere, and enraged by the brutalizing of his son Willie at a prison camp, Dr. Copeland revolts against his vision of salvation through patient striving and demands immediate action. His new vision is expressed in a quarrel with the equally adamant Jake:

> 'I have a program. It is a very simple, concentrated plan. I mean to focus on only one objective. In August of this year I mean to lead more than one thousand Negroes in this county on a march. A march to Washington. All of us together in one solid body.'

But Jake rejects the program, asserting that the answer lies not in an attempt to redress immediate grievances, but in an attack upon the whole capitalist system:

> 'Who cares whether you and your thousand Negroes struggle up to that stinking cesspool of a place called Washington? What difference does it make? What do a few people matter—a few thouand people, black, white, good or bad? When the whole of our society is built on a foundation of black lies.'

" 'Short-sighted bigot!' " shouts Jake. " 'White . . . Fiend,' " answers Copeland. That this prefiguring of our present anguish should take the form of a quarrel between a black man and his white friend, over methods of approach to a problem each needs desperately to solve, demonstrates remarkable insight on Carson Mc-Cullers' part. It would, in fact, come to this.

* * *

It is something, then, the perception of this young Georgia girl. And yet for all her understanding of black and white, and her concern for the little people, she expressed something else in her first novel that is as much a part of contemporary sensibility as it is of the sentimental, reforming spirit of the early forties. Looking back once more at the reactions of early reviewers, one finds such adjectives as "strange" and "queer." It is a strange book, to be sure, especially in the sexual orientations of its characters. Singer, the saintly deaf-mute, devotes himself to the care of another mute, the gross and self-indulgent Antonopoulos, whose death drives Singer to suicide. Biff, the cafe owner, develops distinctly feminine characteristics after the death of his wife, with whom he had long had no sexual relationship. Mick, the tomboy, is seduced by Harry Minowitz, but discovers that this clearly heterosexual experience produces only fear. The implication of these situations appears to be that the loneliness, the alienation experienced by her characters can be mitigated only in some basically homosexual orientation toward human relationships.

The rest of Mrs. McCullers' work bears out this implication, especially *Reflection in a Golden Eye*, but it is not really necessary to go beyond *The Heart Is a Lonely Hunter* to see that she means what she seems to be saying. The transformation of Biff is carefully anticipated in a passage in which he muses upon Mick's adolescent awkwardness:

> She was at the age when she looked as much like an overgrown boy as a girl. And on that subject why was it that the smartest people mostly missed that point? By nature all people are of both sexes. So that marriage and the bed is not all by any means. The proof? Real youth and old age. Because often old men's voices grow high and reedy and take on a mincing walk. And old women sometimes grow fat and their voices get rough and deep and they grow dark little mustaches. And he even proved it himself—the part of him that sometimes almost wished he was a mother and that Mick and Baby were his kids.

Sexual transformation, then, is latent in all of us. Biff's lurking femininity becomes overt when, after his wife's death, he evokes her presence by daubing perfume on his wrists and ears:

> Along with the Agua Florida he found in the closet a bottle of lemon rinse Alice had always used for her hair. One day he tried it on himself. The lemon made his dark, white-streaked hair seem fluffy and thick. He liked it. He discarded the oil he had used to guard against baldness and rinsed with the lemon preparation regularly. Certain whims that he had ridiculed in Alice were now his own. Why?

The obvious answer is that Biff, in his loneliness, has to some extent become his wife, taking on especially her more sensuous and feminine characteristics. We also learn later, in Biff's reminiscences, that a moment of physical coarseness embarrassed and shocked him into impotence once in the past. And near the end of the novel we find him making a delicate flower arrangement in the window of his restaurant, carefully saving out "a freak plant, a zinnia with six bronze petals and two red," presumably for his private pleasure. For all the suggestion of hairy-chested masculinity in his name, Biff is curiously feminine; nor will he be the only character in Carson McCullers' fiction in which a certain artistic sensitivity—indeed, sensitivity of almost any kind—will be linked with either sexual neutrality or transformation.

Nor will the girl, Mick, be the last of the tomboys, with their suggestions of sexual ambiguity. And there is also the corollary matter of "sensitivity" in Mick's love of music and in her recognition of the existence of an inner life:

> With her it was like there was two places—the inside room and the outside room. School and the family and the things that happened every day were in the outside room. Mister Singer was in both rooms. Foreign countries and plans and music were in the inside room. The songs she thought about were there. And the symphony. . . . The inside room was a very private place. She could be in the middle of a house full of people and still feel like she was locked up by herself.

Mick's initiation into adult sexuality comes at the end of a picnic with Harry Minowitz, who has borrowed boy's bikes for them—the kind with "a bar between the legs." After the event, Harry leaves town, and Mick, assailed by "a terrible afraidness," withdraws into herself. Her greatest desire during this period is to confess her sin to the gentle Singer, but she cannot. Only when Mick receives an opportunity to take a job at Woolworth's—to strike out on her own—does she snap out of the near-paralysis brought on by the episode with Harry.

We also note that Mick's compulsion to confess to Singer is an example of the way in which Singer is placed in the role of Christ by various suggestions and devices. Earlier in the novel Mick realizes that "When she thought of what she used to imagine was God she could only see Mister Singer with a long, white sheet around him," and she imagines herself saying to the deaf-mute, " 'Lord forgiveth me, for I knoweth not what I do.' " Equally Christ-like is Singer's position as the center of a group of followers—disciples—made up of Jake, Mick, Dr. Copeland, and Biff. But Biff, lying in bed, also has his chance to be the son of God:

> Biff stretched both of his arms outward and crossed his naked feet. His face was older in the morning light with the closed, shrunken eyelids and the heavy, iron-like beard on his cheeks and jaw.

And so, for whatever it is worth, spirituality is added to sensitivity as a possible concomitant of sexual abnormality.

Is the novel really as naive as all that? In a sense, it is. Certainly the sort of overly explicit allegorizing suggested by the description of Biff quoted above is the work of an immature writer. The diffuseness of *The Heart Is a Lonely Hunter,* both in theme and structure, also suggests inexperience. The real naïvete of the novel lies, however, in certain assumptions already alluded to—assumptions that are primarily a feature of adolescence, although they may not wear away entirely until later in life. The basic assumption is that in order to be sensitive one also has to be "different," a little freakish, perhaps, a little fey. The corollary, of course, is that if one isn't "different," he also isn't sensitive, and all sorts of related propostions cluster around these: that talent and eccentricity are inextricably related; that the sensitive must always by martyred; and that, in general, the world can be divided into the sensitive few and the insensitive many. There is reason enough to suspect that there is some truth in all these attitudes, but when they are used as a basic rationale one is entitled to suspect that a measure of adolescent self-pity or, at least, preciousness is really behind it all.

And yet, to look at another side of the question, Carson McCullers' assumptions about the life of the sensitive have enabled her to explore the theme of loneliness on various levels, and despite the weakness of her premises, to project a certain mood through her material that is quite affecting. Indeed, looking back on the novel now, it may be this quality that strikes us most: that her ambiguous people moving through their inarticulate, dream-like world come remarkably close to the adolescent sensibility of our own time.

*   *   *

Reflections in a Golden Eye is set on a peace-time Army base in the South, and there the dream becomes a nightmare. The basic assumptions are present, but by now there is something a little sinister in them. In the twisted relationships of Carson McCullers' second novel, the only remotely sympathetic characters are the asexual Mrs. Langdon and her effeminate houseboy Anacleto. Both of them have the requisite "sensitivity," both are afflicted by the coarseness of others, but in neither is there anything approaching the charm of a Mick. Indeed, Alison Langdon's response to her situation is self-mutilation, madness, and death in a sanitarium. For the rest of the charatcers, Mrs. McCullers shows little pity. Major Langdon, a boor, is the lover of Leonora Pendleton, a bitch. Captain Pendleton is fascinated by Private Williams, who goes horseback riding in the nude. As someone is reported to have said, "not even the horse is normal." It is all written in a precise, clinical style that somehow makes the novel at once distasteful and suspiciously synthetic. What seems clear in *Reflections* is the author's implication that normal heterosexuality is associated with the coarse and vulgar, and that, once again, any marked degree of sensitivity is likely to have as its corollary a departure, in some direction, from normal sexuality. For Leonora and Major Langdon, the stud and his mate, there is no sympathy. For the Captain, with his fixation on the faun-like Private Williams, there is some. It is a sterile and morbid book, and one wonders why Carson McCullers wrote a novel in which she so obviously felt superiority to and distaste for her characters.

Her humane and comfortable vein returns, however, in *The Member of the Wedding* (1946). The old materials, the old assumptions, are still present: the central figure is a tomboy making an uncertain approach toward the adult world; the same uneasiness about adult, "normal" sexuality lurks around the edges of the story. But there is a good deal less insistence here on the fragile virtues of special people. Compared to the gallery of grotesques who populate the first two novels, Frankie Addams and the magnificent Berenice are comfortingly human, special only in the ways we all are at some point or another.

As in *The Heart Is a Lonely Hunter,* nothing much happens in this later novel. Frances Addams, in the summer of her twelfth year, prepares to attend her older brother's wedding. She talks to the Negro servant, Berenice, pals around a little with her six-year old cousin, John Henry, has a frightening encounter with a soldier who misinterprets her interest in him, attends the wedding and behaves disastrously. John Henry dies, Frances prepares to move to a new house and to take the next, uncertain steps toward adulthood. On this light framework, however, Carson McCullers has constructed an amusing, often touching study of late adolescent psychology. At the heart of the study is a simple, basic symbol: the wedding. For Frances (also called Frankie—her child-name— and F. Jasmine—the pretentious designation she adopts as she begins to struggle free of childhood) the wedding is to be the moment when she joins hands with the world; when, putting childhood aside once and for all, she will be wedded to life and, in life, find herself. Of the bride and groom she says, "They are the *we* of *me*." For this reason Frances is convinced that her brother and his bride will take her with them on the honeymoon and that she will continue to be their companion after. They are the adult world, the world "out there," and Frances is sure she is ready. In reality, she is far from ready. Her encounter with the soldier shows that she is, above all, utterly ignorant of adult sexuality. She is moving toward maturity, but she is not there yet. Frances is, in a sense, unfinished, as is suggested by a brilliantly used symbol that appears in two forms in the novel. In its first appearance, it is a blues song:

> The tune was low and dark and sad. Then all at once, as Frankie listened, the horn danced into a wild jazz spangle that zigzagged upward with sassy nigger trickiness. At the end of the jazz spangle the music rattled thin and far away. Then the tune returned to the first blues song, and it was like the telling of that long season of trouble. She

stood there on the dark sidewalk and the drawn tightness of her heart made her knees lock and her throat feel stiffened. Then, without warning, the thing happened that at first Frankie could not believe. Just at the time when the tune should be laid, the music finished, the horn broke off. All of a sudden the horn stopped playing. For a moment Frankie could not take it in, she felt so lost.

Its other appearance is the unfinished scale played by Mr. Schwarzenbaum as he tunes the piano next door: " 'Do ray me fa sol la tee. Tee. Tee. Tee. It could drive you wild.' " It is not, of course, simply Frankie who is unfinished; it is her life as well that seems always on the verge of some sort of fulfillment. Equally, the unfinished music suggests the frustrating enigma of life in general, the way in which it keeps edging up on an answer, seems about to "lay a tune," but always stops short.

This sense of the awful mystery of life is particularly acute in the otherwise disarming conversations between Frances and Berenice. Berenice's theme is, simply, the prevalance of a random determinism: " 'Things will happen,' " as she puts it, and we are inextricably woven into the patterns that bring those things to us. Our names are part of the pattern, for instance: " 'You have a name and one thing after another happens to you, and you behave in various ways and do things, so that soon the name begins to have a meaning.' " Frances has three names, each symbolic of a stage in the pattern of her life. In one sense, her behaviour in each stage gives meaning to the name; we may impart a certain shape or color to a portion of the pattern. In a larger sense, however, it is the pattern that produces behavior and, through that, controls us. As Berenice says,

> 'We all of us somehow caught. We born this way or that way and we don't know why. But we caught anyhow. I born Berenice. You born Frankie. John Henry born John Henry. And maybe we wants to widen and bust free. But no matter what we do we still caught. Me is me and you is you and he is he. We each one of us somehow caught all by ourself.'

" 'Yet at the same time you almost might use the word loose instead of caught,' " Frances insists, "loose," she seems to mean, in the sense of the existential "absurd." No one knows where the people one sees on the street have come from or where they are going. No one knows why they have arrived in the same place at the same time. They are trapped in the pattern, but the pattern is inscrutable; " 'somehow,' " says Frances, " 'I can't seem to name it.' " Faced with the manifold frustrations of existence, the three —Frances, Berenice, and John Henry—burst into tears. Each blames his outburst on some immediate problem, but the reader knows better: on this "final kitchen afternoon," with Frances's attempt to marry life just a moment in time away, none of them can say what life is all about.

Nor is there to be any real lessening of their bewilderment. Before the novel is done, John Henry dies an agonizing, uncalled-for death on "a golden morning of the most butterflies, the clearest sky." The Addams prepare to move, severing their relationship with Berenice. In the final scene, Frances sits with Berenice waiting for the arrival of a new friend, Mary, who rings the doorbell just in time to prevent Frances from finishing the last sentence she utters in the novel. The symbols of incompleteness, of inscrutability, are carried through to the end.

For all its insistence on the cruel mysteries of existence, however, *The Member of the Wedding* is a gentle, bittersweet book. Among many excellences, its trumph is the portrait of Berenice, a study full of the affection that only a writer from the South—a region that has given the Negro more of pain and more of love than any other—could truly show.

* * *

At the beginning of this essay it was suggested that Carson Mc-Cullers' first novel might have been seen in the somewhat deceptive context of such sentimental novelists of "the little people" as Steinbeck and Saroyan. Deceptive but not altogether misleading, for in *The Heart Is a Lonely Hunter* and in her last novel, *Clock Without Hands* she focuses deliberately and often sharply on those social problems that have been a particular concern of the genre. But it is obvious that in *Reflections in a Golden Eye* and later in *The Ballad of the Sad Cafe* she is as closely associated with the "Southern Gothic" school of Tennessee Williams and Truman Capote, and that the attitudes implied in that phrase are not entirely missing in any of her work.

Carson McCullers makes legitmate claims upon our admiration: the precociousness of her talent, the depth of her sympathy, the courage with which she endured great suffering. These qualities all testify to her strength of character. As a writer, however, she now seems less important than she once did, and we may hope to be forgiven for observing, without malice, how greatly her reputation was enhanced by the time in which she wrote and by her regional associations. Carson McCullers was primarily a writer of the Forties, a period dominated by Southern writers and Southern critics: William Faulkner, Tennessee Williams, Eudora Welty, Katherine Anne Porter, Truman Capote, Allen Tate, Robert Penn Warren, and so on. There was an enormous amount of talent, of genius, embodied in this movement, but there was cultishness too, with a good deal of back-scratching and log-rolling in the literary quarterlies that were the official voice of the movement. In this atmosphere, Carson McCullers was cherished as a kind of *wunderkind,* her talent taking precisely the form that the symbol-oriented proponents of the New Criticism—concentrated in the South—were most adept at explaining. In dealing with Carson McCullers we are dealing with a writer who was favored by a self-supporting coterie that held sway over American letters for a decade. If we should now decide that she was essentially a minor writer, however, this is only to suggest that her vision was often limited and special. Like Biff's zinnia, her art was a kind of hybrid, mixing the familiar and universal with the strange and personal. Within the scope of that vision, she handled her themes of love, loneliness, alienation, and identity with precision and, at her least morbid and most natural, great tenderness.

November 15, 1941

It has been a year and a half since one Southern girl, Carson McCullers, has made good. She has followed up her first novel with a strange second, *Reflections in a Golden Eye.* While the nation drifts reluctantly toward war, other Southerners connected with the increasingly influential Agrarian/New Critical group dominate the literary scene—Caroline Gordon with *Green Centuries,* Andrew Lytle with *At the Moon's Inn.* Faulkner gathers some of his finest stories into *The Hamlet;* soon more will be organized into *Go Down, Moses.*

Surely we have heard enough from the South. Surely we have heard all that there is to be said. "Southern fiction" is becoming a procession of stereotypes. Yet one new voice is still to add a new combination of pathos and whimsy to American literature. Neither Faulkner's lyrical anger nor the New Critics' angry lyricism quite exhausts the paradoxes of a defeated land.

Mississippi—our most backward state—has produced some of our finest writers; one theorizes that great writing is an aesthetic rebellion against a grubby environment. "Among the dogs and dung," writes Wallace Stevens in "The Glass of Water," "one would continue to contend with one's ideas." Even Mississippi is a curious conglomerate. Among its stagnant towns and bigoted "rednecks," fragile, tart-tongued, introspective wits manage to flourish.

They find their artistic embodiment in the handful of superbly crafted stories by a retiring spinster from Jackson, Mississippi's capital. During the 40s, she produced *The Robber Bridegroom* (1942), *Delta Wedding* (1946), *The Golden Apples* (1949) — memorable fables of a world remote from World War II. She collected some of her stories in *The Wide Net* (1943), but many think even they cannot match those in her first small collection, *A Curtain of Green.*

WF

Eudora Welty's
A Curtain of Green

by ROBERT J. GRIFFIN

A Curtain of Green and Other Stories was Eudora Welty's first book. Its publication in the fall of 1941 was, as even *Time* magazine recognized, a "literary event," especially in view of the remarkable range and versatility that this first collection revealed. With a great variegation of theme, mood, style, tone, point of view, pace, and technique of plotting and characterization among the seventeen stories, *A Curtain of Green* was a young writer's record of successes in ambitiously diversified experiments with the form, an apprenticeship that was from the first a proof of mature mastery. As if such cake needed frosting, her first book bore the imprimatur of a shrewd introduction by Katherine Anne Porter, the one mistress of the short story who could properly be called Miss Welty's peer.

This "splendid beginning" was, as Miss Porter predicted, "only a beginning." Before the 40s were out, Eudora Welty had published a number of separate stories and four more books: *The Robber Bridegroom* (1942), a strange humor-horror fable of novella length, combining elements of fairy tale, Southern "color," and the tall story of the American frontier; *The Wide Net and Other Stories* (1943); the novel *Delta Wedding* (1946); and *The Golden Apples* (1949), a sequence of closely linked stories. Her work of the decade—not to mention what came after—provides material enough for at least forty essays. For present purposes, I mean to concentrate

on the first book of stories. I suspect time will eventually tell that
the first volume is the best, and I believe it can be shown that
a special vein of unity runs throughout all that dazzling diversity
in *A Curtain of Green*.

My thesis—which is neither notably original nor for that matter exclusively applicable to Eudora Welty—is that the approach to
the short story represented in the whole of *A Curtain of Green* is
significantly "poetic." Of course the term cannot have precisely the
same meaning applied to each of the seventeen stories; they do
differ considerably as to point of view, tone, and so forth. None
the less, overlapping sets of formal and technical similarities add
up to a distinct congeries or "family" of poetic elements, which
after a while may lead one to wonder why the author didn't choose
verse for her medium instead of prose. Let me try briefly to define
and document the several ways in which Welty's stories may strike
one as poetic.

Perhaps the most obvious consideration is that they simply are
not story-stories. Seldom if ever does a work of hers appear to
exist for the sake of pure narrative values, for the sake primarily
of unfolding a dramatic sequence of events interesting in and of
themselves or pleasurable on account of compact organization and
gripping pace. Instead of centering on some memorable occurrence,
the stories are apt to focus on something that didn't really happen
("A Piece of News") or something that will never happen ("The
Key"). The most interesting plot-like turn of events in "Powerhouse," the wife's gory suicide, is almost surely a "story" in the
sense of a preposterous tale made up on the spur of the moment,
and the most sensational element in "The Hitch-Hikers," the murder of the guitar player, happens offstage and gets reported in such
a way that we never know for sure exactly how it happened. The
truly important action of a Welty story is most likely to be action
of a mind—usually close to "passion" in the classical sense—or
"symbolic action" generated by an overtly imaginative, *authorial*
manipulation of language. Which brings up another poetic aspect,
the prominence of verbal texture, sometimes so prominent that
texture evidently constitutes the structure or the essence of the
story.

Compared to the general run of prose fiction, these stories are
crowded with metaphor and simile, figurative language quite no-
ticeably designed to provide not sensory impressions but ponderable
analogies or twists of imagination. In the first paragraph of "A

Worn Path," for instance, the old Negro woman, Phoenix Jackson, is not simply described; she is said to move "with the balanced heaviness of a pendulum in a grandfather clock," and her tapping the frozen ground with her makeshift cane is said to sound "meditative like the chirping of a solitary little bird." These are not expressions readers can easily pass over unawares. Patterns of repetition, on the other hand, may be more or less unnoticeable on a first reading. The local, unextended repetitions are obvious enough: the quick chiming of "silver," for example, applied within three short paragraphs to winter grass, leafless trees, and weathered cabins in "A Worn Path." But some of the recurrences of certain key words or phrases are less localized and apparently more significant, less immediately manifest and more elusive in their implication; they may ultimately define a kind of figurative subplot, like a cumulative chain of symbolic imagery in a long poem or a Shakespearean play.

"Clytie" is in large part built of such effects, its repetitions at once textural and structural, formal and material. It is a complex orchestration of *faces* (some 53 or more references to faces, facial "expressions," "countenances" and the like), interspersed with the subsidiary motif of *hands* (at least 7 crucial references) and the less unitary set of water images—compounded by the recurring association of Clytie with birds and chickens and various references to her "dream" or "vision" of a happier life—moving from the initial explanation of her pathological fascination with others' faces, through such reinforcing incidents as that of the barber, Mr. Bobo, lamenting the difficulty of shaving Clytie's long-paralyzed father ("The trouble with Mr. Farr was his face made no resistance to the razor. His face didn't hold."), to the pathetic climax of Clytie's reaching out her hand to touch what she takes for a sympathetic face, "the small, doubtful face" of Mr. Bobo. After both recoil in horror, Clytie recognizes the "wavering, inscrutable face" reflected in a barrel of rainwater as her own and drowns herself in irrevocable acknowledgment of her hopelessness. This thick interweaving of texture-structure is not glaringly noticeable if one simply reads the story for pleasure's sake (critics have generally pointed to the story's macabre "Gothic" quality as its most outstanding feature). But when one deliberately scrutinizes the plaiting of verbal repetitions, it does begin to reveal patterns of organization analogous to musical composition, the sort of patterning of language we usually associate with poetry.

At any rate, the multiformities of "Clytie" coalesce; the patterning holds and signifies, it works. Motifs in some of the other stories do not lend themselves so tolerably to analysis. In "A Curtain of Green" there are six specific yet ostensibly random or incidental mentions of the neighbors' windows, usually stressing the presence of the neighbor ladies at these upstairs windows which overlook Mrs. Larkin's garden, her private haven. We can see well enough a part of the windows' significance. Since Mrs. Larkin has totally isolated herself after the accidental death of her husband, the separate upstairs windows represent the neighbors' distance and the fact that they can only see, or may even no longer bother to see, the solitary widow working in her strange over-lush garden. But, considering the main present-tense event of the story, Mrs. Larkin's near-murder of her occasional Negro helper (she raises the hoe but does not strike), we may wonder why the author obliquely insists that these are *upstairs* windows from which the neighbors *can see* what happens in the garden. Are we meant to suspect that Mrs. Larkin's private act is not really private—implying, say, that she cannot completely set herself apart in her sorrow and desperation? Should we infer some connection between this implication and the fact that the Negro has somehow sensed her standing behind him (this fact and the windows are in adjoining sentences at the close of the story)? How exactly do the recurrent references to windows relate to the phrase, never actually used in the story, "*curtain* of green"? We cannot be sure. Apparently we are left with a motif that doesn't quite serve, a recurrence frequent enough to indicate a fairly complex significance but without any reliable clue to what it may signify. This would not be the only instance in Miss Welty's fiction of an unserviceable obscurity or a use of rhetoric merely rhetorical. But of that more later.

A special feature of Miss Welty's mastery of language is an ingenious connectedness of metaphor and fictional "fact." In the phrases from "A Worn Path" quoted above we may note how the "grandfather clock" metaphor underscores both the heroine's extreme age and, in the implication of steady regularity, her indomitability in her periodic mission, and further how the image of a "solitary little bird" connects with both the physical condition and the connotatve name of Phoenix Jackson, not to mention the subliminal suggestiveness of applying "meditative" to an arational creature. Probably "The Whistle" is the work in which this technique is most thoroughly and impressively carried through.

Depicting a poor, elderly couple's desperate efforts to save their young tomato plants from a late freeze, and then to keep themselves warm, the story abounds in figures like the following: the darkness of night is "thin, like some sleezy dress that has been worn and worn for many winters and always lets the cold through to the bone"; a flickering fire is described as "exhausted" like the old couple; later, when the wife dreams of luscious ripe tomatoes, her vision comes "only in brief snatches, like the flare-up of the little fire" now burned out; her farm-worn body is "as weightless as a strip of cane"; and in the context of so generative a texture of cross-references, Welty can enliven such a dead metaphor as comparing the husband's thinness to that of a bean.

There is, admittedly, something rather problematical about "The Whistle." More so than most of the pieces in *A Curtain of Green,* it is not so much a story as a mood piece, a tone poem in which the affective atmosphere very nearly blots out the narrative line. There is a story in the common sense: something happens, to credible characters, and it matters. Yet the story is not so much told as embroidered. Clearly it is not its own excuse; it is more an occasion. If we chose to be snippy, we could say it is the occasion for a great deal of fancy writing. But the truth is that elaborate manipulation of language justifies itself when the interpenetration of "factual" circumstance and figures of speech makes every aspect of the poetic story intrinsic. "The Whistle" may not be one of Miss Welty's greatest stories, but it is, like the otherwise very different "Clytie," of a piece. And observing the way a Welty story may define its own special integrity, I am reminded how many of her most successful poetic turns are spoken or thought by—or directly associated with—a particular individual character who has a touch of the poet. "A Memory," the most openly autobiographical of the stories, has for its young heroine an incipient artist, and has thus a natural climate congenial to idiosyncrasies of expression that might elsewhere seem too florid. The extravagance of language used to evoke Powerhouse's wild inscrutable jazz is—aside from its spectacular feat of imitating another medium—somehow guaranteed by the fact that Powerhouse is also a master at making fictions. Of course the writer enjoys a certain convenience of place: Southern colloquialisms are more picturesque than most idioms, and Eudora Welty may have the keenest ear for Southernisms recorded in print. And often leading characters are uneducated, afflicted, or simple-minded in such a way as to allow them a kind of primitive vividness of imagination and figurativeness of language: old Phoenix Jackson treds on past cabins "with the doors and windows boarded shut, all like old women under a spell sitting there. 'I walking in their sleep,' she said. . . ."

Phoenix Jackson, the name of an old, old "bird" who at the end of the year manages almost miraculously to walk into town to renew the prescription for her ailing but undespairing grandson—the name is typical of Welty's fondness for unobtrusive allusion or hints at mythic resonance, as if to signal quietly that these eccentric-seeming characters or circumstances have universal point. Contributing to the dense atmosphere of "Clytie" for example, are the references to an ironic statue of Hermes and such character names as "Octavia," "Clytie" (short for "Clytemnestra"?) , "Lethy" (probably short for "Alethia," but reminiscent of "Lethe") . Critics have shown how the matter-of-factness of "A Visit of Charity" faintly reverberates with echoes of established fairy-tale and fantasy-literature figures, Little Red Riding-Hood and Alice through the looking glass, and how "Death of A Traveling Salesman" intimates background references to the Hercules and Prometheus stories. "A Curtain of Green" is similarly charged with reminiscences of Eden, or more broadly, of the general pastoral-garden or "green world" myth. Very simply, the story is about an eerie though down-to-earth version of Eden-paradise, lush and in need of constant tending (one thinks most specifically of Milton's teeming garden) ; the eerie, or pathetic part is that Mrs. Larkin must tend it alone, with a kind of compensating compulsion. Jamey, her sometime helper, is an intruder in this queer pastoral world which in its excessive fertility ironically images Mrs. Larkin's loss of innocence, her enforced solitude and sterility resulting from her husband's having been crushed by an enormous "fragrant china-berry tree." Like the frequently cited Gothic element in the stories, these lurking allusions and mythic echoes are further components in the general impression that imaginative atmosphere may count more than mere event; they participate, in other words, in the poetic way in which Miss Welty's fictions typically take form and convey meaning.

I should mention also her way with natural emblems and symbols. Sometimes they are big and, for Welty, blatant: however many satellite emblems it may claim, "Petrified Man" revolves around the multiple implications of its symbolic title freak, and "The Key," a story about symbolism, also centers on a kind of visual pun. Perhaps more impressive on a close reading are the seemingly casual parallels, inserted without any authorial comment yet yielding, once we notice them and take thought, rich implicit comment on the persons or events they parallel: in the midst of the hilarious chaos at the railroad station in "Lily Daw and the Three Ladies," "a crate full of baby chickens got loose on the platform" (a great many chickens and birds populate these stories) ; the old dog in "The Hitch-Hikers" is not a little like the salesman, Tom Harris, in his exhausted "slowness and hesitancy"; finally, for two heavy-handed instances, "Flowers for Marjorie" features a broken clock and a snow-scene paperweight.

Now obviously, in these technical and formal elements I have loosely labelled "poetic," as representing a general aesthetic principle that favors suggestiveness over plain statement and forthright narrative reporting, Eudora Welty is not extraordinarily singular. These or similar devices have been welcomed into the far-reaching realms of short fiction at least since the time of Henry James. Whatever else recent criticism of imaginative prose may have taught us, it has surely shown that new-critical techniques of interpretation are not the exclusive preserve of poetry readers. And it can be very misleading to assume a simple distinction between poetry and prose; though prose and verse make a cleaner dichotomy, even that presents problems. Yet we do have ordinary notions that bask in a time-honored simplicity, notions that critical terminology might sensibly take account of. We do conceive (if that isn't too intellectual-sounding a term) of poetry as the kind of writing that gives us imaginary gardens, perhaps preferably with real toads in them, and of prose as offering gardens so unartificially "real" that there may seem to be no gardener. Miss Welty may start with real gardens—or, as in *The Robber Bridegroom* and some of the stories in *The Wide Net,* the actual fields and forests of history —but the flowers of language soon enter, and the toad may turn out to be some peculiar sort of frog-prince. If prose be thought of as essentially the straight-line medium, the mode of language best fitted for getting us from one simple point of action or argument to another in the shortest distance, then clearly the language of her stories is straining against the mode. I would argue—though I cannot now go into such matters as her concern for the cadence of her prose—that Welty's technique is much more consistently poetic than most story writers'. Her various experiments with point of view, for instance, her attempts to make point of view a form of metaphor, indicate her desire to force the medium beyond its customary bounds and to have us read the stories with the kind of attention we might devote, say, to a tough metaphysical lyric. Moreover, many stories deal centrally with problems that are at the very heart of literary expression: the difficulties of perceiving and knowing and sharing, the gap between knowing and being able to say what we know.

Aside from those works whose themes relate obliquely to the nature of literature—"The Key" and the problems of personal symbolism, "A Curtain of Green" and the possibility of cultivating one's private garden as a stay against the confusions of solitude, "Keela, The Outcast Indian Maiden" and the paradox that the meaning of the action or circumstance is greater than the persons involved can comprehend or effectively cope with—several stories focus pretty forthrightly on the nature of the artist. "A Memory" presents a metaphor for the confrontation of the ordering artist with the vulgar disorder of the "other," the life outside neat art and captivating fantasy; while the strangers intrude noisily on the satisfactions of the young girl's daydream visions, she imposes on them a framing scrutiny and a great weight of interpretive metaphor. That the story does not sentimentalize the girl's delicate sensitivity would appear to signify Miss Welty's awareness of the perils in condemning experience for failing to be nice art. "Powerhouse" is another of her stories in which something quite vital is bursting or threatening to burst out of the reasonable confines of craft and convention. It is more specifically a tale about the character and power of an artist or entertainer: apart, fascinating and even somewht frightening, very enigmatic; he is "in motion every moment," one of the exotics who "give everything" and communicate "in another language," the language of creative "hallucination." In "A Still Moment," to cite a later story from *The Wide Net*, Audubon the artist seems to synthesize the contraries of the other two prototypal characters: murderer and minister, hater and lover, destroyer and saver. It is hardly an unqualified glorification of the artist that Audubon, who alone fully appreciates the transfixing beauty of the great white heron, kills the heron so that he may patiently capture the details of its beauty in paint. Whatever the individual implications of the artist stories, collectively they exhibit the self-conscious involution of exploratory aestheticism: not art for art's sake exactly, but definitely art examining its own nature, power, and malleability—dramatizing such issues as identify a poet's poet.

One final source of evidence for the general, multiplex poetic quality I have been trying to sketch can be found in Miss Welty's explicit statements about her craft. She has spoken, for instance, of her conviction that it is "the *way* of writing that gives a story. . . . its whole distinction and glory" (her italics). In the same essay, "How I Write," she speaks also of a connection between her kind of "regional" story and lyric poetry, in their shared concern with "place," and of how the one sure unifying factor in the whole of a writer's diverse works is "their lyric quality," which I take to mean fundamentally their expression of a sensitive self. Further, she asserts that "one of the short story's finest atributes" is its ability to capture—not to interpret or explain away but imaginatively to shadow forth—some ineffable mystery. Here and elsewhere she has expressed a firm belief that the best story writers are inventive obstructionists; beauty, she says, is "associated with obstruction—with reticence of a number of kinds." There are dangers in these deeps.

One is the danger of over-indulged lyric sensitivity. Welty is so expert at dramatizing the human tendency to indulge in fancies, to dream up finer worlds of one's own, that earth feels the wound when she seems to take pride not in showing her characters doing this but in doing it grandly on her own, as though she were saying "observe and admire *my* delicate creative soul." The poetry of her prose (in particular the striking use of figurative language) is usually at its best when used as a technique of characterization, a key to characters' thoughts and feelings. "Flowers for Marjorie" is the one major disaster in *A Curtain of Green,* and partly so I think because of an inadequate agreement between subject matter and technique. In the first paragraph, describing a group of unemployed laborers sitting on a park bench: "Beyond was the inscribed base of the drinking fountain which stemmed with a troubled sound up into the glare of the day. The feet were in Vs, all still. Then down at the end of the bench, one softly began to pat. It made an innuendo at a dainty pink chewing-gum wrapper blowing by." This surely is "poetic style" getting the better of apt perception of life. The inclination toward, in Isaac Rosenfeld's phrase, "an aesthetic of presentation," visible now and again in the stories of *A Curtain of Green,* becomes almost an artiness for artiness' sake in the second collection. Too many of the stories in *The Wide*

Net have the air of showpieces, proud verbal *tours de force*; they have a syrup which pours but cannot satisfy the appetite for nourishment.

Another danger, likewise a fault through excess of a sometime virtue, lies in the philosophical commitment to true-to-life obscurantism. Some ambiguities may be inadvertent and may not matter much. The mystifying frequency of reference to the neighbors' windows in "A Curtain of Green" is not a serious impairment because it is peripheral and the story is otherwise excellent; it amply rewards re-reading. "Powerhouse," too, endures; it earns the right to its mysteries by virtue of its fantastic yet credible title character and its faultless adjustments of style to content. "Old Mr. Marblehall," however, though bizarrely captivating at first glance, defies re-reading. The closer we look the more puzzling it becomes, till finally it seems more garble than riddle. For example, a contradiction emerges between the narrator's gossipy interest in Marblehall's affairs and the recurrent assertions that "nobody cares." Is Mr. Marblehall just dreaming? or is it the teller who has made it all up from the mere stimulus of seeing a smug old gentleman who appears to pride himself on some personal secret? The story provides no clear hints on such matters; it so teases us out of patience that we may feel justified in turning on Miss Welty her own metaphor for cheap terror stories, "richness without taste, like some holiday food."

"We must confess the faults of our favorite," said Samuel Johnson, "to gain credit to our praise of his excellencies." I could cite other instances of muddle or excess, but my real regret is over how little I have shown of the excellencies of this gifted, inventive, and venturesome writer, not least her great humor, which seems to me as excellent an accomplishment as the finest accesses of her poet-like imagination.

In the essay introducing *A Curtain of Green* Katherine Anne Porter said that Eudora Welty might "very well become a master of the short story." Looking backward, we may wonder what further evidence Miss Porter could have required. *A Curtain of Green* is a very masterly collection; already several of the stories have, in their several ways, established themselves as secure classics. And if I say that this first book still seems to me the best of Miss Welty's works, I mean the best of an excellent lot.

November 18, 1942

Almost exactly one year after the appearance of Eudora Welty's first collection of stories, the first great theatrical event of the decade occurred.

In the meantime, the United States had at last been forced into World War II by Japan's treacherous bombing of Pearl Harbor while its emissaries were talking peace in Washington.

The war struck a devastating blow to literary activity, except for the kind of flag-wavers discussed in the first three essays in this volume. Who cares about books when escapism is shirking one's duty and facing the truth is too horrible to contemplate? (One of the most enduring consequences of the abrupt switch to war-time thinking was Americans' inability to look one another in the eye for two decades.)

Yet when our war was almost a year old, a literary bomb burst on Broadway that still sends reverberations around the world when the military bombs have been defused. Thornton Wilder was already on his way to work in military intelligence in the war zone when *The Skin of Our Teeth* opened on Broadway. He had also already produced four brilliant novels and the Pulitzer-prize winning play *Our Town* (1938). This new unparalleled cross between *Hellzapoppin* and the *Book of Job* was to crown his theatrical efforts and to bring a lusterless season to life.

Despite scintillating performances by Mr. and Mrs. Frederic March—as the progenitors of the human race—and Tallulah Bankhead, giving one of her finest country ham performances as the principal antagonist of hope and progress, audiences predictably found the play "difficult." Yet enough were excited by its message of guarded hope in a time of despair, to keep it going until—especially after the war in liberated Europe—it gained the recognition it deserves as one of the great dramatic tributes to the unconquerable human spirit.

WF

111

The Skin of Our Teeth
and the Theatre of
Thornton Wilder

by GERALD RABKIN

Wartime—*real* wartime, not the grim twilight zone of police actions and unratified escalation—is, for obvious reasons, rarely productive of serious drama. Drama is a public art and all too clearly must join in the general mobilization. That exhortation and escapism tend to become its major aims may be confirmed by a brief glance at the American theatrical record from 1941 to 1945. The years immediately preceding American entry into the war had produced such plays as *The Time of Your Life* and *The Little Foxes,* but the theatre of the war years gravitated between escapist concoctions of the *Junior Miss, My Sister Eileen, Over Twenty-One* variety and "serious" declarations of faith in our fighting men and our democratic principles such as *Winged Victory, The Eve of Saint Mark,* and *Tomorrow the World.* The social concerns of the Depression were absorbed in the universality of the war effort—a generalized anti-fascism remained the prime dramatic legacy of the 1930s. After the war new voices articulated new concerns. The most significant dramatic events of the 1940s are clearly the emergence of Miller and Williams and, after a decade of silence, the reemergence of O'Neill with *The Iceman Cometh.*

One play from the war years, however, did succeed in speaking both to the public need of its time and beyond. Thornton Wilder's *The Skin of Our Teeth* was presented in 1942 at a moment in history when it seemed quite possible that all civilized values—indeed, all human existence—were endangered by a barbarism greater than any the world had ever known. We need only think of the fortuitous outcome of the desperate race for atomic power to surmise how close that dread night came to being reality. Wilder's parable of man's capacity for survival spoke directly to this fear by placing contemporary catastrophe in the perspective of all human history and by pointing out that however close his possible annihilation man has always come through by the skin of his teeth. Despite its articulation of a grim moment in our history, the play, unlike so many works reflective of a period of convulsive social change (one need only cite the dramatic record of the 30s), succeeds in transcending the events which inspired it. Indeed, its continued stage popularity, particularly in Europe, indicates that the need for reassurance which it expresses did not disappear with World War II.

It is for these reasons curious to look back at a controversy which attended the successful original production of the play, a controversy which, some claim, prevented the New York drama critics from awarding it their annual prize for Best Play (although the Pulitzer Prize committee was not so inhibited). In brief, the controversy involves the claim that Wilder plagarized *The Skin of Our Teeth* from Joyce's *Finnegans Wake* (which had been published in 1939), a work so profoundly different in both form and scope as to make comparison appear almost gratuitous. Shortly after the New York opening of Wilder's play on November 18, 1942 Joseph Campbell and Henry Morton Robinson, who had been working on a "skeleton key" to Joyce's complex work published an article in the *Saturday Review of Literature* entitled "*The Skin of Whose Teeth?*" in which they claimed that the play was "not an entirely original creation, but an Americanized re-creation, thinly disguised of James Joyce's *Finnegans Wake*." They pointed out quite clearly and irrefutably Wilder's indebtedness with regard to plot elements, characters, devices of presentation, and thematic motifs: that *The Skin of Our Teeth* borrows *Finnegans Wake*'s circular form, opening and closing with the cycle-renewing, riverrunning thought stream of the chief female character; that the main divisions of the play are closed by periodic catastrophies, devices similar to the comic dissolution of *Finnegans Wake;* that the character of Antrobus is strongly reminiscent of H. C. Earwicker who has endured through all the ages of the world despite periodic confrontations with disaster; that other characters (Sabina, Henry) and incidents (the letter in the sea) clearly show Wilder to be an avid student of Joyce.

The resemblances pointed out by Campbell and Robinson are undeniable, indeed quite helpful in revealing Wilder's dependence upon Joyce's complex experiment in mythmaking. What strikes one as extremely curious, however, is the alternation of attitude by Campbell and Robinson between admiration for the skill with which Wilder assimilated Joyce's complexities and outrage similar to having caught a bright freshman with a plagiarized theme. In this and in a later article written after the publication of the play, the Joyceans acknowledge Wilder's immense skill in transmuting Joyce for his dramatic purposes; they admit that Wilder has adapted the four books of *Finnegans Wake* to the exigencies of a three-act play "skillfully and without essential dislocation." And they praise his "creative re-interpretation" of H. C. Earwicker's dream of a future ideal and its dissolution into workaday toil into Antrobus' determination to persevere. In short, they show that Wilder has used Joyce as many other dramatists have creatively used their sources. Why then the tone of accusation as though Wilder had cunningly counted upon the complexity of *Finnegans Wake* from ever revealing his shameful indebtedness? One has not to read far to sense the reason for their outrage. Joyce's work, which now has achieved the status of unchallengeable classic despite its obscurity, had been dismissed by many contemporary reviewers as a "literary abortion," needlessly and pedantically puzzling. Robinson and Campbell were obviously furious that the same kind of critics who had contemptuously derided Joyce "today hail with rave-notices its Broadway reaction. . . . The banquet was rejected," they lamented, "but the Hellzapoppin's scrap that fell from the table they clutch to their bosom."

The tone of condemnation born of the injustice of it all (which seems now, of course, ironic) inevitably bred reactions. Woolcott Gibbs, who had praised Wilder's play highly, responded with characteristic *New Yorker* tongue-in-cheek: "The truth of the matter is that, instead of being partially borrowed from Mr. Joyce's work, *The Skin of Our Teeth* was actually taken almost in toto from an early novel of my own, called *Nabisco*. It is, of course, obvious from this title and the name of Mr. Wilder's heroine, Sabina both stem anagrammatically from the root word 'basin,' a circumstance that I regard as suggestive to say the least." Gibbs went on to claim that his heroine, stolen by Wilder, was "sometimes Mrs. Roosevelt and sometimes Mae West but always Lilith."

Edmund Wilson in the *Nation* maintained that Gibbs was wrong to ridicule the possible indebtedness of Wilder to Joyce: it was so evident as to have been clearly conscious on Wilder's part. Wilson quoted from a letter he had intended sending to Wilder before the controversy erupted: "What pyorrheotechnical edent and end of the whirled in comet strip (a) brings dionysaurus to Boredway . . . translimitates polyglint prosematics into plain symbol words . . . disinflects Anna Livia and Americanizes H. C. Earwicker." No, Campbell and Robinson are right in their facts but wrong in their conclusions. Indeed, far from trying to put Joyce over to the middlebrow audience, "what Wilder is trying to do is quite distinct from what Joyce is doing." In fact, Joyce often gets in Wilder's way: ". . . the state of saturation with Joyce in which the play was written has harmed it in certain ways, precisely in distracting Wilder from his own ideas and effects. . . ."

To demonstrate that literary wounds heal slowly, Mr. Robinson returned to the attack fifteen years later after the success of another Wilder play, *The Matchmaker*. In *Esquire* of March 1957 he notes how carefully Wilder has attributed the sources of his latest play to Johann Nestroy and John Oxenford. After close analysis which implies that apart from the character of Dolly Levi all the real humor in the play is taken from Nestroy's version, Robinson returns to the unattributed source of *The Skin of Our Teeth*. Despite the passage of time the injustice to Joyce still rankles. Wilder credited Terence and Menander in *The Woman of Andros*, Catullus and Suetonious in *The Ides of March*, Nestroy and Oxenford in *The Matchmaker*, Robinson notes, but for *Finnegans Wake* "he was content to take the cash and let the credit line go." Indeed, until such time as Wilder publicly speaks on this question his reputation will be "clouded by puzzlement, controversy and contempt." The fact is that although Wilder never engaged in public debate with his detractors he has on many occasions given voice to his debt to Joyce. In the Introduction to *Three Plays* (1957) he replied to the charges in his own manner, acknowledging that *The Skin of Our Teeth* "is deeply indebted to James Joyce's *Finnegans Wake.* I should be very happy if, in the future, some author should feel similarly indebted to any work of mine. Literature has always more resembled a torch race than a furious dispute among heirs."

From the vantage point of time this controversy seems hardly to have raised questions as serious as those evoked by the awarding of the Bollingen prize to Ezra Pound later in the forties, and one cannot help feeling that Wilder was wise to remain above this particular battle. *The Skin of Our Teeth* may be discussed more meaningfully in relation to the rest of Wilder's plays than to *Finnegans Wake.* For Wilder's vision of the theatre has remained remarkably consistent, and the virtues and vices of *The Skin of Our Teeth* are, in large part, those of his entire canon. His unabashed theatricality, for example, is a source not only of strength but of weakness. Emerging as a playwright in a period in which social realism dominated the stage, Wilder correctly pointed out that realism is itself a convention and a relatively new one at that in dramatic history. The great periods of drama—ancient Greece, Elizabethan England, the Spanish Golden Age—never attempted to create the illusion of reality. On the contrary, they affirmed the theatrical basis of their art, exploiting the very nakedness of their stage environments rather than masking them. Had Wilder emerged dramatically a decade earlier during the period of the experiments of O'Neill, Lawson, and Rice he might not have had to assert his case so forcefully. Nor might he have been as tempted to have rested so much of his case on theatricality itself. In many of his plays—"The Happy Journey to Trenton and Camden," "The Long Christmas Dinner," "Infancy," "Childhood"—he seems to feel that theatrical innovation can itself carry the dramatic burden (cars created by chairs, ninety years in thirty minutes, babies played by adults, etc.) .

Our Town is a case in point. Theatrical simplicity is basic to its dramatic intent: to abstract the universality of human life from the experiences of individuals in a microcosmic American town. That the style *is* the play can be seen from the disastrous film version which fleshed out the audience's imaginative participation naturalistically and consequently destroyed Wilder's metaphor. But surely the film's failure demonstrates *Our Town's* dependence upon the theatrical impact of the bareness of the stage and the absence of properties. In a letter to producer Sol Lesser, Wilder pointed out that "realistically done—your wedding scene won't be interesting enough, and . . . will reduce many of the surrounding scenes to ordinary-ness." Which raises the disturbing question: divested of stepladders and chairs and umbrellas and Pirandellian interjections from the audience does not *Our Town* reveal an ordinary-ness, a banality born of folksiness, which its theatricalism fails to obscure? Wilder assumes the audience's unfamiliarity with his technique and his play leans heavily on the evocation of delight in his cleverness. It is the obverse of such early naturalistic dramas as James A. Herne's *Shore Acres* in which commonplace events are made theatrically attractive by the *innovation* of the accretion of naturalisfltic detail; in *Our Town* the commonplace is supposed to be rendered interesting by the very absence of this detail.

The Skin of Our Teeth seems to me more effective as a play because its theatricality is not as self-sufficient. Indeed, so wedded is form to theme that it is impossible to conceive of a naturalistic version in any medium. Wilder is successful in assimilating a whole range of influences—Olsen and Johnson and German Expressionism as well as Joyce—and in subordinating them to his thematic affirmation of faith in man's ability to survive the disasters, natural and self-inflicted, which assail him. As Mary McCarthy pointed out in the *Partisan Review,* part of the theatrical enjoyment of the play derives from the familiar mainspring of the anachronistic joke, "a joke which insists . . . that Neanderthal man with his bearskin and his club is at heart an insurance salesman at a fancy-dress ball." (The joke is still being exploited in such mass-art concoctions as *The Flintstones.*) But Wilder does not rely solely on this comic device. When Antrobus banishes his pet Dinosaur and Mammoth to the oncoming ice we enjoy the playwright's skill in reducing their biological extinction to a simple theatrical gesture; when Sabina cries to the audience to "Pass up your chairs, . . . Save the human race" at the end of Act I the breaking of the proscenium barrier creates direct involvement in the incipient disaster; when the pre-flood frivolities of mankind are equated with "Fun at the Beach" at Atlantic City we admire the skill with which Wilder infuses contemporary comedy with mythic apprehension.

Indeed, so numerous are the virtues of *The Skin of Our Teeth* that one is particularly disturbed by what seems a crucial failure of nerve on Wilder's part. At various times during the action he has the actors drop character and express their bewilderment or annoyance at what is going on. Sabina reveals herself as Miss

Somerset, an actress who laments the economic necessity of appearing in obscure pieces like the present one. "Why can't we have plays like we used to have—*Peg O' My Heart,* and *Smilin' Through,* and *The Bat*—good entertainment with a message you can take home with you?" Undoubtedly Wilder is having fun at the expense of the tired businessman's taste in theatre, but one wonders if the interjection is not really meant to assuage this philistinism by anticipating—and hence undercutting—hostile objections to the play's unconventional style. Similarly, the intense confrontation scene in Act III between Antrobus and Henry, now the embodiment of fascist violence, is terminated by Sabina (Miss Somerset) because of its potential violence: "Stop! Don't play this scene. You know what happened last night. Stop the play!" But the scene is too important to be resolved in this manner; if violence is to be stopped it cannot be by theatrical fiat.

Now it may be argued that Wilder has added another level of complexity by revealing the actors beneath the roles, that he has increased the relevance of past to present by exploiting the dimension of stage time through the play-within-a-play. But *The Skin of Our Teeth* is neither a Pirandellian journey to the no-man's land between reality and illusion nor a Brechtian parable of social exploitation. Whatever metaphors used to describe them, the catastrophes which confront man are real and the struggle of the Antrobuses through history demands empathic response not alienation. That the breakaways exist as concessions to middle-brow taste can be seen by the scene at the beginning of Act III in which it is revealed that the actors who are to play the hours at the end of the play are ill and that backstage help must therefore be pressed into double duty. The real point of the scene is that it enables Wilder to articulate unambiguously the thematic complexities of his finale wherein humanistic philosophical values are shown to prevail over desolation. When the stage manager fails to explain why the author wants to show the hours of the night appearing as philosophers, Wilder democratically has the Negro wardrobe mistress point the moral: "Just like the hours and stars go by over our heads at night, in the same way the ideas and thoughts of the great men are in the air around us all the time and they're working on us, even when we don't know it." And so when the hour/philosophers *do* appear at the end of the play the audience can sigh collectively because it knows *who* are being quoted—Aristotle, Plato, and Spinoza as we've been told—

and what the scene is supposed to mean. One is reminded of Stan Laurel's comment on Red Skelton's tendency to drop character: "Just dreadful. I love his talent but I hate the thing he does with it when he does that deliberate breaking up."

Perhaps this is somewhat unfair to Wilder. Is it his fault he has had the dramatic sense to anticipate his audience's objections? The answer is that more than in any other art first-rate drama demands first-rate audiences. Perhaps Wilder has been overly conscious of his role as mediator between highbrow sensibility and middlebrow taste, perhaps he has too strenuously adapted his intellectual proclivities to the demand of the bourgeois theatre's "group mind." "A group mind," he has written, "presupposes, if not a lowering of standards, a broadening of the fields of interest." Unlike the other arts, the drama cannot "presuppose an audience of connoisseurs trained in leisure and capable of being interested in certain rarefied aspects of life." Note the qualifying clause in the first sentence. The greatest of modern dramatists enlarged audience taste precisely by not conceding to it. But Wilder in play after play feels compelled to underline the obvious or provide a graspable theme "nugget." Two instances will serve. The stage manager in *Our Town*: "There's something way down deep that's eternal about every human being"; Officer Avonzino in "Infancy": "Babies acting like growed-ups; growed-ups acting like babies." Wilder's almost maddening tendency to aphorize contradicts his avowed aim, articulated in the Introduction to *Three Plays,* to disturb middleclass complacency: the theatre he rejected was "not only inadequate, it was evasive . . . it aimed to be soothing." He is enmeshed rather in the snares of what Dwight MacDonald has termed "midcult," the submerging of complexities in the tepid ooze of a cozy universality and folksiness. Even *The Skin of Our Teeth* ends on a note of coy optimism at odds with the spirit of much of the play as Sabina counsels the audience, "This is where you came in. We have to go on for ages and ages yet. . . . Mr. and Mrs. Antrobus! Their heads are full of plans and they're as confident as the first day they began." One notes these tendencies with regret, for Wilder's dramatic instinct and theatrical inventiveness are undeniable. Most of his plays, particularly *The Skin of Our Teeth,* hold the stage despite their defects. One keeps wishing that he hadn't played it so safe and that along with Joyce's ideas he had been more influenced by the Irishman's artistic intransigence.

March 31, 1943

The height of a war is hardly the time to look for a great dramatic innovation. Yet just two months after the securement of Guadalcanal, three months before the beginning of the Italian campaign, the American musical theatre was transformed in a single night from a frivolous wedding between the old burlesque "wheels" and the British music hall into—in popular terms—a twentieth-century equivalent of the nineteenth-century Italian opera.

The occasion was the premiere of *Oklahoma!*, a musical version of Lynn Riggs' play *Green Grow the Lilacs*. The original play was a Southwestern sentimental melodrama by a prolific writer who has never produced another work to attain any widespread prominence. The lyrics were by Oscar Hammerstein II, grandson of an opera impresario, who had already turned out the memorable words for the songs in such light operatic successes as *Desert Song* and *Show Boat*. The key difference between *Oklahoma!* and its predecessors lay in the music by Richard Rodgers, who had produced, in collaboration with another collaborator Lorenz Hart, a succession of musical comedies culminating in the unique *Pal Joey* that had nearly reformed a divertissement into a serious vehicle of social criticism.

The added ingredient was the choreography of Agnes DeMille. The United States—the world, in fact—had never seen anything like *Oklahoma!* It loved it. The old types of musical and revue were as dead as Mussolini's fascism, and for a quarter of a century the Rodgers-Hammerstein type of sentimental musical theatre remained unchallenged. Whether even *Hair!*—the American tribal love-rock musical—will make a difference remains a problem for the literary historians of the future.

WF

"A Nightly Miracle":
The Early Musical Dramas
of Rodgers and Hammerstein

by Jackson R. Bryer

> The greatest eras in the theatre have reflected some-
> thing beyond literal imitation of life. They have been
> dominated by nobility of spirit, as in the Greek period,
> or the beauty of the word, as in the Elizabethan period.
> The theatre, at its best, is a nightly miracle.
>
> —Oscar Hammerstein II

It may well be that, in the almost two-hundred year history of
the American stage, the unique contribution of our theater to
world drama is the musical play. Surely the giants of our modern
dramatic history—O'Neill, Miller, Wilder, Williams, Saroyan,
Anderson, Albee, Barry, and others—are following in the footsteps
of such British and continental antecedents as Ibsen, Chekhov,
Strindberg, Wilde, and Shaw. And the first one hundred and fifty
years of our theatre were not characterized by native originality,
stretching as they do from Royall Tyler's thoroughly English Res-
toration comedy, *The Contrast,* through the melodramas of the
briefly transplanted Irishman, Dion Boucicault, down to Clyde
Fitch and his Pinero-like "comedies with a thesis." Although the
subjects often were—and still are—American, the techniques were

123

usually highly derivative. Paradoxically, the American musical has often looked to far-off shores for settings (less so within the last twenty-five years, although the 1960's has had its *Fiddler on the Roof, Man of La Mancha,* and *Cabaret*) but the treatment has increasingly become original and, in that sense at least, American.

This line of argument may be open to dispute; not disputable is the fact that the American musical theater came of age in the 1940's and that the leaders in that maturation process were Richard Rodgers and Oscar Hammerstein II. Although the 1940's was a "golden age" of the musical, it is incorrect to assume that the musicals of that decade—and more particularly those of Rodgers and Hammerstein—sprang full-grown from the ashes of a dead tradition. It is true that, deriving as they did from vaudeville and the light operas of Gilbert and Sullivan and old Vienna, American musicals in the '20's and '30's were usually either revues, foolishly plotted romantic operettas, or light-weight shows with memorable songs and lyrics.

But the '30's and, to a lesser extent, the '20's also saw several musicals which in their inventiveness and seriousness of purpose laid much of the groundwork for the advances made in the '40's. Rodgers and Hammerstein, working with other partners, were involved in some of these and thus were moving toward the type of musical drama which they would perfect as collaborators. Hammerstein wrote the book and lyrics for *Show Boat* (1927), the first American musical with a logical and dramatic plot line and credible characters; and he contributed importantly to *Rose-Marie* (1924) and *Music in the Air* (1932), early attempts to integrate music and story (The authors even placed a note in the program of *Rose-Marie* that "The musical numbers of this play are such an integral part of the action that we do not think we should list them as separate episodes.").

Meanwhile, Rodgers, working primarily with Lorenz Hart, did *Peggy-Ann* (1926), which was built around the dream life of its heroine, had no singing or dancing for its first fifteen minutes, and concluded with a slow comedy dance performed on a darkened stage; *Chee-Chee* (1928), described by its creators (Rodgers, Hart, and Herbert Fields) as "a new form of musical show, in which all the songs were a definite part of the progress of the piece, not extraneous interludes without rhyme or reason"; *On Your Toes* (1936), the first musical to integrate ballet sequences with plot;

and *Pal Joey* (1940), which helped transform the American musical theater from mere escapism into a medium where unglamorous characters could be portrayed successfully.

Pal Joey is the musical which paved the way for the work of Rodgers and Hammerstein; but there were other shows in the late '30's and early '40's which helped do so. The left-wing musicals of Marc Blitzstein, *The Cradle Will Rock* (1937) and *No For an Answer* (1941), combined operatic musical techniques with a strong and bitter social message. Similarly, Kurt Weill and Paul Green's *Johnny Johnson* (1936) was a biting anti-war play-with-music, and Weill and Maxwell Anderson's *Knickerbocker Holiday* (1938) attacked Fascism and autocratic rule. In *Lady in the Dark* (1941), Weill collaborated with Moss Hart and Ira Gershwin, using the interest in dream psychology which Rodgers and Hart had been concerned with fifteen years earlier, but producing the greatest integration of music and play to that date. The show, built around the dreams of its heroine, Liza Elliott, an emotionally disturbed fashion-magazine editor, reaches its climax in the second act Circus Dream, where Liza's inability to make up her mind (about which of three men to marry, what cover to use on the current issue, and about what sort of woman she wants to be— "the executive or the enchantress") is portrayed by a three-ring circus-trial presided over by a ringmaster-judge. In this scene, it is impossible to separate the songs from the play: the musical sequences flow into one another to form more than fifteen minutes of continuous music-drama, not only a technical achievement of overwhelming originality but also a carefully designed study of the intricacies of Liza's mind. Infrequently revived and often slighted in histories of the American musical, *Lady in the Dark* deserves more attention as a pivotal event in the evolution of that form.

When Richard Rodgers and Oscar Hammerstein finally came together in 1942 to write *Oklahoma!*, they fashioned a show which was not nearly as daring in subject matter as *Pal Joey* or as technically ingenious as *Lady in the Dark*. They adapted Lynn Riggs' successful play, *Green Grow the Lilacs* (1931), about farmers and cowboys in the Oklahoma territory at the turn of the century. Neither setting nor characters were novel, nor was the situation—two sets of triangles, the major one of which revolved around who would take Laurey Williams to the Box Social. It is the treatment of this banal material which gives *Oklahoma!* its historic importance. This is suggested by the show's opening: turning their backs on a hundred years of musicals which opened with choral numbers, Rodgers and Hammerstein began with a fifty year old woman, Aunt Eller, sitting alone on stage churning butter, while, offstage, a cowboy, Curly, was heard singing "Oh, What a Beautiful Mornin'."

After Curly finishes two verses of his song, he pauses and three lines of dialogue take place. Aunt Eller asks what he is doing at her house and he replies, "Come a-singin' to you" and then continues his song. This interlude integrates dialogue and music, a feature which Rodgers and Hammerstein were to perfect; but, more importantly, it establishes the plausibility of Curly's song—he really is singing and, as soon becomes apparent, he is a man who likes to sing. Throughout their partnership, Rodgers and Hammerstein carefully placed their musical numbers at moments in the book where music could enhance the effect, could believably expand or define a character, and could advance the story line. Hammerstein's lyric here—simple and appropriately colloquial, yet almost poetic ("The breeze is so busy it don't miss a tree/And a ol' weepin' willer is laughin' at me!")—combined with Rodgers' soaring melody defines Curly as a simple lover of nature with a homespun eloquence which he enjoys putting into song. This first impression is reinforced by subsequent episodes, for example "The Surrey With the Fringe on Top" in which he tries to convince Laurey to go to the Box Social with him by melodically conjuring up for her a magnificent conveyance in which he will take her there. This song again weds effective music—the "clip-clop" of the horses' hooves—with Curly's own brand of persuasion —"The wheels are yeller, the upholstery's brown,/The dashboard's genuine leather,/With isinglass curtains y'c'n roll right down/In case there's a change in the weather—." But it also functions in the plot because it is his success in describing this "rig" which leads to her decision—short-lived though it may be—to go to the Social with him. Again, the song is broken by dialogue: Laurey starts to weaken, and the music continues under the text (another favorite Rogers and Hammerstein technique) as an indication that, while she is denying her willingness, she is really thinking of the picture Curly has drawn for her.

There are only twelve basic musical numbers in *Oklahoma!* (*Show Boat* has twenty); but each one is an important part of the show's total design. Some, like "I Cain't Say No" and Jud's soliloquy, "Lonely Room," define the persons who sing them; others— "People Will Say We're In Love" and "All er Nuthin' "— advance the love stories; and there are songs which do not seem as necessary but which are appropriate for the persons who sing them and the occasions on which they are sung. An example of this is "Kansas City," the rollicking number which Will Parker sings upon his return from that wickedly progressive metropolis. As a country boy, he has clearly been impressed by a place where "You c'n walk to privies in the rain an' never wet yer feet!" and it is natural that he should be moved to sing about it. Further, the fact that he is fascinated by these modern conveniences shows him to be inexperienced and immediately sets up the contrast between Will and the worldly-wise peddler, Ali Hakim, both of whom are involved with Ado Annie. The show's two great chorus numbers, "The Farmer and the Cowman" and "Oklahoma!," develop very naturally out of the occasions on which they are sung, the former as a hoe-down at the Box Social and the title song as a celebration of Laurey and Curley's wedding at a time when Oklahoma is about to become a state.

Oklahoma! obviously "works" on stage because it takes a simple story about uncomplicated people and tells it simply, using music where appropriate and fitting songs and lyrics to characters and situations. But, despite this, there remains a disturbing element in the show which probably makes it the least satisfactory of Rodgers and Hammerstein's four great musicals. In *Oklahoma!*, as in their later works, they were trying to combine romance, comedy, and the sheer enjoyment of life with something more complex and thought-provoking. The latter is represented in the figure of Jud Fry, the twisted and tormented ranch hand who is in love with Laurey. Through songs like "Pore Jud" and "Lonely Room," they skillfully develop a portrait of a lonely and frustrated figure who dreams of recognition and love. Unlike many of the other characters in the show, Jud is not a stereotype; his evil instincts result from an understandable feeling of inadequacy. When, late in Act Two, he breaks in on Curly and Laurey as they are about to leave on their honeymoon, we are prepared for the serious consequences. Jud is killed after falling on the knife he has drawn on Curly and this seems to be the natural continuation of the "serious" part of the story. If Jud had not attempted to forestall the wedding, we would have accused the authors of introducing a character and then not following through with him. But what fails is the manner in which this episode is disposed of. To be sure, Rodgers and Hammerstein were handicapped by the ending of *Green Grow the Lilacs;* but, in transferring their second show from an earlier source, they made a significant and successful change in the ending. Here, at the insistence of Aunt Eller, Curly's "trial" is held on the spot and when the judge, Cord Elam, admits that he feels "funny" about such a breach of normal procedure, the following dialogue takes place:

> AUNT ELLER. And you'll feel funny when I tell yer wife you're carryin' on 'th another womern, won't you?
> CORD ELAM. I ain't carryin' on 'th no one.
> AUNT ELLER. Mebbe not, but you'll shore feel funny when I tell yer *wife* you air.

Curly is acquitted, and the couple leaves as planned. This corny ending is in keeping with the tone of much of the rest of the show, but it is not faithful to the tone of Jud's story which it concludes. There is a lack of integration between Jud's really rather complex personality and the rest of the book. We feel cheated when what has been built up as a matter of considerable seriousness is disposed of so easily and unconvincingly.

Rodgers and Hammerstein's second musical, *Carousel* (1945), carries forward many of the innovations of *Oklahoma!* and, in fact, has many similarities to the earlier show; but it also evidences considerable artistic advance. Like *Oklahoma!*, *Carousel* is a close adaptation of a successful play, in this case Ferenc Molnar's *Liliom;* but here there are more alterations made in the original, the most important being the change of setting from Hungary to New England. The opening scene, a pantomime done to "The Carousel Waltz" in which many of the leading characters are introduced as they cluster around Mullin's Carousel and its handsome barker, Billy Bigelow, is even more unconventional than the beginning of *Oklahoma!* But it is entirely plausible (the music is that of a carousel) and very functional. Many of the characters in the two shows are similar. The female leads in *Carousel*, Carrie and Julie, are like Laurey and Ado: one of each pair is comic, naive, and superficial, while the other is introspective and more complex. But while Laurey's serious side is only implied in ballads like "Out of My Dreams" and "Many a New Day," Julie's is an integral part of her relationship with Billy. It is overtly introduced by

Carrie's song, "You're a Queer One, Julie Jordan," and is further defined by Julie's own "What's the Use of Wonderin'."

Nettie in *Carousel* is like Aunt Eller—both are strong and wise older women and confidantes of the leading lady. Both shows center around large festive gatherings, the Box Social in *Oklahoma!* and the Clambake in *Carousel*. There are also parallels between the Ali-Ado-Will triangle in *Oklahoma!* and the Enoch Snow-Carrie-Jigger triangle in *Carousel*. In both, one of the men is straight-laced and devoted to the object of his affections; while the other is an adventurer, a man of the world out to get what he can without becoming permanently involved. But, while Ali is a very funny character, Jigger is a villain. Unlike Jud, however, he is not complex; he is merely a bad man, but one who provides a great comic moment when he tries to teach Carrie some wrestling holds. Much of our dislike for Jigger is undercut by this scene: it implies that Billy's brief but fatal criminal career is not due to Jigger's influence but rather to Billy's own frustrated desire to make something of himself so that his child will not be raised as he was. This is made explicit in Billy's "Soliloquy," Rodgers and Hammerstein's most radical musical innovation in *Carousel*. Theatrical soliloquies, while often beautifully written, are often awkward interpolations in the action. Here, though, Billy's thoughts are smoothly set to music and show us the gentleness and compassion of this externally rough man, at the same time demonstrating his stubborn determination to bring his offspring into a better world than his own. This number, which goes much further than Jud's soliloquy in *Oklahoma!,* shows again how much Rodgers and Hammerstein developed between the two shows.

Similarly sophisticated integration can be seen in the love scene between Billy and Julie in Act One, when dialogue alternates with song, most particularly "If I Loved You," which reveals their love to them and to the audience. The Carrie-Enoch relationship is also suggested in a similar scene. But the most daring aspect of *Carousel* is the death of the hero four scenes before the final curtain. Death was not a subject previously treated—much less emphasized—in musicals; but Rodgers and Hammerstein were to use it prominently in three of their four great shows. Significantly, too, they were to confront it more directly each time. In *Carousel,* the finality of Billy's death is considerably eased by his reappearance in Heaven and by his return to Earth fifteen years later to do a good deed. In *Liliom,* he fails; the play ends when he slaps his daughter after she refuses to accept the star he has brought her. Realizing that this conclusion would have been out of keeping with the tone of the rest of their show (a realization they had not come to with *Oklahoma!*), Rodgers and Hammerstein wisely added another scene in which Billy attends his daughter's high school graduation and urges her to believe the words of the song being sung at the ceremony, "You'll Never Walk Alone," the same song Nettie sang to Julie as they knelt beside Billy's body. It now takes on added meaning because, although Louise cannot see her father, she can hear him. When she joins in, we recognize her awareness that she is not alone and never will be.

Carousel does not suffer from the same flaw as *Oklahoma!* The more serious aspects of the book—Jigger's villainy, the attempted robbery, Billy's roughness with Julie—are not left unassimilated. Jigger's character is softened by his scene with Carrie; no one is hurt (or robbed) at the robbery—except Billy who kills himself; and Billy's true personality is well-defined in his soliloquy. The sentimentality of the end also is fitting. It does not assure us, in the phony terms of *Oklahoma!*, that everything will be all right. Billy is dead, after all; but, in Nettie's words, the important thing is "to keep on livin'—keep on keerin' what's goin' to happen." This ending is in the best tradition of the theater: it takes normally unacceptable material and by surrounding it with the magic of the theater creates what Oscar Hammerstein has called "a nightly miracle" by making us accept it.

Allegro (1947), Rodgers and Hammerstein's third and least well-known Broadway show, is worthy of mention because it is technically their most innovative work. The book—the first original text which Hammerstein wrote in collaboration with Rodgers—is deceptively simple: it begins on the day in 1905 when Joseph Taylor, Jr., is born to Dr. and Mrs. Joseph Taylor, and it follows his life through childhood, adolescence, college, and his early career as a country doctor, until, under the influence of a materialistic and social-climbing wife, he leaves his father to take a position at a large Midwestern clinic. At the end of the show, as he is about to become head of the clinic at the age of thirty-five, he refuses the promotion and returns to assist his father at a small rural hospital. As even this brief outline makes clear, *Allegro* is heavily satirical and didactic; it is this bitter tone which probably accounts for its relative lack of success in 1947. A nation just emerging from a World War did not want to be lectured. Today, it might well get a fairer hearing. But it does suffer from a diffuseness, including as it does simple and direct ballads like "A Fellow Needs a Girl" and "You Are Never Away From the Home in My Heart" along with caustic numbers like the title song which uses the musical term to describe the pace of modern city life and "Money Isn't Everything" ("As long as you have dough"). There is also at least one instance where the authors seem to retrogress to the gratuitous insertion of a song: it occurs when Joe, in college, dates a loose girl named Beulah who tries unsuccessfully to get him to make love to her. Beulah is a crude type and when she bursts into song with "We have nothing to remember so far," the lyrics and music seem inappropriately tender and poetic—even if they are satirically so—for this character and this moment.

But these limitations of *Allegro* may well be overridden by its originality. No scenery, in the conventional sense, is used. Instead, small scenic pieces on a moving stage and light projections provide the background. A singing chorus is introduced, as the stage directions tell us, "to interpret the mental and emotional reactions of the principal character," and, occasionally, to narrate the plot. Music and dialogue fit together more completely than in any other Rodgers and Hammerstein show, with many of the episodic scenes reminiscent of *Lady in the Dark*. One of the best is a posh cocktail party given by the Taylors in their Chicago mansion. The recurrent refrain of the chorus—"Yatata yatata yatata yatata"—is punctuated by snippets of vacuous conversation in an indictment of society's superficiality.

Allegro has other revolutionary features. The major character, Joseph Taylor, Jr., does not appear until well into the middle of the first act; he doesn't sing until almost the end of the act; and he only has one solo in the entire score. In fact, with the exception of Joe's one number, all of the solos are handled by minor characters and the other songs are done by the chorus. But to speak of musical "numbers" in *Allegro* is misleading; because, in this show, Rodgers and Hammerstein achieved together the total integration of music and book they had sought independently in *Rose-Marie* and *Chee-Chee*. While there are only sixteen basic numbers in *Allegro*, there are forty-four music cues, that is, occasions when music is played. *Oklahoma!* and *Carousel* have twenty-nine and thirty-one such cues, respectively.

If *Allegro* was not a total success (to the end of his life, Oscar Hammerstein wanted to revise it for a revival), its serious and, at times, harsh criticism of society was carried over into Rodgers and Hammerstein's next musical. *South Pacific* (1949) introduced more unconventional and increasingly uncomic material for the musical stage. In its two love stories it depicted the theme of intolerance based on differences of background. This is explicitly stated in Lieutenant Cable's bitter song "Carefully Taught," a very daring number, in which he says that prejudice is learned not inbred. The same point is implied in the relationship between Nellie Forbush, the happy-go-lucky nurse from Little Rock, and Emile de Becque, the worldly middle-aged French planter, whose disclosure that he has fathered two children by a Polynesian mistress horrifies Nellie.

What is most unconventional about *South Pacific,* however, is the male lead. For years, the male romantic lead in a musical had invariably been a young handsome tenor who was vapid and uncomplicated. Rodgers and Hammerstein had begun to chip away at this tradition in *Carousel* where Billy was not without flaws. In *South Pacific,* they attempted the seemingly impossible by making him a fifty year old basso with two illegitimate children. They suceeded because they were able to make the love of Nellie and Emile believable in a marvelous opening scene which is built around two perfectly conceived contrasting musical numbers. "Cockeyed Optimist" characterizes Nellie as "stuck/(Like a dope!)/With a thing called hope" and ready and willing to meet the world on its own terms. After a brief interlude of dialogue, music returns as both soliloquize as to the improbability of their falling in love as well as to the excitement they feel. As this song ends, they silently drink brandy together and, as they do, according to the stage directions, "the music rises to ecstatic heights," making us aware, in a technique reminiscent of Wagnerian opera, that they are in love. Emile tries to explain his feelings in dialogue but can do so adequately only in "Some Enchanted Evening," which characterizes him as effectively as Nellie's song has her.

This is the major achievement of *South Pacific,* a show not without weaknesses (the lack of a musical number during the second half of the second act is one). More than any other Rodgers and Hammerstein effort, it contains a variety of types of musical numbers; but, unlike in *Allegro,* they are extremely well-assimilated in the book. The two earthy male choruses—"Bloody Mary" and "There Is Nothing Like a Dame"—emerge logically from the presence on a Pacific island of a large group of rough, fun-loving enlisted men. Nellie's songs—"I'm in Love With a Wonder-ful Guy" and 'I'm Gonna Wash That Man Right Outa My Hair" —are peppy and perfect expressions of her personality. In contrast, the simplicity and sincerity of Joe Cable are conveyed in "Younger Than Springtime" and the sophistication of Emile is suggested in "This Nearly Was Mine." Bloody Mary's two songs, "Bali Hai" and "Happy Talk," reveal something of the exotic and romantic aura of the Tonkinese natives, an aura which tragically captures Cable in the person of Liat, Mary's daughter. In fact, the three major love songs in the score—"Some Enchanted Evening," "I'm in Love With a Wonderful Guy," and "Younger Than Springtime" —all express the same emotion, but they are very different melo-dies with very different lyrics, each perfectly fitted to the character who sings it.

The King and I (1951) is in many respects the culmination of Rodgers and Hammerstein's growing artistry. Again, there are innovations and risks: as in *South Pacific,* the theme centers on intolerance; as in *South Pacific,* the male lead is middle-aged and not a tenor, but this time he has many wives and sixty-seven chil-dren. The female and male leads never kiss and never sing a love song (he only sings once in the show; the male lead not only dies in the end, but his death is the climactic final scene). There are no choral numbers and the secondary love story—of the Burmese girl Tuptim and Lun Tha—also ends in death for one of the pair (in *Carousel* and *South Pacific,* at least one of the two love stories had ended happily). Finally, the cast of *The King and I* includes only one major character whose native language is English; and the action takes place entirely in Siam.

But the show meets the challenges of these innovations and consolidates the best elements of Rodgers and Hammerstein's four previous musicals, adding the two most engrossing characters they ever created. It is, above all, a tightly-written and carefully-plotted show. Each of the songs defines character and advances plot and is plausibly located in the action.

The opening scene depicts Anna Leonowens and her son Louis arriving in Siam where she is to become governess to the King's children. In the conversation between Anna, Louis, the captain of the ship carrying them to Siam, and the Prime Minister who has been sent to meet them, we learn a great deal about Mrs. Leon-owens. She is the widow of an English army officer; she is a woman of refinement who is disturbed when Louis blurts out that

134

the Prime Minister is naked; she displays courage and pride in insisting on her right to a house of her own rather than a room in the palace; she shows a sentimental warmth in commiserating with the Prime Minister over the death of the queen; but the one song in the scene, "Whistle a Happy Tune," implies that Anna's bravery is partially forced. As with the opening numbers in *Oklahoma!, Carousel,* and *South Pacific,* this is a believable situation for a song: Louis and his mother *are* singing to keep up their courage. This scene also presents a good deal of implied information about Anna's antagonist-to-be, as when the Prime Minister remarks that the King does not always remember his promises and does not like to be reminded that he has broken his word. This very brief scene, then, fully draws one of the major characters, suggests the other, and indicates the areas of probable conflict between them.

The second scene presents the King and also quickly establishes the sub-plot. The King is everything we expect: he does not remember his promise of a house for Anna; he is suspicious of a gift from the King of Burma. When he walks off, Tuptim, who is the gift, sings "My Lord and Master," which is occasioned by the Prime Minister's remark that the King is pleased with her. She picks up this line and repeats it sarcastically, for "What does he know of me . . .?" Though he is her Lord and master, he will never know that she loves another man. This song introduces the secondary love story but it also defines Tuptim as an introspective, sensitive, and proud girl, qualities which she will display through her actions later in the show.

In the first confrontation between Anna and the King which follows, both reiterate their previous positions about the house but we begin to see hints of other personality traits. The King shows that, at times, he can be an overgrown child when he boasts about the fireworks at the queen's funeral and then asks eagerly "How you like my acrobats?" Anna is predictably appalled by the King's bad manners and horrified by his attitude towards his wives; but she is impressed by his forcefulness and won over by the children. The two musical numbers in this scene function in the book. "Hello Young Lovers" defines Anna as a romantic, but one whose love for her late husband is sufficient to keep her happy forever. This information becomes very important later when she defends Tuptim against the wrath of the King. The second musical number, "The March of the Siamese Children," is a masterpiece in which Rodgers suggests the music of the Far East without parodying it. The tempo of the march matches the movements of the children as they are presented to Anna; and it is this parade which makes her decide to remain in Siam.

The remainder of the book and score elaborate and develop the characters and situations introduced in these two scenes. The King's "Soliloquy" serves much as Billy Bigelow's, but the King is revealed as a more complex figure. We see the doubt that lies beneath his autocratic exterior: "There are times when I almost think/I am not sure of what I absolutely know." He realizes too that times are changing and that he cannot bring up his son as he was reared. This number thoroughly humanizes the King. Similarly, Anna's later "Shall I Tell You What I Think of You?" reveals the ambiguities of her attitude toward the King and her experiences in Siam. It is brought about when he calls her his servant and she storms from the room, vowing to leave the country. In her room, she pretends to address the King and begins by indicting him as a "conceited self-indulgent libertine"; but then she thinks of the children, especially the Crown Prince whom she sees as "very like his father"—"stubborn—but inquisitive and smart." This, in turn, causes her to tone down her criticism of the King and she admits, "You're a conscientious worker/But you're spoiled." Her initial total rejection has altered considerably through this number which concludes with her concession that "There is much I like in you." This soliloquy is followed by Lady Thiang's moving "This Is a Man," which reinforces Anna's softening appraisal and wins her over to helping the King. This song works where Lady Thiang's words do not. Through two musical selections, then, Anna's attitude towards the King has changed completely.

The best example of the tightly-knit structure of *The King and I* is the way the ballet scene is integrated with the book. Dance had never played a very significant role in the previous Rodgers and Hammerstein shows. But, as with the musical numbers, they made an effort to have whatever dancing there was be part of the action. The one major ballet in *Oklahoma!* is a dream sequence and the other briefer dances in that work as well as in *Carousel* and *South Pacific* are introduced naturally as part of choral numbers, at the Clambake in the former or in the "Honey Bun" amateur-night performance in the latter. But, in *The King and I,* the only dancing is a "set-piece" ballet performed for the visiting British ambassador. For many an earlier musical, just the plausibility of the occasion would have been sufficient; but Rodgers and Hammerstein have gone much further. The ballet is instrumental in proving to the ambassador that the Siamese are a cultured civilized people; and it also is important to the sub-plot, for it is Tuptim who adapts *Uncle Tom's Cabin* as "The Small House of Uncle Thomas." Her reasons for choosing this story are explained in an emotional outburst at the end of the narration, when she draws a parallel between Topsy and Eva's predicament under Simon's domination and her own enslavement by the King. The ballet is her way of protesting her condition and position. It is not only a charming and stylized interlude; it plays an important part in the plot and in character definition. That Rodgers and Hammerstein conceived of it in this way is indicated by the care with which they set up Tuptim's adaptation. When she first meets Anna, Tuptim asks her if she has a copy of *Uncle Tom's Cabin;* and, later, during a classroom session, Anna tells her students, Tuptim among them, about ice, about how people can walk on frozen rivers, and about snow. All of these "miracles" later reappear in the scenario for the ballet.

In *The King and I,* more effectively than in any previous American musical, music is used dramatically, both with lyrics and under dialogue and action. It represents the high-point of Rodgers and Hammerstein's evolution of a serious musical drama in which music supplements, reinforces, and enhances a strong book, rather than dominating it as it had in the '20's and '30's, when a musical comedy plot was usually merely the excuse for the songs. In this respect and in its depiction of a subtle relationship between two absorbing and untraditional (for musical comedy) characters, it looks forward to the great musical dramas of the '50's and '60's like *My Fair Lady, West Side Story, Fiddler on the Roof, Cabaret, Gypsy,* and *Man of La Mancha.* In these shows, believable and often off-beat characters and effective integration of music, dialogue, and dance combine to produce what we regard as the best of our musical theater. These more recent works may well go beyond the innovations we have discussed (and it is only fair to mention that the '40's saw great musicals by others—*Finian's Rainbow, Kiss Me Kate,* and *Brigadoon,* to name just three) ; but it is undeniable that Rodgers and Hammerstein were the trail-blazers who defied the conventions of fifty years of American musical comedy. They loosened the bonds which had restricted the form for so long and foreshadowed many of its potentialities. It is no small additional measure of their significance that they realized many of these potentialities in their own work: they not only tried new approaches, they were successful in doing so.

August 6, 1945

The one date that is inescapable in any history of the 40s or of mankind. A single explosion proved that men can indeed change the world and that they are fanatically obsessed with changing it for the worse. The atomic bomb affected writing as profoundly as it did every other human activity.

WF

American Apocalypse: Notes on the Bomb and the Failure of Imagination

by KINGSLEY WIDMER

The murderous glare of the American Hiroshima Bomb, the single most destructive moment of that part of the twentieth century Eurasian barbarism quaintly labeled World War II, casts a peculiar light on some literary as well as moral faiths. Surveying the writings linked to the atomic bomb must impress us with how dimly literature reflects and comprehends the actual. Even the obvious symbol of the mushroom-cloud rising above a hundred thousand dead humans (and another hundred thousand dying and crippled) —rather a better sign of the end than anything in *Revelation*—carries but small affective power. At best, the art of the word can only provide a paltry, and probably falsified, reality.

Many of the inadequacies of our forms of imagination apply, of course, to the related experiences. How memoralize, extend into moral dialects, or in any way humanly realize the fate of the millions of Jews (and the forgotten Gypsies) murdered in the Nazi "Final Solution"? And the similar millions of the Stalinist Russian slave-labor exterminations? How, indeed, comprehend any major fact of the continuous sanctioned violence of our century and its victims, of which the killed and wounded (a hundred

141

million?) indicate only a part of the man-made suffering. Nor do the integral and pervasive political terror, social exploitation, technological dehumanization and moral viciousness find appropriate expression. When our actualities provide the standards, the study of our culture must mostly note inadequacy and mendacity.

One way to reduce the vast horror to recognizable scale takes the form of the documentary-novel. This fusion of journalism and fictional art now provides the stock genre for exceptional events— invasion, the fall of a city, technological exploits, rural murder, and other man-made catastrophes. Refusing the individual integration of the personal "memoir" or the responsible factual organization of the public "history," the documentary-novel uses fiction's devices of vivid description, curious anecdote, character sketch, imagined dialogue and stylized narrative. Yet it claims literal truth. Most of these documentary-novels come out too patently artful, not least in their indebtedness to the cinema for multiple and cross-cut narration and visual heightening. Perhaps more damaging, the view of character tends to the reductive; persons appear as random and representative topical figures, diverse only within a normative evaluation of the event and almost never as commanding and exceptional individuals. People serve as manipulatable material for an author whose superior editorial stance, professionally masqueraded as disinterested sympathy, inherently implies contempt. The economy and polish and consistency of the documentary-novel (in contrast to true documents) indicates a drastic editing down, and out, of much of human response.

Given the scale of the events and the refusal of individual focus, the fictional verisimilitude (right down to brand names and a nearly surreal over-exactness on odd details) must falsify the reality. The author's pose of merely recording and reporting allows him to obscure personal evaluation, attenuate intellectual reflection, abstain from moral argument and abnegate poetic meditation. Such decorous and unthoughtful fictionalized reportage illustrates not only the limitations of commercial authorship but of the popular audiences and our standard exploitative publication which combines over-indulgence with undernourishment. The documentary-novel is itself a technological exploit; it expertly and vividly "communicates" but at the price of a considerable reduction in human response and relevance.

Such is John Hersey's *Hiroshima*. In its dozens of editions and millions of copies, this montage of half a dozen recitals of victim-survivors seems to have been crucial, even to many Japanese, in setting the attitude—most essentially the lack of adequate attitude—to the American atomic bombing of Hiroshima and Nagasaki. *Hiroshima* is, of course, competently written, blandly sympathetic, reasonably vivid and weirdly understated and depersonalized in its synthetically interwoven narratives and pathetic anecdotes of destruction and shock. Artful detail substitutes for moral intelligence. The unreflective and finally rather decorous treatment, part of which may be blamed on the parochial sophistication of the *New Yorker* audience for whom it was written (and perhaps on the editing of Harold Ross and William Shawn), manages to suggest some of the commonplaces of horror but loses fuller individual response as well as any larger issue.

Many lesser technicians than Hersey have done documentary narratives of and around the Bomb. And still continue to, two decades later. Some are rather quirky, as with Robert Trumbull's imitation, *Nine Who Survived Hiroshima and Nagasaki*. The assumption of this montage of narratives and rather thin reflections is that if surviving one atomic bombing is something special, then surviving two is profundity. But the most profound response reported there may be that of the one double survivor who was too "bitter" to provide human interest data.

The related atomic events (building the Bomb, testing the Bomb, poisoning Japanese fishermen, rebuilding Hiroshima, etc.) appear in similar narrative reportage (by Daniel Lang, Ralph Lapp, Lansing Lamont, and others). Even some poets fell back on heightening documentation. For example, Thomas Merton's *Original Child Bomb*, "Points for Meditation to Be Scratched On the Walls of a Cave," simply and awkwardly takes forty-one paragraphs of commonplace facts about the bombing as constituting a poetic indictment. Is the horror and guilt so great that no thought and imagination can be made relevant? While a factual narrative can be valuable when based in an individual sensibility and commitment (thus Lester Atwell's *Private* provides some of the more insightful literature about American army experience in Europe in World War II), psuedo-objectivity ends quite inadequate.

Literature, we sometimes forget because of our "positivistic" bias, cannot achieve awareness by merely describing. The documentary fictions, for all their exactingly dramatized reportage, must miss many of the crucial experiences. In the *naif* accounts of survivors (for example, those presented by Takashi Nagai, *We of*

Nagasaki) appears an insistent theme little found in the documentary novels or hardly any of the American discussions: "survival guilt." As we also find in the European "death camp" literature, this guilt remains pervasive and scarring. The fear and shock and brutalization in the bombing made kindly people walk away from the thirsty screams of their friends, mothers abandon their children, sensitive men ignore the women they loved. This permanently crippling revelation about one's self and about others separates the remembering *hibak'sha* from those who did not undergo the experience. One knows, then, that man is not a worthy creature. No mere detailing and dramatization will explore this guilty knowledge, this bitter human dimension basic to so much of our warfare.

In more indirect ways, of course, guilt may be the dominant force behind much of the Bomb literature. Several commentators note that even much of the Japanese moral outrage (including the widespread view that the United States should have officially apologized for the Bomb) resulted from the guilty American concern over what had been done. As later accounts (such as Rafael Steinberg's *Postscript from Hiroshima*) indicate, American pacifists helped bring out, in Japan as well as in America, a fuller consciousness. Only one and two decades later did Hiroshima take on its symbolic resonance, as did the European death camps. Other meanings of the Bomb may be yet to come.

But I cannot yet find much literature of guilt from official figures—President Truman later wrote that he regretted nothing; American public life may be distinguished by its absence of a style of honor and expiation. The atomic scientists provide a partial exception, though one which did not take much in the way of literary form, in their later debates and in that ardent minority who struggled for "civilian control" of the atom, for "test bans" and for the limitation of the American nuclear weapons obsession. Yet the key scientific attitude, then and now, may well be that expressed by Robert Oppenheimer: "when you see something that is technically sweet [such as developing the Bomb] you go ahead and do it and you argue about what to do about it only after you have had your technical success" (as quoted in the excellent study of Robert Jungk, *Brighter Than a Thousand Suns*). A similar mystique of doing the technical job for its own sake can also be found in the accounts of the military and political figures connected with the Bomb. That piety towards the "technically sweet" may go far beyond the scientists and executioners to serve as a dominant contemporary moral ideology, or its substitute. Certainly our religiosity of technology requires quite a warping of imaginative awareness.

One of the few serious fictional attempts to deal with a guilty scientist appears in Vance Bourjaily's *The Hound of Earth* (1955). This centers on an atomic physicist in the army who worked, unknowingly, on the production of the Bomb. (That a two-billion dollar enterprise employing tens of thousands of people for several years could have been kept so secret even from those in it provides one of the threatening legacies of the Bomb, though one little explored.) When he learns of the Hiroshima bombing and his own culpability, Bourjaily's physicist deserts the army and his conventional family and self-punishingly lives as a fugitive for seven sad years. He lets himself get caught and falsely punished for additional crimes. His guilt, he argues, takes the atomic Bomb as a proper symbol for the whole destructive and decadent American civilization. Yet the somewhat forced revelations of this neo-naturalistic novel seem to insist rather more on a special curse of character. As presented, this masochistic sense of defeat seems a special characteristic of the despairing generation maturing during World War II. (Bourjaily's epochal theme relentlessly continues in his later novels, such as *The Violated,* but some similar sense of betrayal and curse of a generation appears in a number of the WW II writers.) For such writers the Bomb and its implications are less explored than simply assumed to be the proper images of our moral and civilized end.

Not much direct and adequate American literary response to Hiroshima seems available from the immediate post-Bomb years. Quite a number of teachers in that period, I have discovered, felt it necessary to add to Hersey's *Hiroshima* the commentary of appropriate stories, such as W. V. T. Clark's "The Portable Phonograph." This sardonic little tale of the loss of civilized feeling assumed a country devastated by "conventional" weapons. It also suggested the moral barbarism inhering in our ways of warfare. Though written in 1942, it was appropriate since much of our conduct of the war, and especially the "saturation" bombings (which helped convince Robert Lowell and others of the immorality of the American war so that they chose imprisonment rather than military service), were of a piece with the morality of atomic bombing Hiroshima and Nagasaki.

To follow some of the other responses to the Bomb requires looking a decade or more beyond the first Bomb. The subject, of course, then becomes compounded with the "advance" of nuclear weapons and computerized attack systems and sensibilities. I suppose some basic American attitudes find popular fictional form in Pat Frank's serial magazine melodrama, *Seven Days to Never.* There the fatuously good guys in the army save America from a nefarious Russian atomic attack and, with simple-minded lower middle-class virtue, kill the subversives, terrorize the Russians, put down the intellectual snobs and skeptics, and domesticate a pretty lady military scholar. This sentimental viciousness, plus the rococo gamesmanship about American "defense systems," provided an acceptable fantasy way around the fears of the Bomb.

Probably more important were the later popular novels, which were also made into movies: Peter Bryant, *Red Alert,* and Eugene Burdick and Harvey Wheeler, *Fail-Safe.* I suggest that these reveal obvious displacements of Hiroshima-guilt; for instance, they both show the United States, the only country ever to use the Bomb on people, making unprovoked bombings. In *Red Alert* a madly arrogant general orders the attack; in *Fail-Safe* a madly arrogant "defense" system "orders" the attack. The Bryant book, weakly mechanical in style, intelligence and perception, blames a sick anti-Communist General for the evil but pretties up its mannequin President and other paper figures in order to support our official orthodoxy that apocalyptic terror will "secure peace on earth." Curiously, the rewriting of *Red Alert* into the movie *Dr. Strangelove,* by novelist Terry Southern and director Stanley Kubrick, kept the official piousness intact. Though adding some brilliantly satiric and surreal humor, a nuclear Armegeddon instead of sentimental conclusion, and a badly parodistic Nazi-American scientist, the movie continued the same dubious politics. The "liberal" prejudice that a sick anti-Communist General will cause the final war contravenes most of the evidence, including that in the story. The "deterrence" system of finally uncontrollable power and aggression was created—and is commanded—by ostensibly rational and liberal men. It seems probable, and fits the images given of the political and technical leaders, that just such men would trigger the "nuclear holocaust," as was true for Hiroshima and the gratuitous addition of Nagasaki.

Even non-pacifist historians of the moral development of the atomic bombings, such as R. C. Batchelder (*The Irreversible*

Decision), show that "inadequate and dangerous concepts" about war and the role of America, and an ethos that fundamentally lacks the appropriate "discriminations and restraints"—not any lack of liberal rationality—sanctioned such destruction. Revisionist historians (such as Gar Alperovitz, *Atomic Diplomacy*) suggest that "liberal" ideology, the rationalizations of American anti-Soviet diplomacy, and the competitive power ambitions of the United States gave political impetus to the use of the Bomb. The works of popular fantasy will not stand up to such moral and political truths—not, especially, since they receive significant confirmation with the extensive and brutal destruction of civilians and the political ambitions revealed by the American war in Viet Nam.

Literature may properly explore other dimensions than the political. Within the limits of popular topical fiction, *Fail-Safe,* an obvious imitation of *Red Alert* but far more intelligent, falteringly does. It attacks part of the accepted technological system. Human control has been replaced by computers. The similar imperial rulers of both sides in the Cold War agree that—as the atomic scientists said of the Bomb—these "automated systems became technologically possible, so we built them." And so the destructive technology takes over. Early in the story (though the point is later lost) one minor character notes the dehumanization which provides a more fundamental cause: "Man has calculated himself into so specialized a braininess that he has gone beyond reality. And he cannot tap [any more] the truth of his viscera. . . . The two evil forces he has created—science and the state—have combined into one monstrous body." The authors argue, in a mixture of scientific and apocalyptic imagery, that the "laws of probability assure us" that these technological-state "monsters [will be] playing out the last act of their cataclysmic tragedy."

Fail-Safe uses this apocalyptic awareness to excuse its bland military and political figures of authority from any responsibility. Without any conscious irony, a stock and mildly liberal politics thus gets compartmentalized away from cataclysmic reality. But the recurrent Bomb guilt shows through. After the "fail-safe" system destroys Moscow, the handsome and fatuous young President has his beloved General tit-for-tat murder ten million Americans and both men's families. Thus the authorities prove they properly play the "peace" game. Good men, all, whose insane "rationality" and psychotic "liberal decency" can only be understood, I believe, as the final moral logic and sado-masochistic guilt resulting from the persistent Hiroshima-style destructiveness and dehumanization.

While I have been considering such fictions (and films) as the popular art response to what was involved with the Bomb, this may not be altogether fair. In this post-literate age there might be equally authentic popular expression in another medium. The several Guthrie-style sardonic protest ballads about Hiroshima, the later "hit" song "On the Eve of Destruction," and, perhaps the best of the genre, Bob Dylan's "It's A Hard Rain's a-Gonna Fall," may reach a deeper sense of nuclear apocalypse.

Naturally, poets do not achieve consensus. The post-political W. H. Auden suggests, in a rather off-hand meditation ("The Bomb and Man's Consciousness" in *Hiroshima Plus 20*), that the bomb has had little practical or emotional effect. He does grant it "great significance" as a "symbol" (which doesn't affect men?). For Auden, the Bomb stands for the reversal of man's relation to nature because it replaces what used to be called "acts of God." Thus any sense of natural order and relationship has been destroyed. Curiously, he does not draw the implicit conclusion that man thus loses the sacramental sense of the value of life. Religious poets, especially the American "guru school" of post-WW II, do, as with the shrill Neo-Christian rhetoric of Brother Antoninus. His accusing *mea-culpa* insists that Americans did in the bombing what the Germans did in the death camps. Allen Ginsberg apocalyptically extends the effect of "the bomb that's slaved all human consciousness/ and made the body universe a place of fear" (*Witchita Vortex Sutra*). For those who openly respond to the Bomb, such as the public confessional poets, we usually find fearful rage for the end, the sense of the last of days.

The eschatology, however, can take some odd forms. In the popular fantasies, nuclear Armageddon becomes curiously blissful. Nevil Shute's *On the Beach*, a sentimentally trite and stilted portrayal of an American suburbanite and a few Australians in the last six months of human life on earth as radiation poisoning completes its work, insists that nothing really changes. The usual feelings and social arrangements go on right to the total retching end. Though we rather deserve it, because of irritating newspapers and some vague lack of virtuous appreciation of things as they are, people go on the same, only a bit nicer. This absolute faith in the relentless middle-class commonplaces is, if one can ignore for the moment its stupidity and triviality, almost awesome. Frank's *Alas,*

Babylon provides a bouncier version as the small town stalwarts play at do-it-yourself recreation of American civilization, including a vigilante hanging of the bad city-guy survivors, in optimistic spite of "the thousand year night."

Amongst these vulgar fantasies we should probably include not only many official manuals (such as those once put out by U. S. Civil Defense) but the farther reaches of subsidized learned imagination. For example, Herman Kahn, in *Thinking About the Unthinkable,* praises the relevance of "imagination" to our most overwhelming problems, and then goes on to practice it in the war and post-war games he calls "scenarios." (Some of them naturally employ elements from the pop-novels discussed above.) With a social and psychological sense almost as complex as that of juvenile adventure stories, some of these scenarios end happily. That is, a good half of the population is left "alive" and, after a bit of gung-ho work to straighten things out, American civilization goes rocketing merrily along. Fortunately, I suppose, some more primordial awareness somewhere still partly limits the "cool rationality" of the big-bomb-game artists and other giants of orthodox frozen fancy. A similar mentality helped murder hundreds of thousands, and may do even better next time.

But the apocalyptic optimism of such fantasies may also point to something beyond technological religiosity and the American pathology of positive thinking. Apocalyptic awareness has been with us for a long time, though never before in such a practical way as in the post-Bomb period. Historically, apocalypse usually links with utopian images and efforts. Paradise lies on the other side of Armageddon. The destruction of the old order makes possible a new one. True, our totalitarian technology, combined with a naturalistic world view, complicates the utopian reach. However, Science Fiction, whose extension and contemporary "seriousness" seems intimately related to the Bomb as well as the lunacies of rocketry, proposes different worlds after we finish ruining this one—preferably millions of light years away.

Science Fiction may reach high levels of intellectual ingenuity, like the technology it reflects, and the appropriate emotional and social mechanism. More insightful use of it, and the apocalyptic-utopian vision, appears in the exacerbated utopias of the contemporary imagination (such as William Burroughs and John Barth). These seem to bring to Swiftian and Sadean dreams a universal scope and automated horror, and perhaps a guilty nausea and self-cannibalism, that seem relatively different from the past. Similarly, our guilty confessional poetry, whether the Whitmanian ramblings of a Ginsberg or the academic baroque of a Lowell, both of whom responded strongly to the Bomb, discover terror in the technological rather than the redemption of scientist fantasy. More generally, the widespread utopian form in current novels as well as the angry reemergence of political utopian ideology in the New Radicals and of social utopianism with the Beat and Hippy movements suggest the other side of the apocalyptic awareness. As many of the utopians insist, they find part of their sanction under the aegis of the mushroom cloud.

On the apocalyptic imagination, fashion-mongering critics, whether skittish liberal pedants such as Frank Kermode (*The Sense of an Ending*) or professional mavericks such as Leslie Fiedler (*Waiting for the End*), strangely ignore most of our traumatic actuality. No doubt literature feeds on literature, but there is also a world outside. What Kermode calls our "de-mythologized apocalypse," so plain when compared with Joachimite and other ornate prophetic modes, may have been stripped by our violent technology and explosive competitive ethos. Granted, the Bomb may be less important as a thing in itself than as a mark of the watershed point of our dehumanization.

Was that Bomb so truly different? Literature, which may just as often serve to guiltily obscure actuality as to comprehend it, cannot provide the answer. If, as most of those who think about it seem to assume, atomic bombing is indiscriminate destruction, then, in almost all moral arguments, its use must be an American crime. The pretty Ahabs who pursue the Bomb don't disagree so much as not recognize the issue. Therefore, wherever our moral imagination appears, and I assume it does get into literature at times, it would be guilty. So I have argued. Yet a question remains, the old one: At what point did a change in quantity become a change in quality? Most of the reflective literature takes the culminating destructions of WW II as indiscriminate and inhuman, the edge of the ultimate abyss.

But if we are in the final fall, not Hiroshima and Nagasaki, not the actually more destructive "death camps" and "saturation" bombings, not even the more general horrors of the twentieth century Eurasian war and its related falsities and anxieties and terrors, provide an adequate moral edge. The technological dehumanization, including the use of literature as mere technical document or game, go back much further and more broadly. The loss of human dimension and autonomy and community seem basic to our whole corruptingly powerful and mass-technical civilization. Perhaps the original atomic bombing of August 6, 1945 should serve as an apocalyptic portent of an older and larger doom— not "the promised end," which may be far advanced, but "image of that horror." Our literature seems quite inadequate to any such knowledge and reality. If American man fortunately achieves a new Neolithic Age, whether before or after a nuclear Armageddon, the atomic mushroom-cloud may become an exotic trope in bardic legend. That would be the real achievement of the post-Bomb imagination, though it require the radical change of our inadequate civilization and culture.

December 28, 1945

A political era had ended in August, 1945; a literary age ended four months later with the death at 74 of Theodore Dreiser, the man who had literally dragged American literature kicking and screaming into the twentieth century with his sensational *Sister Carrie.*

The kind of mystical naturalism that Dreiser specialized in dominated in the serious fiction of the first four and a half decades of this century. Ironically, the man who had shaped much of the creative thinking of the period died at almost precisely the time that events forced recognition of the inadequacy of his vision.

Yet, though he died in his seventies after a strenuous life, Dreiser left two of his most ambitious works behind him to be published posthumously. *The Stoic,* not published until 1947, rounded off at last the trilogy depicting the career of financier Frank Cowperwood, which Dreiser had begun to publish 34 years earlier. The final embodiment of Dreiser's vision is probably to be found, however, not in this work that looks back across the century, but in *The Bulwark,* a story—unexpected from Dreiser—of profound religious experience.

Dreiser's posthumous works were received with respect and considerable curiosity, but they attracted few readers. They seemed too much voices from the past. They sharpened the realization however, that their author's death had marked a distinct break in our literary development exactly half-way through the decade. The post-war era was about to begin. At first, it was a hopeful period; but hope yielded to despair before five more years had passed.

WF

Dreiser's Bulwark:
An Archaic Masterpiece

by Jonas Spatz

The case of Theodore Dreiser is relevant to the question of how we read the literature of a recent but rapidly receding past. That is, what demands do we make on works too far removed from contemporary concerns to provide the immediate experience but too close to us to be excused as "classics"? Literary historians are fond of classifying writers according to stylistic or ideological movements, relegating each to his proper place as a "giant of realism," "the embodiment of the classical spirit," or, in more doubtful cases, a neglected precursor or decadent leftover, forced by an accident of birth into "an age of transition." A refinement, or rather a vulgarization of this practice, chops history into even smaller pieces for easy digestion and transforms complex personalities into symbols of a decade, a country, or a social class. This tends to "date" writers, to remove them from our centers of interest as soon as the mood which once made them popular disappears. More important, it stuffs them into narrow categories which blind new readers to other, less fashionable facets of their work.

Dreiser is an example of a writer who has suffered from misplaced classification. In courses in American fiction, he is regarded as the first of the modern novelists, implicitly the rival of such

156

products of the modern movement as Hemingway, Fitzgerald, and Faulkner with whom he has little connection and of Algren, Steinbeck, and Mailer, who have adapted his naturalism to a new era. In the present collection, Dreiser is dragged into the Forties as the grand old man of American fiction whose last two novels look crude and naive—artifacts of a dim and forgotten past —next to the subtleties of Trilling, Warren, Lowry, and Welty.

Much of this is attributable to the fact that Dreiser has always been associated with the rebellion against the Genteel Tradition, looked upon as a revolutionary who almost single-handedly brought American literature into the twentieth century. The power of his greatest work derives from his disillusioned approach to the romantic myths of the nineteenth century. Yet, the modern movement meant more than the brutally honest treatment of sex, poverty, corruption, or religious disillusionment. It also brought the poetic treatment of the structure and language of the novel: the development of symbolism and point of view, the subtle rendering of internal reality, and, perhaps most relevant, the search for the correct word and a tendency toward selectivity rather than inclusiveness.

Dreiser, however, wrote for almost fifty years without abandoning or even amending the stylistic lessons of his nineteenth century masters. His novels — full of the stark contrast between the grime and frustration of poverty and the glittering, overstuffed luxury of the heedless upper class world — smell of Balzac, Dickens, and Zola. Like them, he was obsessed with the sense of what it is like to be alive in a particular time and place. He overwhelmed the reader with endless details — names, faces, figures, rooms, houses, streets, foods, clothes — piling them all into a seemingly formless mass. He ignored all principles of selectivity because life itself seemingly ignored them. To Dreiser, life was a brutal physical struggle, and the narrative subtleties of Conrad, James, or Virginia Woolf, could not begin to suggest its crude and strong taste.

All of this is confirmed by the progress of Dreiser's career. *Sister Carrie,* written in 1899, was a bombshell so far ahead of its time in attitude and subject matter that it was partially suppressed and did not achieve its full impact on the public until 1911, when *Jennie Gerhardt* was published. Large portions of *The Genius* (1915) were written in 1903. The events of *An American Tragedy* (1925) had taken place in 1906, and despite its great achievement the novel already seemed slightly archaic at the time of publication. *The Stoic* (1947) was the lame conclusion to a trilogy which had been begun in 1911 and described scenes from the 1890's. Finally, Dreiser had completed an early draft of *The Bulwark* (1946) as far back as 1910. Thus, after 1925, Dreiser was finished as a contemporary novelist. Through the thirties he was revered, imitated, and discounted. By the time he decided to complete the unfinished business which had been bothering him since the period before World War I, two literary generations had passed and a third would shortly be born in the aftermath of World War II. It is in this context that Dreiser's last works must be read. To read him with sympathy we must see him as a contemporary of Tolstoy, not Nelson Algren or Truman Capote.

Not that he needs defenders. Even as far back as 1946, Lionel Trilling felt it necessary to combat what he considered the pervasive and unhealthy admiration of Dreiser's work. And his reputation has grown steadily in the twenty or so years since his death. Yet, for the reasons I have mentioned, his last great novel, *The Bulwark,* has been underestimated. Although it lacks the overwhelming realism of *An American Tragedy* and *Sister Carrie,* it has an archaic poetry that takes it back beyond the nineteenth century to the simplicity of Aeschylean tragedy and The Book of Job.

The Bulwark is a straightforward chronological account of the decline and fall, through three generations, of a Quaker family overcome first by ignorance and later by desire. Symbolically, it traces the fall of American innocence before the temptations of an increasingly urban and materialistic society. The framework of this innocence is Quakerism, a faith which demands simplicity, love, generosity, and selflessness. Arrayed against it is the spirit of capitalism, a system that engenders greed, ambition, and the glorification of the individual ego. In "The Trilogy of Desire," Dreiser embodied this spirit in the person of Frank Cowperwood, whose death in *The Stoic* emphasized the ultimate futility of his constant search for power. But in *The Bulwark, Dreiser* attempted to re-tell Cowperwood's story and to find meaning in the blind cycle of man's struggle for existence.

As in *Sister Carrie,* Dreiser's story begins at a moment of unrecognized crisis. Rufus Barnes decides to move his family from an isolated farm community in Maine where they have been protected from the temptations of the outside world to another Quaker society near Philadelphia, in which money has begun to undermine the simplicities of the old faith. Rufus prospers almost in spite of himself. Although his wealth has come through virtue and although he generously aids the needy, he realizes that the Book of Discipline condemns "an inordinate love and pursuit of worldly riches." He finally decides that God has made him one of His earthly stewards to preserve and distribute His riches. This adulterate compromise, brewed out of a cup of sincerity and a drop of desire, initiates a process which will finally poison the lives of his descendants.

The hero of the novel is Rufus' son, Solon Barnes, who, unlike his father, grows up in two worlds. At home he is irrevocably formed by the Quaker discipline and a childhood incident which recalls by contrast Cowperwood's formative experience with the lobster and the squid in *The Financier*. Solon accidentally kills a catbird while carelessly playing with a slingshot, and after a sleepless night he confesses to his mother who absolves him of blame and impresses him with the need for conscience and belief. Yet she herself is troubled by the fact that so much evil can result from ignorance or accident. Later this problem will plague Solon as he seeks to reconcile his faith in God's justice with the disasters that overtake him. Thus, as he enters the world of business, where "lust for wealth and power are in the air," he carries with him a belief in the honesty of men and the virtue of women and a set of moral principles that he later finds are "too high for these days." Unlike Cowperwood, he is unprepared to face the ugly realities around him. The novel traces Solon's gradual recognition of the deceit and ruthlessness of American capitalism and the greed which drives men to trade their integrity for quick fortunes. He finds his part in this process morally unacceptable and after exposing a scheme which in effect would defraud his bank's depositors, he retires defeated and disillusioned about the nature of man.

But the childhood incidents in *The Financier* and *The Bulwark* underscore a far more significant difference between Cowperwood and Solon Barnes. Cowperwood learns not only that he must always be stronger and more ruthless than his competitors if he is to survive but also that he must follow his impulses and desires wherever they take him. Solon, however, learns that his impulses are not to be trusted and that to indulge his desires is to risk disaster. Cowperwood proceeds to refine his sense of pleasure and to seek new methods of gratifying it. Solon shuts off his senses and even tries to deny their existence. Although at an early age he witnesses a violent war between the religious community and the town's brothel keepers, he is untouched by it. He idealizes his rather weak sexual urge into a worship of women. He falls in love and marries but, alone for the first time with his wife, his ardor is "tempered by a yearning, voiceless desire to be mothered" He watches uneasily as his fellow Quakers desert their vows of simplicity to participate in the sensuous luxury around them. At one point, he allows a young employee at the bank to go to prison for embezzlement although the boy's father, a fellow Quaker, pleads for another chance. But Solon cannot sympathize with the boy's motives (to abandon his strict and colorless home life and "embark on a freer, happier existence") because he has never felt the same emotions. In his old age Dreiser created for the first time an innocent and undersexed hero whose tragedy is partly a result of his inability to understand and experience human desire.

The Bulwark is a powerful confrontation between a beautiful, naive faith and the unfathomable experience of life. In the third generation of the Barnes family, the delicate balance that has both blinded and protected Solon Barnes is completely upset. Times have changed. In a society where happiness seemingly depends only on money and where success comes to those who most cynically pursue it, honesty, abstinence, and a belief in the divine order appear outdated. Solon raises his five children to be good Quakers, to deny their passions and ignore the temptations of materialism. Yet to his amazement, one by one they go their separate ways to failure. Isobel, the oldest, is sensitive but unattractive. She finds herself rejected by men and even by her prettier classmates. She drifts into despair and takes refuge in her studies and in pathetic romantic fantasies about her favorite teacher. Isobel is doomed to loneliness despite her need for love, and Solon is powerless to help her. He begins to ask himself how life could so frequently run counter to divine justice or even mercy. Orville and Dorothea both marry well and achieve the respectability Solon has always valued. But they are snobbish, selfish people who have no use for their religion except as a means of social advancement. They are grotesque caricatures of what Solon thought he wanted for his children.

The two youngest, Etta and Stewart, are most painful and mystifying to Solon. Etta is a dreamer, a believer in the beautiful and the ideal, who has an inordinate need for affection. Stimulated by her secret reading of Flaubert and Daudet, she enters a mental world of unrestrained passion. She rebels against her narrow schooling, running away from her parents, first to the University of Wisconsin with stolen family jewels and then to Greenwich Village, where she has an affair with an artist who finally deserts her.

Stewart, even more than Etta, is oversexed. He is "cursed" with "an overwhelming urge for physical sex gratification, and, like Clyde Griffiths whose story his resembles, he is attractive to women. He needs only the opportunity and the money. At first he borrows from his aunt and then in desperation he begins to steal from his parents to continue his romantic adventures. But his sexuality destroys him. One of Stewart's companions administers a tranquilizer to a young girl in order to seduce her. The girl, however, has a weak heart and dies. All the boys involved are arrested, and Stewart, overcome with shame, commits suicide in his cell. Solon's wife, overwhelmed by this series of disasters, collapses and dies soon after. The tragedy is complete.

Dreiser skillfully weaves the two stories together, stripping the layers of Solon's innocent beliefs from him until he stands like Job, naked before his God, crying out against his undeserved fate. And to a great extent Solon is justified. He has done his best to live according to the Inner Light and to warn his children against the dangers of the flesh and the selfish spirit. Moreover, despite its failure to prevent disaster, Dreiser leaves little doubt that the Quaker faith is the answer to many of the questions he had asked himself in earlier novels. He suggests that the Committee of Sufferings, formed by the society of Friends to care for less fortunate members of the community, is the kind of cooperative solution to the excesses of capitalism for which he had searched throughout the Thirties. Moreover, Dreiser endorses Solon's denial of the sensuality that drove some of his earlier heroes to destruction. Etta admits to herself at the end that she has fed her romantic imagination too greedily and as a result has become enslaved to an erotic dream of ideal love that can never satisfy her. In Stewart, as in Clyde Griffiths, sex becomes identified first with the need for freedom, then with the desire for luxury and power, and finally with death. As in Dreiser's other novels, sex is a symbol of the capitalist ethic — summed up by Cowperwood's laconic dictum, "I satisfy myself."

But if Solon is really guiltless, if the impersonal forces of destiny and social environment have been too much for him,

then the situation just before the final chapters of the novel takes
us no further than *An American Tragedy. The Bulwark,* however,
is not merely a reworking of earlier themes. Dreiser attempted,
in the last few years of his life, to reconcile himself to the problem
of living in a vast and incomprehensible universe in which man
is little more than the servant of social and psychological forces.
After the initial stages of his grief, Solon suddenly assumes the
blame for the fates of his children. By seeking to control them
through anger and will, he has misunderstood the Book of Discipline, which counsels love and patience. Perhaps his punishment
has been out of proportion to his crime, but Solon accepts responsibility for his acts rather than question God's providence.
We are more than the sum of what the world makes us. And love
is the difference.

Solon falls ill and retires to wait for death, cared for by Etta
and Isobel. He begins to look at nature again, as he had in childhood, and discovers a purpose in the continual cycle of mutual
destruction by which all beings live. Two incidents, also selected
as obvious contrasts to Cowperwood's observation of the lobster
and the squid, complete Solon's spiritual development. Observing a beautiful green fly which must devour a flower in order to
survive and is itself destined to be devoured, he senses the mystery
and order of existence. Beauty, harmony, variety, even tragedy
have their places in this divine order, and man is ignorant and
insignificant before it. He then sees an adder, and, by com-
municating his good will, he is able to make it drop its defensive
and menacing posture. To Solon, this is God's revelation of "His
universal presence and his good intent toward all things — all of
His created world." Where Cowperwood found in nature's chaos a
license to destroy other men in order to glorify his own ego, Solon
finds that nature is not "red in tooth and claw" but harmonious
and morally edifying. He finds new meaning in the Quaker in-
struction to annihilate the self and to love all things. And, as
Etta finally realizes, this religion is one of love, not for one man
but for the poor, the weak, the oppressed, and for nature itself.
It is "an intimate relation to the very heart of being."

In the final analysis, Solon's encounter with reality has not
been disillusioning. The old beliefs, which were once to be obeyed
because they were written, are now living impulses tested by experience. Dreiser implies this development by characterizing his hero
as a "bulwark." The word appears four times in the novel, each

time with a different meaning. First, at the height of his prosperity, Solon is regarded as "one of the nation's bulwarks," courteous, kind, generous — a good man untouched by misfortune. Later, the directors of his bank see him as a respectable and conservative front behind whom they can hide from prosecution for their manipulations. Reversing these suggestions of complacent respectability, Dreiser next uses the word to describe Solon after he has repudiated his partners: he is a representative of an older time when money was not so important. Finally, in death, he is a bulwark of the faith whose memory will inspire his descendants. He has traced the classic pattern of tragedy, from ignorance through suffering to knowledge, in order to understand for the first time what he has always believed.

The Bulwark manages, despite its primitive style, to achieve an authenticity that transcends current conventions of language, characterization, and narrative technique. The novel was born long after its time, but it is not an anachronism. It is almost as if Dreiser, bypassed by the mainstream of modernism, was attempting to demonstrate what could be done not only with the assumptions of nineteenth-century fiction but also with the simplicities that have formed the basis of tragedy from the beginning.

May 17, 1946

Wallace Stevens published several important books during the 40s: *Parts of a World* (1942), *Notes Toward a Supreme Fiction* (1942), *Esthetique du Mal* (1944), *Transport to Summer* (1947), *A Primitive like an Orb* (1948); but this is not the date of the publication of these or any of his works. It is the date of his induction into the National Institute of Arts and Letters at the age of 66. This date is chosen as a forceful reminder of the long neglect that Stevens suffered.

Literary attitudes did change markedly after World War II and the bombing of Hiroshima, and one of the most striking of these changes was the revaluation of Wallace Stevens. Almost ignored and occasionally abused during the fatuously wicked 20s and the noisily righteous 30s, Stevens began to win at last in the 40s respect and acclaim as one of the half-dozen greatest poets of the century.

This change could accompany only a growing sophistication in the audience. Stevens' work was simply incomprehensible to all but a handful of admirers before the horrors of the 30s and 40s made man look deeply and fearlessly into himself. As Kingsley Widmer argued in a preceding essay, no thoughtful man could maintain the posture of innocence after August 6, 1945. Stevens had known for years what others were only just discovering: "We live in an old chaos of the sun," he had written in *Sunday Morning* in 1915, one war earlier.

Stevens knew, too, that "guilt" was not an adequate reaction to the loss of innocence, but only another sentimental evasion. If enlightened man is not to succumb to chaos, he must asscept responsibility for ordering it. "I placed a jar in Tennessee," Stevens had written in 1919; "The wilderness rose up to it/And sprawled around, no longer wild." There is no sense of guilt in Steven's poems, but a clear, cool, ironically objective sense that if the end of innocence is not to be the end of everything, there must follow not guilt, but responsible, imaginative action. If we discover only chaos, we must imagine order. As Donald Sheehan points out, Stevens asserted in an essay in 1942 that the poet "creates the world to which he turns incessantly and . . . gives to life the supreme fictions without which we are unable to conceive of it." In the work that stands to his own career and vision as the jar to the Tennessee wilderness, Stevens left us his "notes" towards such a supreme fiction.

Whether "they will get it straight one day at the Sorbonne" remains to be seen; the omens are not hopeful. But at least at 66, Stevens' voice was honored by his fellow artists. He was taken into the National Institute of Arts and Letters along with Lillian Hellman, Robert Peter Tristram Coffin, Franklin P. Adams, and Simon Strunsky.

WF

The Ultimate Plato: A Reading of Wallace Stevens' "Notes Toward a Supreme Fiction"

by DONALD SHEEHAN

"Isn't it ridiculous to make every
effort after precision and accuracy
in other matters of small importance,
and yet not demand supreme accuracy
in subjects of supreme importance?"
　　　　　　　—Plato, *Republic*
"Does not philosophy carry us to a point
at which there is nothing left except
the imagination?"
　　　　　　—Stevens, *Opus Posthumous**

---

* Wallace Stevens, *Opus Posthumous* (New York, 1957), p. 200; the volume hereafter abbreviated in text as *OP*. Quotations from "Notes" are from *The Collected Poems* of Wallace Stevens (New York, 1954), pp. 380-408; no abbreviated indication of this volume will appear in text. Stevens' collection of essays, *The Necessary Angel* (New York, 1951), will be abbreviated in text as *NA*. Arabic numbers in text will refer to pages of the volumes in which quoted matter occurs. Finally, the quotation from Plato is from the *Republic*, Book VI; the phrase in my title, "the ultimate Plato," is from *Collected Poems*, p. 27.

Taken emblematically, the publication history of Wallace Stevens' "Notes Toward a Supreme Fiction" illuminates the poem's argument. First printed in limited edition in 1942, "Notes" did not reach an audience until 1947, when it was included in the trade volume, *Transport to Summer*. This half-decade pause between major poetry and significant response now looks something like prophetic fulfillment of the poem's own proposition that:

> We reason of these things with later reason
> And we make of what we see, what we see clearly
> And have seen, a place dependent on ourselves. (401)

So our minds work, Stevens says in "Notes," seeing and accepting the world, yet recreating it imaginatively so as to know and understand fully what we see and have seen. The "imagination's Latin" (397) makes its *fictions* (cf. the Latin *fingo, finxi, fictum,* meaning "to order," "to imagine") and, through them alone, we come to know and understand our world. In the fictions which give us knowledge, we make the world a human place and ourselves on a human scale; consequently, we respond to world and self with neither a god's pity nor a demon's despair but with the "easy passion, the ever-ready love/Of a lover" (394). Yet this knowledge and affirmation are never permanent since, as they involve fiction, they are subject to change — the Latin also means "to feign," "to deceive." Thus, since change characterizes everything, we must continually abandon our fictions at the point where they change from knowledge into lie. Accepting both the visible world and the duality of fiction, we can see, know, and constantly create the world we live in; and thus our relation to the world is alternately passive, active and both simultaneously.

And all this, "Notes" says, is the absolute and final truth about ourselves and the world; and so it is the *supreme* fiction. That is, the poem's complicated argument about truth, reality, and our creative relation to them is, in its own terms, a fiction; and the point of all the metaphysics and epistemology is not philosophic certainty but poetic feeling. The philosophy in the poem is thus constantly carrying us to the point where only imagination exists; and the philosophic fiction acts primarily to elaborate and reveal a central poetic feeling. So viewed, "Notes" is an extended lyric poem whose order and progression are not rational and general but, like any lyric poem's, emotional and particular. Put another way, the poem's emphasis is on the speaker and his responses and not on the generalized "content" of his ideas. Rather than writing original, or even interesting, philosophy in "Notes," Stevens is writing poetry. And in the poetry is both the interest and the value of the poem.

The poem's structural technique is related to its lyricism. As in earlier poems, Stevens in "Notes" relies not on the logic of narrative causation but on the mere probability of the sequence itself to provide order and progression. That is, instead of, say, section IV of the first part being *caused by* events in preceding sections, the fourth section is simply *probable* as it occurs within the sequence. Thus, there is little or no causal relationship between the poem's various parts (evident in the fact that selected sections can easily stand alone in anthologies) ; and so the sequence itself acts as the agent of coherence. Probability results when a given section can be grasped as relating *in any way* to preceding sections. Repetition is, therefore, the basic device for creating the probability of the sequence — which, again, creates the overall order and progression. The advantage of this structural technique is obvious: materials unconnected within a logical narrative can easily be incorporated without damage to the total order. That "Notes" is for Stevens a summation of his past poetry and a projection of his future work is partially the result of its structural design.

Yet Stevens imposes an "artificial" order onto this sequential structure: the poem is divided into three equal parts of ten sections each, with every section made up of seven unrhymed tercets of 21 lines each. The relationship between the "artificial" and actual structure of the poem, though, is functional; for just as the poem's philosophic argument is a lyric "fiction," so the neat, precise divisions embody a structure without apparent logical order. And the surface precision reveals the poem's true order in the same way the surface philosophy yields its deeper lyricism: through the speaker's mind and emotions within a specific lyrical situation. Thus, the similar end of both sequential probability and superficial precision is to emphasize, embody, and reveal the speaker himself: his moods, beliefs, quirks, niceties, and passions.

The speaker and his situation, then, are crucial. To begin with, the speaker may be seen as a university lecturer whose topic is the nature of poetry; with elaborate precision, he instructs an ephebe on the subjects of abstraction, change, and pleasure in poetry. Working from notes and not a prepared essay, he delivers succinct maxims and illustrative parables, occasionally jokes (often with a professor's imposing silliness), asks and answers questions, and insists on certain truths. A genuine scholar, he intends to find the truth of his subject, assured that it lies not simply through but in words. His greatest disdain is thus for blurred or imprecise speech just as his deepest love is for accurate and illuminative words. Neither complacent nor desperate, he is both passionate and deeply civil since he knows beforehand at least the proper questions about poetry, though he initially knows neither the truest answers nor the best order of his ideas. The drama of the "Notes," then, is best seen as a lecturer's exercise in extended definition. And what is to be defined is, of course, poetry — and in two senses. First, he means to tell the ephebe the truest and most useful things to know about writing poems; second, and more deeply, he intends to speak of those emotions and ideas which create in oneself that peace and love without which there is no poetic creativity nor any imaginative life at all. And just as the academic voice is inseparable from the speaker's emotional discoveries, so the academic pursuit of definition is consistent with the intuitive lyricism and quick imagination: that is, the first is the framework or fiction that reveals the second. *It Must Be Abstract.* Each major division opens with a denial of certain ideas about poetry, either because they are now irrelevant or because they never were true. Throughout the first part, the speaker elaborates a concept he calls the "first idea," which, in turn, leads to an idea of "major man":

> The major abstraction is the idea of man
> And major man is its exponent, abler
> In the abstract than in his singular . . .

> *   *   *   *   *

> The major abstraction is the communal,
> The inanimate, difficult visage. (388)

This visage is his whose figure sums up the "separate figures" we daily see; and our task is, first, to feel his existence as truly human—

> . . . Give him
> No names. Dismiss him from your images.
> The hot of him is purest in the heart (388)

—and then to "sing for this person accurate songs" (388) :

> It is of him, ephebe, to make, to confect
> The final elegance, not to console
> Nor sanctify, but plainly to propound. (389)

This man is poetically truer and more useful because, quite simply, he is all of us who are "looking for what was, where it used to be" (389) and who find ourselves living in a place that "is not our own and, much more, not ourselves" (383). Major man, in other words, represents and enacts the comedy of consciousness: our minds separate us from the world, thereby creating the imagination that will, in its fictions, rejoin self and world. Without mind, we have no need for imagination; with it, we recreate imaginatively the very unity we lost in giving birth to imagination.

This comedy is, in a general sense, Platonic. And so the speaker is concerned throughout the first part to distinguish his Platonism from any religious Neo-Platonism: the first idea, he says, does not predicate "an inventing mind as source / Of this idea" (381). The speaker therefore insists, as does Plato in the *Republic*, upon the non-hypothetical nature of his first principle. Any concrete instance of the first idea, that is, has in it literally and not hypothetically the idea itself — otherwise, we could not know the instance for what it was. Furthermore, like Plato, the speaker thus claims superiority for the first idea primarily in terms of knowledge: "More fecund as principle than particle," the first idea leads us to "see these separate figures one by one, / And yet see only one" (388, 389). (In an essay also written in 1942, Stevens asserted that the poet "creates the world to which we turn incessantly and . . . gives to life the *supreme fictions without which we are unable to conceive of it*"; *NA*, 31, my italics.) Thus, for both the speaker and Plato, one's movement toward greater knowledge is paralleled by an increasing difficulty in *naming* the things one discovers. Referring to Plato's "cosmic poetry in prose," Stevens wrote:

> Certainly a sense of the infinity of the world is a
> sense of something cosmic. It is cosmic poetry be-
> cause it makes us realize in the same way in which
> an escape from all our limitations would make us
> realize that we are creatures, not of a part, which is
> our everyday limitation, but of a whole for which,
> for the most part, we have as yet no language. (*OP*,
> 189)

Just as for Plato no image equals its original, so for the speaker of "Notes" no name is equal to one's truest and most comprehensive insights. And the problem is above all a poetic one, perhaps the most crucial, since it involves, on the one hand, "the whole, / The complicate, the amassing harmony" and, on the other, the "bluntest barrier" beyond which no speech exists (403, 397).

Pure parodox, this problem is insoluble in its own terms and so is shifted from reason to sensibility. Major man is thus not so much pure form as a feeling for form. The philosophic question—"He is and may be"—dissolves in the excitement of assertion; and what is impossible as thought is fully possible as feeling: "but oh! he is, he is" (388) Unlike Plato, then, the speaker urges not better reason but better emotion as the solution. The first idea, we are told, can occur in a number of ways:

> It must be visible or invisible,
> Invisible or visible or both:
> A seeing and unseeing in the eye. (385)

Plato's theory that the invisible world of ideas *causes* the visible world of things is here reconceived fully. That is, sometimes visual perception causes the first idea to take shape (section VII) while at other times the first idea causes perception (VIII) or both can occur simultaneously (X). Very simply, causality must be a casual affair, both because the world changes constantly and because one's imagination is bored by repetition. (Besides creating the need and context for the poem's second and third parts, this view of causality grounds the technique of sequential probability in the poem's substance.) In refashioning Platonic causality, the speaker gives as much value to thing and sight as to idea and thought; and what subtly emerges is an intellectually serious defense of poetry that is itself brilliantly poetic. *It Must Change.* As intellectual inquiry, the lecturer's attempt at definition is scarcely completed. Having isolated and related idea and thing, thought and sight, he has implied that a full explanation of the supreme fiction that is poetry entails consideration of change and pleasure. Change is thus the subject of the second part, and the major ideas involved are love, marriage, and participation. The major conclusion is:

> Two things of opposite nature seem to depend
> On one another, as a man depends
> On a woman, day on night, the imagined
>
> On the real. This is the origin of change. (392)

Dependency generates change because the "partaker partakes of that which changes him" (392) : that is, as a man loves a woman and is thereby changed, so the imaginative world is transformed through its love for the real. The relationship between imagination and reality is always one of correspondence and similitude, never one in which either fully absorbs and so negates the other. And the reason absorption is impossible is simply that the imagination's processes of change are essentially different from those of the real world. Change in reality is merely repetition and so is "blunt, not broken in subtleties" (390) ; and, because of boredom, we are tempted to legislate permanence to our old perceptions of the world. Yet this temptation is "rubbish in the end" and represents one of "our more vestigial states of mind" (392). The only genuine response is an "easy passion and . . . love" for the possible harmony between the real world and our imaginative knowledge of it. Only this love, and its harmonies, are of "our earthly birth and here and now," for only they are accurate and subtle enough to yield true and faithful fictions (395).

And what is true of the imagination generally is true of poetry particularly:

> The poem goes from the poet's gibberish to
> The gibberish of the vulgate and back again.
> Does it move to and fro or is it of both
>
> At once ? . . . (396)

The poet "tries by peculiar speech to speak / The peculiar potency of the general," thereby infusing the power of generalization into the particulars of perception and so harmonizing the two capacities (397). Abstraction is thus put back into change and is grounded simultaneously in the imagination's transformations and in the world's repetitions. And the poem, then, partakes of both the general and the particular, reflecting change by being abstract even as its abstractions are constantly changing.

This meditation on change seems, the speaker says, "To be an evasion, a thing not apprehended or / Not apprehended well" (396). That is, since the thought *qua* thought is either philosophic banality or nonsense, the mediatation is really an emotional and not rational matter. Again, the attitude is, I suggest, quite Platonic: the deepest truths cannot be directly grasped by the mind but can only be glimpsed by the imagination in myth and story. The poet is therefore the "spokesman at our bluntest barriers" who tells us stories in "a speech only a little of the tongue" (397). Perhaps the poem's most beautiful and complicated myth is the eighth section of the second part (395-396), beginning "On her trip around the world, Nanzia Nunzio / Confronted Ozymandias." Nanzia Nunzio is the spiritual messenger of reality, her name derived from the Italian *nunzio*, "papal ambassador." Her demand for the imagination's speech triggers a miracle: for even when poetry is divested of its gaudy glitter and artifice, reality in it is "never naked" but is always clothed in a perfecting love. In this story of transformation, the speaker's words must evade the truth that is the miracle simply because, once reduced to words, the truth and miracle would lose their reality. That the imagination transforms, perfects, and completes reality is both deeply true and fully mysterious; thus, the poem is a "fictive covering" that reveals as it veils the world.

Again, what is rationally disjunctive is imaginatively harmonious. That is, on a purely rational level, the speaker could never solve the philosophic problems involved in creating and then relating two distinct spheres (imagination and reality), each with its unique processes of change. Yet, in the story of Nanzia Nunzio, he has simultaneously solved and dissolved the problem: the imagination is superior to reality in the way that a perfective power is superior to the thing perfected; and, at the same time, the imagination is dependent upon reality for its life in the way that any power, to exist, is dependent upon an object of power. Though logical nonsense, the assertion combines perfectly a balance of opposites with a hierarchy of values, with the result that the two spheres' processes of change become one:

. . . The freshness of transformation is

The freshness of a world. It is our own,
It is ourselves, the freshness of ourselves. (397-398)

Self and world are thus wedded, and the poems about it become
the necessary "rubbings of a glass in which we peer" and see ourselves, our world, and our lives in the world constantly anew (398).
And in the poem about these poems, "Life's nonsense pierces us
with strange relation" to disclose truths that philosophy never
could (383). *It Must Give Pleasure.* In both preceding parts, the
speaker as lecturer has destroyed the purely rational pattern of his
definitions. The question of irrationality itself is therefore para-
mount: if a decrease in rationality is justified by the truths of the
human imagination, then an increase in irrationality must represent a gain in imaginative value. Yet the *value* of irrationality is
difficult to prove since it is scarcely possible to demonstrate intel-
ligibly even the *fact* of irrationality:

> . . . the difficultest rigor is forthwith,
> On the image of what we see, to catch from that
>
> Irrational moment its unreasoning,
> As when the sun comes rising, when the sea
> Clears deeply, when the moon hangs on the wall
>
> Of heaven-haven. These are not things transformed
> Yet we are shaken by them as if they were.
> We reason about them with a later reason (398-399).

The difficulty begins when first we understand that what we see
is an image of what is, then is increased when we discover that
the relationship between image and object is irrational in that it
is habitual, conventional, and artificial — i.e., an affair purely of
our words. The difficulty deepens when the real world undergoes
momentous change: "the sun comes rising, . . . the sea / Clears
deeply." For these moments of natural change, though they of
course "are not things transformed," nevertheless force us to transform our prior image-object patterns so as to keep pace with
the change. The total process thus involves shock ("we are
shaken") and adjustment to it ("We reason . . . with a later reason"); and it is difficult to *know* much about the process since
knowing is itself more than mere adjustment and is free from
shatterings and shocks. How, then, can rational knowledge know
its own irrationalities?

The answer is, through pleasure. The speaker's idea of pleasure
resembles Plato's idea of the philosopher as a lover of wisdom:

174

that is, the process of the mind's search for order is for both the love of "the whole, / The complicate, the amassing harmony" (403). And while the speaker insists that the process has no fixed sequence, he does claim that it has certain pleasurable shape. The search can begin with simply the sense that things resemble and so depend upon one another, and it can end in a meditation upon cosmic coherence. Or it can start in certain meditation and end in uncertain perception. Either way, the shape — and the pleasure — derives from one's discovery of his own capacity to know and the belief that one's imagination will yield the final truth of everything. This search is irrational in that it is unpredictable, and it is pleasureable in that it affirms as it exercises one's greatest powers. Pleasure thus provides knowledge of the irrational simply because it is itself a knowledge of the process of knowing.

The idea of pleasure thus transforms the earlier meditation on change into a discourse on imaginative processes, and thereby makes fully explicit the poem's central implication: that given the capacities to abstract and to change, man's imagination is not only adequate before reality but is itself more interesting and delightful. Made explicit, the idea thus further implies that man's pleasure is his greatest abstraction and that his imaginative power is his deepest fiction:

> . . . To find the real,
> To be stripped of every fiction except one,
>
> The fiction of an absolute — Angel,
> Be silent in your luminous cloud and hear
> The luminous melody of proper sound. (404)

By virtue of the idea of a capable imagination — this pleasurable "fiction of an absolute" — we can say: "I have not but I am and as I am, I am" (405). Though irrational, this assertion of self creates man at the center of truth, just as his pleasure in it affirms the assertion through knowing it as it is. The imagination, then, asserts, exercises, and validates itself in such a way that its circularity comes to resemble the world's:

> And we enjoy like men, the way a leaf
> Above the table spins its constant spin,
> So that we look at it with pleasure, look

> At it spinning its eccentric measure. Perhaps,
> The man-hero is not the exceptional monster,
> But he that of repetition is most master. (406)

Natural repetition thus provides a basis for imaginative transformation, and vice versa. And the key to poetry, then, lies in the capacity to love the earth's dizzying whirl and to affirm the repetitions of merely "going around" as a final good because it is change imaginatively enjoyed. (Repetition as a technique of esthetic coherence is thereby grounded in the poem's substance.) We thus reach the final marriage of self and world in which abstraction and change together "comprise / An occupation, an exercise, a work, / A thing final in itself and, therefore, good" (405), and we find it pleasurable.

In the final three sections, the speaker goes beyond his lecturer persona. Tentatively as an angel filled "with expressible bliss" (404), then confidently as an "I" who not only can do "all that angels can" but can moreover enjoy angels (405), the speaker at the end gives flesh and voice to the poetic spirit he has all along been discussing. This "I" is major man infused with the speaker's own reality, and the "fictive hero becomes the real" with miraculous simplicity (408). Yet this final transformation is the most complicated in that, because of it, poetic language now goes beyond knowledge to become "the bread of faithful speech" that gives us life as well as the "proper words" by which we gladly die (408). This vision of poetry as sacrament represents, as does Plato's vision of the next thousand years at the end of the *Republic,* a spiritual augmentation of an intellectual injury, a deepening into belief of the mind's discoveries. And, like any belief, the vision requires an emotional leap: "That's it: the more the rational distortion, / The fiction that results from feeling" (406). The measure of the leap, as well as the witness to the miracle, lies in the fact of this final poetic transformation: like Plato become Socrates, so the speaker has become his greatest creation.

And thus, in the last six lines, a completed Supreme Fiction is glimpsed beyond these Notes:

> They will get it straight one day at the Sorbonne.
> We shall return at twilight from the lecture
> Pleased that irrational is rational,

> Until flicked by feeling, in a gildered street,
> I call you by name, my green, my fluent mundo.
> You will have stopped revolving except in crystal. (406-407)

Class over, walking home, the lecturer and ephebe are pleased, even slightly smug, about the insights they have gained. Then, with the merest feeling, the structure of insight becomes the intense experience of seeing and knowing the real world. The completed Supreme Fiction is thus found there where it has always been: in one's response to the world and one's attempt to master but not deny it through accurate speech. The "crystal" of pure knowledge is the imagined future at the same time it is the present fiction that, through feeling, creates that future. The complete Supreme Fiction, like Plato's Form of the Good, therefore involves "a war that never ends" (407) since, in a sense, one constantly moves toward but never reaches it and, in another sense, one is constantly reaching it simply through moving toward it — "up down, / Up down," the speaker concludes (407), thereby restating (as did Plato) the darkest Heraclitean truth, that the two modes of operation are finally the same. And here, as throughout the poem, Stevens' genius lies in the easy humor and ever-ready wit with which his speaker restates such complicated metaphysics: "Fat girl, terrestrial, my summer, my night . . . Civil, madam, I am, but. . . ." (406).

The poem's epilogue is perhaps one of Stevens' boldest strokes. Addressing first the "Soldier" and then "Monsieur and comrade," Stevens briefly sketches the major fact of the world of 1942: "a book in a barrack, a letter from Malay," the Second World War (407). This introduction of the historical moment is crucial in that Stevens ties the dynamics of imaginative argument to the conflicts of literal war: the "war between mind / And sky . . . depends on your [i.e., the soldier's]. The two are one" (407). For just as in the *Republic* Plato's perfect city could not have taken shape without the pleasure of Athens' actual decay, so in "Notes" Stevens' struggle toward imaginative knowledge cannot be understood apart from the pressures of the war. In 1942, Stevens wrote: "To sum it up, the pressure of reality is, I think, the determining factor in the artistic character of an era and, as well, the determining factor in the artistic character of an individual," asserting that the present "war is only a part of a war-like whole" (*NA*, 22, 21). The cool elegance and urbane wittiness of "Notes" thus ultimately implies a view of experience as violent and savage. Yet the "single, certain truth" the poem insists upon as man's fully possible solution to his mind's and his world's wars is stated in the prologue's address to the spirit of the Supreme Fiction: "The vivid transparence that you bring is peace" (380).

May 27, 1946

Scholars tend to take a supercilious view toward "popular" literature; yet the admittedly light-weight works that are runaway best-sellers can tell us a great deal about the actual values and dreams of an era. Certainly an analysis of Ayn Rand's *The Fountainhead* (1943), a longer and more ponderous work than most best-sellers, could tell us a great deal about the distortions of the pioneer spirit in an urban age.

The appeal of Miss Rand's book, however, has obviously not been just to readers of the 40s, but to a certain kind of continually recurrent personality that is unreconciled to the demands of civilization. We can get closer to the distinctive qualities of the period itself by considering one of those books that was enormously popular, but clearly has "had its day."

As the *New York Times'* reviewer pointed out (in a Monday column; the novel was not dignified with space in the influential Sunday *Review*), Frederic Wakeman's *The Hucksters* was perhaps the book during the decade that was looked forward to most eagerly by those in the advertising, public relations, and communications businesses who fancied that they created American tastes and shaped the nation's image of itself.

Surely the late 40s were a Golden Age of advertising, with a public weary of war-time rationing, eager to pounce upon new consumer goods as they became available and television about to begin bringing not just disembodied voices praising products, but the very products themselves into the home. *The Hucksters* is a kind of prose folk ballad about the heroic figure of the period. Although Frederic Wakeman wrote other novels, he was never so precisely to put his finger on the public fancy as in this novel of the forging of post-war America.

David Pugh, in the following essay, gives us an unusual insight into the fate of a "best-seller," by describing the reactions it provoked in the generation that was just being born as it was scoring its great success.

WF

179

Reading an Old Best-Seller: The Obvious and the Unobtrusive

by DAVID G. PUGH

Reading popular novels is often colored by the peculiar mind-set that the book will be simple, obvious and full of cliches. The responses made by some readers born since 1946 to an old best-seller of the forties show that what seems the simple and obvious will vary for them, unmarred (or unaided) by any nostalgia or sentimental journey that an older reader or re-reader experiences. To unleash English majors armed with Literary Interpretation on a twenty-year-old novel results in some surprising responses to style and structure.

Reviews of Frederic Wakeman's *The Hucksters* frequently summed it up as interesting sociology and a good exposé of radio and advertising, but flat in characterization and weak in formal structure. Recently it has been referred to as a bench-mark, the Ur-success myth, a prototype for the organization man in the gray flannel suit. Interestingly enough, the references in the last phrase to the commonly-held image of corporation employees filter down to us over the last two decades in sociological exposition, sometimes in *Fortune*-style prose, as well as in fiction or movie versions. Now that the sociologists are writing sprightly and vivid interpretations themselves, what can be the profit in returning to a

181

best-seller of the forties? Since it no longer seems an exposé, what will a look at structure, characterization and diction tell us now?

One question (here gently passed by) is often phrased, "What on earth did we see in that novel then?" Instead, the inquiry posed is "What gets through to the next generation?" At those points where responses vary, how do they illustrate the complex of experience which a reader must furnish to the suggestive details given him by the writer; how do they illustrate, in the interval between the forties and sixties, the development of different expectancies, different taken-for-granted images or patterns?

When John Updike, for instance, uses a small detail in "Tomorrow and Tomorrow And So Forth" to show that Mark Prosser, the teacher watching his last class of the day enter the room, is interested in one of the young high school girls because he predicts that she will walk through the door wearing "that ember-pink angora sweater," he depends upon a ground for believability much more easily reached for those who attended high school in the thirties and forties than for those more affluent younger readers whose complex of experience triggers the interpretation that there is something wrong with Gloria Angstrom if she wears the same clothes often enough for a teacher to notice them. In reading *The Hucksters,* do readers of the sixties misinterpret patterns which are no longer taken for granted?

Much of the discussion of the machinery of radio programming, Hooperatings, and soap advertising is easily transferable to our viewpoints about TV. Nielsen has replaced Hooper, sight gags now are used instead of being avoided, but the joking bandleader, the stooge, the ritual of "Thursday night is Figaro Perkins (or Jack Benny) night" are all still current. Twenty years have made the Internal Revenue Service rulings on capital gains and corporations built around the entertainment stars much more familiar, and Wakeman's explanations come through clearly. It is not too hard for readers familiar with TWA advertisements showing costumed hostess flights for the tired businessman to make sense of Vic's desire to travel only with reserved space on the Santa Fe Super Chief to Hollywood, or to realize that a Dunhill lighter or Countess Mara ties used to be very "in" things. In these areas of social history, the patterns and the cliches are still close enough to the cues used by the writers so that readers pick up details meant to influence their attitudes toward the characters.

When singer Jean Ogilvie spends much of her time smoothing her skirt, fondling her legs, mentioning that her left breast is a little lower or offering to sleep with Vic, the cues are standard enough (and obvious enough!) to be interpreted now, this side of the Miniskirt, the Maidenform Bra, and the Pill, as they would have been in 1946. It is with the minor characters that any novelist may run the greatest risk of having his characterizing detail become dated: Carnaby Street fashions may interfere with the effect intended in describing a British talent agent who wears a wide apple-green tie, hand-painted with orange-yellow carrots.

Most troublesome, however, are likely to be those references which depend upon some knowledge of political or social history. A younger reader who remembers Truman's dismissal of MacArthur during the Korean War will interpret the description of E. L. Evans as "The Gen. MacArthur of the Ad Game" slightly differently than Wakeman intended, and he may also find that the description of future rocket and missile warfare written in 1946 can jolt someone who remembers the Cuban Missile Crisis of 1962, but not the V-2's over London. Late TV reruns of old movies seem to keep some of the wartime references alive: nylons being scarce, Parisian women hiding shaved heads in turbans after the Liberation, the drunken major on the club car coming back to an unfaithful wife.

The drunken major's behavior is a vignette which serves to sharpen the crucial point of sympathy and identification with the two main characters in the novel. Can a reader coming to the novel in the 1960's, even with servicemen in Viet Nam, vicariously experience the emotional situation which pulls Kay, with a husband in the OSS (what's that?), to have an affair with Vic, and to predict from social attitudes (as well as novelistic foreshadowing) the inevitability of a separation rather than a "happy ending"? Can a reader identify and sympathize with characters, even in a social or historical setting which he is able to visualize, if the details furnished for their behavior and actions seem unrealistic to him?

The board room scene where Vic recognizes that he fears E. L. Evans seems now to be a movie-script set-piece, as full of familiar details as a Henry Fonda jury-room scene or a Perry Mason courtroom, but out of place stylistically in a "novel." What might possibly have been fresh detail then is, two decades later, formula machinery. What kind of a car does Vic rent in Cali-

fornia to drive to the beach? A convertible, natch. The same is
true for some aspects of the language used. To name the actress
who sleeps with Vic on the Super Chief "Constance Linger" can
slip by unnoticed just as Updike can name a high school fullback
"Brute Young" or an ex-basketball player "Flick Webb"; after all,
The Huckster's main character is "Victor." However, when Connie
Linger pleads, afterwards, "Please don't think I'm wanton" — as
the last line closing a chapter, yet — the use of "wanton" can
cause more twitches in a reader these days, providing it is even in
his or her vocabulary.

It is a little hard for readers who acquired their skill in the
era of Nick Adams and Frederic Henry to accept the notion that
the climactic beach scene, with the waves crashing and Kay urging
"Now, Now, Now," could cause readers to giggle that the dialogue
and love scenes are — as in Hemingway — corny and mushy, or
that lines like Kay's "hold my foot, darling. It feels so good when
you hold it," (said as they lie in bed in a third-rate hotel) might
be possible in real life, but can only cause a snort when — as in
Hemingway ? — it is printed on a page of a novel.

Whenever Kay is passionate, her hair is flowing down her back,
but when she is reserved, "regal" in fact, it is done up, braided
into a crown. The reaction to this as an unrealistic cliché is based
upon the frequency with which it is mentioned and its use as a
shorthand editorializing symbol, a reaction to the way the words
are handled within the small units of the book, not to the basic
plot or chapter structure. Repeated references to the skaters in
Rockefeller Center make their use obviously "symbolic," but other
elements tightly linked together in the novel are much more
unobtrusive.

Here the reading of any novel from any era can come to grief.
If a detail is so unobtrusive that it is missed, only a subliminal
coherence can possibly remain; if it seems spelled out too broadly,
the reader may be put off by the artifice. Wakeman built a tight
framework in his 300 pages. The first third of the book establishes
the main character, his job goals, his antagonist, E. L. Evans, and
the reason for the trip to Hollywood via the Super Chief. The middle third introduces Kay, her children (complications) and the
lovers' commitment (on the beach) followed in the last third by
the increasing pressure to stop the affair before her husband returns. Here are some of the symbolic touches or foreshadowings

which are easy for a reader who approaches the novel as a "best-seller" to overlook:

1. Vic buys a Sheraton desk for his "home," an apartment on Sutton Place in New York, and notices the inlaid wood shining in the morning sun before he leaves for the coast. At the end of the novel, when he sits down to phone Kay that it is all over, it is a dark gloomy evening in the foyer as he surveys the desk and all the "junk" he bought for the apartment. That seems obvious enough.

2. At one point Vic and Kay park and light *one* cigarette. "At some point over the weekend they had gotten into the habit of smoking the same cigarette." Later, after Vic indicated he must leave and return to New York, the chapter ends, in the waterfront hotel, with this line: "Their bodies were quiet as they lay side by side in the healing darkness, thoughtfully smoking their cigarettes."

3. At least three times during the train trip the theme and actions of the final chapters are foreshadowed. Vic indicates that he gets no kick out of success and that people have a great deal of trouble because they become scared and fearful; he says that Hollywood is a place where people fall in love for reasons other than love (he says this, by the way, in answer to Kay's conversation opener, "Tell me about Hollywood.") ; Ellen, Kay's small girl, foreshadows her mother's behavior when the girl fusses over Vic, and is told by Kay, "Don't love him to death, dear."

4. And yet again. Vic, throughout the novel, "schemes," in at least three subplots which contrast with and support the behavior of the principal characters at the end. In one of these smaller segments, Wakeman balances Vic's bad writing of Dos-Passos-style prose about "the real America" on the back of telegraph blanks (he tore them up when rereading them the next morning), with his skill at phrasing a contract with a theatrical agent, a real contract, with power and bite, not just empty emotional wordage.

These four items may seem obvious, possibly obtrusive. Yet they were overlooked by readers born since 1946 coming to the novel this last year, readers trained as English majors or graduate students to observe symbol, structure, foreshadowing. The reason the novel was easy for them to put down had more to do with the style and characterization than with creaking plot or symbolic structure. Finding a flatness or staleness in diction apparently turned off their awareness of over-all contrasts in form, too.

Some materials Wakeman used in the novel did affect them, however. Some behavior patterns seem still to be true, to speak to readers a generation later. The objections usually are made to the way things are phrased. A girl, even now, in an upswept hairstyle (never mind the technology of falls of hair) will feel more of a need for distance, for a "don't touch" pattern of behavior. She may not react positively to the word "regal," however. Again, people in love may still enjoy cheeseburgers more than fancy meals, talk of exotic dishes to be impressive, try to make love while worrying about their kidneys, and men may still give women slow infuriating once-overs when they first come into view. The "infuriating" quality seems to be in the unsubtlety, the obviousness, which is exactly the complaint most often voiced about best-sellers like *The Hucksters*.

Wakeman overcomes the woodenness of some of the rest of his dialogue in his ability to evoke suggestively the special cruelty which in a lover's quarrel causes each to tear at the other, "to give back the hurt," to experience both the peaks and the valleys. Does the culturally-expected behavior of women in love, both "appealing and commanding" as Wakeman phrases it, seem a reversal of roles or oddly Victorian now? Apparently, "scheming" men are still taken by young women readers as a fact of life, but without any adverse reactions being evoked by the word *scheme*. It may now be read to show *premeditated planning*, but not an unethical, unfair, unusual design "to take advantage" of a girl.

This ability to share emotions, to feel a common pattern of experience with others vitalizes certain portions of the book, but not frequently enough to keep newer readers involved in its "corny Hemingwayish love scenes." It cannot compete with *TV Guide* as an exposé or sociology, or even compete as a vicarious lark with a 35-year-old superman who never blows his cool. Vic Norman is no James Bond. Its style is too uneven to enable readers to concentrate on the interconnected structure, and it looks and reads like many movies made since then.

Even as a picture of life in 1946, it lacks a certain aura of accuracy. For those who remember the shouting style of the singers on the old Lucky Strike Hit Parade, for those who happen to recall the song "Linger Awhile" as they read the name "Constance Linger," for those who would know what's funny about Don

Ameche inventing the telephone, *The Hucksters* is not a mirror of 1946, but a chance to recall equally distorted images of their own. Like the shrill, glossy, slightly vulgar women in minks riding the Super Chief, the novel's surface is too sleek, especially in the dialogue.

In a sense, Wakeman schemed; he set up a tight narrative and then to show a segment of social life, built in formulas like "Tell me about Hooperatings." You were supposed to see at the time that the "sincerity" was schemed. Two decades later, we react even more strongly to the tone of sarcasm in the word "sincerity," and Wakeman's attitude becomes all the more obvious. Only when the novel happens to use materials still commonly experienced does it sound straightforward enough for readers in this decade to keep interested in it. Even here, there are some grave limitations. To use the opening question again, how can one expect the following incident to get through completely to the next generation?

When Kay has decided to use all her remaining seven days before her husband returns to stay in the sleazy hotel with Vic, he is forced to tell her that he must return to New York the next day. They have been lying on the bed, and she has just had a hysterical shuddering crying spell, after which he has held her close to him. She turns to him, holding herself on her elbows above his body, and he notices she is trembling again. When he says sharply, "Stop it, Kay," she replies, "It's only from leaning on my elbows, that's all it is."

Any one under 30 is likely to think this is an obvious feminine trick and has just got to be an excuse. Linger awhile, kiddo, just linger a few years longer.

August 19, 1946

Because of Faulkner's recent reputation and the success of *Gone with the Wind,* people tend to think of the 30s as the great decade of the Southern novel. Yet scarcely anyone read Faulkner in the 30s; nor had any other Southern writers scored enormous successes. Even the great vogue for Erskine Caldwell's scandalous backwoods romances did not arise until they became available in inexpensive, paperbacked editions in the 40s.

Actually the great age of the Southern novel, quantitatively and (except for Faulkner) qualitatively, was the 40s when the best work of Eudora Welty, Carson McCullers, Caroline Gordon, and Truman Capote appeared. Towering over even all these was the first post-war novel to be greeted with great critical enthusiasm, Robert Penn Warren's *All the King's Men.*

Warren had published novels earlier — *Night Rider* (1939) and *At Heaven's Gate* (1943), but he was still best known at the end of the war as a poet, essayist, and collaborator with Cleanth Brooks on the revolutionary textbook, *Understanding Poetry.* He was to publish many novels after *All the King's Men;* but none have achieved its reputation, and his stories have become increasingly ponderous. In his story of a backwoods demagogue risen to high political estate, Warren was providing the archetypal fictional form for one of this country's most characteristic success stories. Others were attracted to the same material; but Hamilton Basso's *Sun in Capricorn* (1942), John Dos Passos' *Number One* (1943), and Adria Locke Longley's *A Lion is in the Streets* (1945) lack the breadth, intensity, and staying power of Warren's meditation on history.

The relationship of the story to the career of Louisiana's arch-demagogue Huey Long remains controversial. Warren has repeatedly denied that the story was inspired by Long or reflected upon his career; but the parallels between the notorious public figure and Warren's Willie Stark certainly accounted for a great deal of the popularity of the book and the motion picture based upon it. Clearly, however, in detail, *All the King's Men* is not the story of Huey Long; successful fiction is never the unaltered record

189

of one man's life. Perhaps it puts both life and literature in clearest perspective to regard Huey Long as one of the best-known examples of the mythical archetype that Robert Penn Warren creates in *All the King's Men*. As James Justus suggests in the following essay the novel is not even so much *about* Willie Stark as about the influence that this figure exerts upon others.

WF

All the Burdens of
Warren's All The King's Men

by JAMES H. JUSTUS

When *All the King's Men* appeared in August, 1946, it was not the first time that Robert Penn Warren had published his version of such a hardy American theme as the conflict between the public and private self, the real and the ideal, commitment and disengagement. By concentrating on the uses of political power, he had made this theme his own in two previous novels, *Night Rider* (1939) and *At Heaven's Gate* (1943), in which he explored the nature of big-bossism both in its corporate and individual forms. Nor was it the first time he had tried to transform these relatively abstract embodiments of power (the tobacco growers' association in one, Bogan Murdock in the other) into a particularized, sensuously immediate politician whose motives and acts both are examined in a context of rich circumstantiality.

Warren tells us that worrying this politician into shape began in the winter and summer of 1938 in Louisiana and Italy — in a verse drama called *Proud Flesh* — continued in the summer of 1940 and, later, in the spring of 1943, only gradually emerging through what he calls "the coiling, interfused forces" that go into literary decisions as the protagonist of *All the King's Men*. Into this story of a southern demagogue, whose name had now changed from Willie Talos to Willie Stark, went not only the example of Huey Long, the cornpone *tyrannos* whom Warren's governor superficially resembled, but also his wide reading in Dante, Machiavelli, Elizabethan tragedy, American history, William James, and his observation of the very real day-to-day melodrama of depression in Louisiana and fascism in Italy. But Warren was not yet done with his politician. The urge to dramatize the Willie Stark story was not lessened by the enormous critical and popular response to the novel nor by Warren's winning of the Pulitzer Prize. The tinkering and reshaping of the by now multi-versioned drama resulted in numerous theatrical performances, most of them unsuccessful, from 1946 to 1959. Finally in 1960 *The Sewanee Review* published the text of *All the King's Men: A Play* — presumably in the dramatic form which satisfied Warren. The weaknesses of these versions were readily apparent: stilted dialogue, old-fashioned artiness in the Eliot manner, abstract moralisms imposed upon the action, belabored antitheses too categorically parceled out. But the most obvious reason for the dramatic failures was the generic necessity to deëmphasize Jack Burden, the narrator of the novel. This diminishment looms over all, changing all; Burden's transformation from a nearly undifferentiated bystander to chief among the king's men, from mere observer of the spectacle to narrator of and participator in the Willie Stark story, is, as most critics now agree, the peculiar strength of *All the King's Men* as a novel.

The fleshing-out of Burden was from the start, as Warren himself has pointed out, a technical choice. The novel fairly cried out for a more sensitive self-consciousness than that of the politician whose story had to be told. Call him Ishmael or Carraway, Burden is another in a long line of American narrators who by dint of their special positions in the stories they tell end by telling their own stories as well. In the case of Willie Stark, the substance readily invited naturalisitic treatment, and, as Warren saw, remembering the evolution of novelistic form, the "impingement of that material . . . upon a special temperament" allowed him "another perspective than the reportorial one"; it also provided the basis for "some range of style." Both author and narrator finally agree that the story of Willie Stark has been also the story of Jack Burden.

Most of the earlier hostile critics of the novel concentrated their fire on what seemed to them Warren's lax or worse, favorable, attitudes toward a home-grown fascist; most of them regarded Burden, an innocent aristocrat who is disquietingly ambivalent toward corrupt politics, as simply his author's mouthpiece. The implications were grave. If Willie Stark was a fictionalized Huey Long, Jack Burden was a fictionalized Robert Penn Warren, who had taken Long's money, first to teach at Long's university and then to edit the state-subsidized *Southern Review*. It took Warren's introduction to the Modern Library edition of *All the King's Men* (1953) to expose what he called the "boneheadedness" of equating Stark with Long, but slower-pac't evils have a longer day's dying, and we must probably depend only on continuing good sense to see the irrelevance of the second equation. Almost alone among the earliest critics, Norton Girault was able to see the focus of the novel in the character and sensibility of Burden, in his language of rebirth, in his halting, stumbling movements from ignorance to knowledge. Though the progress from Cousin Willie to Governor Stark may be the tale told in the book, it is Burden's revelation of that progress which is the experience of the book. And *revelation* in two ways: first, his discovery of the meaning of Stark's rise and fall and of his own identity through these events, and second, his articulation of those meanings in a long I-narration. Perhaps no other modern novel so clearly demonstrates the fact that a happy technical choice, a fictive device, alters the very meaning of materials which it must shape. Nothing is more naturally dramatic or susceptible of significance than the Willie Stark story, the hard narrative facts isolated and untouched by a consciousness other than the author's. But both the drama and the meaning of that story are significantly redirected and heightened by having those narrative facts experienced and related by an intervening consciousness. In Burden this consciousness belongs to a man of imagination and intelligence whose own drama, as James observed of Lambert Strether, is, "under stress, the drama of discrimination," the shucking off of first one, then another, alternative to meaning until he *sees* and in the seeing allows the reader to follow the painful progress to moral awareness. From the desire to remain innocent, to resist the costly maturity of rebirth, Burden moves through even more costly immersions into experience, which he misinterprets and revises until he is forced to acknowledge his portion of evil.

* * * * *

Burden is a most unlikely learner when we meet him. Smug, intelligent, world-weary, he could almost pass for a New South variety of Conrad's Decoud in *Nostromo*. But the empty *boule-vardier,* who scribbles his self-regenerative letter in the focus of battle, has pushed a habit of vision to its limits; Burden's memoir is itself the symbol of regeneration, a product of, not an ingredient in, his moral education. Such a memoir, then, is *All the King's Men,* produced by a man who, after having arrived at a certain stage of self-knowledge, reënacts the costly process. We are constantly aware of growth as something both achieved and being achieved. But however insistent the interweaving of product and process — the necessary impingement of present attitudes on past beliefs and acts — the shaping perspective is that of the educated Jack Burden, the "legal, biological, and perhaps even metaphysical continuator" of the earlier king's man.

Burden's change has sometimes been thought phony or self-deceiving. And it is true that Jack Burden is no Cass Mastern; neither is he a Scholarly Attorney. He has nothing of the humility of the one nor the radical spirituality of the other. But in his learning, Burden does achieve a measure of both humility and spirituality which is lacking earlier. There are conversions and conversions. If we are tempted to think of Burden as non-changing because he does not become either a Mastern or a Scholarly Attorney, we might well speculate on the failure that would result if Burden's conversion had taken on the obsessive coloration of those other two. One of the thematic constants in Warren's fiction is that single-mindedness, of whatever sort, destroys human balance; it leads to a warping of man's need for community as well as for personal identity. Hence, the narrator's slower progress. If Burden calls Trollope "Anthony," it is only good craftsmanship to make the new Burden in certain tangible ways consistent with the old. Even the disasters tumbling in profusion about him cannot rout the tendencies of a lifetime — the easy cynicism of the newspaperman grafted onto the floating romanticism of the graduate student.

It is also true that the narrator seems callous in episodes which, upon proper assessment, require sensitivity; and he turns unduly sensitive at times when we would prefer less verbalization from The Hurt Young Man. But we are *properly* offended by his on-again off-again, hard-boiled detective stances interspersed by debilitatingly romantic fancies. There is, in short, in Burden an esthetically functional split that Warren articulates by making his narrator vacillate between pretentious philosophizing and wise-guy witticisms. To wish away such weaknesses is to prefer a more simplistic character than the one which Warren created. The split in his narrator serves in fact as an exemplum, a trope, compacted and made interior, for the entire novel. If a study of its theme and structure shows anything, it is that *All the King's Men* is a meditation on "the terrible division of [our] age," explored not only through explicit antitheses (man of idea-man of fact, means-ends, science-nature) but also through the subtle and pervasive doubling of characters: Stark-Burden, Burden-Duffy, Stark-Irwin, etc. It is natural that Burden, with his problems of integration, should become the front-and-center figure within the play of larger, if not more meaningful, antitheses; we know him better than any other character, and we do so only through a narration that reveals qualities which in real people we could do just as well without. Tough guys and ersatz philosophers in our own time can be just as tiresome as efficient housekeepers and virtuous companions of Victorian fiction.

As the twentieth-century wise guy who has put his learning to work for him, Burden must take shape, more imperatively even than Stark, literally through his own words. As public figure, he is in-the-know; as private figure, he seeks to know. His rhetoric, both as narrator and as character, reflects this split, appropriately embodying the strain between Burden as Sam Spade and Burden as Stephen Dedalus. He is alternately garrulous and non-committal; he is cynically efficient, always prepared to "deliver" or to "make it stick." Privately, he belittles his efficiency, and we become increasingly aware of his real distaste for the particular person he has become. He chides himself frequently, referring to himself in the third person. With cocksure stridency he announces "the curse" of Jack Burden: "he was invulnerable." But even as he talks, he shows how vulnerable he is — to nostalgia, sentimentality, and tangential events which nudge him into newer versions of himself and of reality.

The Burden who remains after the fall of the king is a different person from the king's man; indeed, after those ambivalent and tentative loyalties, he takes a stand similar to Cass Mastern's. Partially responsible for at least three deaths and several lesser disasters, he comes to accept them fully in the "awful responsibility of time." He ends with a healthier respect for flawed humanity, extending to both Judge Irwin and Willie Stark, and with discomfort even sees his connection, spiritual as well as physical,

196

with Tiny Duffy. As acting son and stenographer, he cares for the Scholarly Attorney in his last days; and instead of condescension toward his husband-prone mother he shows a thoroughly admirable, if low-keyed, compassion. He devotes himself to the long-delayed editorial task of publishing the diary of Cass Mastern. He refuses to say the word to Sugar-Boy that would destroy not only Duffy but Sugar-Boy as well. He marries Anne Stanton which, even in the afterglow of passion, still represents a belated victory over the paralyzing image of purity which he holds of her throughout much of the novel. Perhaps most important, he even hints of his return to active politics under the aegis of the honest Hugh Miller.

Burden is a conscious artist scrupulously constructing his story from an open position, manipulating the early image of himself from his newer stance of control, growth, and moral self-evaluation. Though he perceives more at the end than at the beginning of the novel, he is careful in his verbal reconstruction to permit his earlier self full rein to maneuver within those limited terms. If he sounds occasionally hysterical or often absurd to us, that impression is one that the narrator who reconstructs himself is the first to recognize. Such is the risk that the educated Burden willingly takes to present the learning Burden honestly. Certainly the final position at which he arrives is neither absurd nor hysterical. It is, in fact, a measure of his integrity that he can submit an imperfect image of himself with only such sporadic glossing as "that was the way I argued the case back then."

His rhetoric throughout maintains certain characteristics: wise-cracks, fancy metaphors, self-irony, the mingling of the elegant and colloquial. His general diction and syntax do not change in any substantial way, since the entire story is a memoir of events from 1922 (and occasionally earlier) to 1939 in the language of the latest stage of his growth. Just as there is no dramatic physical alteration in Burden — he presumably looks much the same in the late 1930s as he did in the early 1920s — so there is no obvious change in the physical shape of his words. The changes in Burden are philosophical and psychological, and the changes in his language are largely tonal.

It is one thing to see the mature Burden still clinging to the wise-guy idiom of his Great Twitch days, but more important is the fact that the tone of that idiom shifts perceptibly. Here is the typical early Burden style:

> In a town like Mason City the bench in front of
> the harness shop is — or was twenty years ago before
> the concrete slab got laid down — the place where
> Time gets tangled in its own feet and lies down like
> an old hound and gives up the struggle. It is a place
> where you sit down and wait for night to come and
> arteriosclerosis. It is the place the local undertaker
> looks at with confidence and thinks he is not going
> to starve as long as that much work is cut out for
> him. . . . You sit there among the elder gods, dis-
> turbed by no sound except the slight *râle* of the one
> who has asthma, and wait for them to lean from the
> Olympian and sunlit detachment and comment,
> with their unenvious and foreknowing irony, on the
> goings-on of the folks who are still snared in the
> toils of mortal compulsions.

This subject — courthouse characters — is not an unusual one for
the narrator at any time; neither is the feeling of bemused superiority which seeps out of his own Olympian syntax and the
brash imagery. But if the subject and the observer's clear-eyed
view of it do not vary greatly, the tone does. Here is a similar
passage from the last chapter:

> And I sat for hours in the newspaper room of the
> public library, the place which like railway stations
> and missions and public latrines is where the catar-
> rhal old men and bums go and where they sit to
> thumb the papers which tell about the world in
> which they live for a certain number of years or to
> sit and wheeze and stare while the gray rain slides
> down the big window-pane above them.

In his final phase the narrator's wisecracks become muted, the
tough line grows flabby, the naturalistic observations become a
trifle lame, the superiority itself undergoes chastening: all these
changes reflect the sadness and near-inertia of an exhausted man.

* * * * *

One of our pleasures in following the narrator's efforts to
close his emotional and intellectual gaps is, I think, our detection
of the extraordinary resonance of that struggle throughout the
novel, the way in which this interior trope is reinforced by every

aspect of the larger context. Consider, for example, the title of *All the King's Men* and its Dantean epigraph. In these Warren establishes, almost anterior to the novel itself, two apparently contradictory positions which suggest the basis of the conflict in Burden's difficult progress to self-knowledge. The title, with its nursery-rhyme allusion, connotes a pattern of thought and behavior dominated by acquiescence to the phenomenal, the factual, the way things are. The factual motif is posited by Stark's own proverb: "Man is conceived in sin and born in corruption and he passeth from the stink of the didie to the stench of the shroud." Burden's own discovery in his Case of the Upright Judge ("There is always the clue") is reinforced by Cass Mastern's final vision of the "common guilt of man" and the Scholarly Attorney's tract statement that "the only way for God to create, truly create, man was to make him separate from God Himself, and to be separate from God is to be sinful." This pattern, in short, asserts the natural depravity of man, the way, whether he likes it or not, man is.

Against the shattered world of Humpty Dumpty, Burden comes to juxtapose his own experiences in that tragedy and to conclude from them that he has not only been affected by the tragedy but that he has also affected it. As a Student of History, Burden must accept Cass Mastern's insistence on personal involvement in the guilt of others; as a student of human nature, he must share the blame in an affair that takes the lives of his two best friends and almost wrecks the life of the woman he loves. The deterministic resonance of the title, however, is counterpointed by the fragmentary epigraph from the *Purgatorio*: *Mentre che la speranza ha fior del verde*. The hope that survives the Willie Stark story may appear more gray than green, but it is hope nevertheless.

Acceptance of the way things are may, without hope, be merely sentimental complacency. As a graduate student, Burden had flippantly visualized his future in some junior college "long on Jesus and short on funds" where he would have watched "the slow withering of the green wisp of dream," but later he can find a green wisp in the most basic fact of all: "there were some of us left." Survival is earned. He and Anne read Trollope together, uncurious about how equilibriums are changing; caught in a "massive and bemusing tide," hardly speculating on the "happiness which it surely promised," they accept that tide's own "pace and time." Acceptance is earned. Burden, seeing the grandson of

Stark, agrees with Lucy that she has to believe that Stark had been a great man even though the "greatness and ungreatness" had been so mixed even he could not tell them apart. History is neutral, but man, working through history, is not. For all the ruck of irresistible fact that impinges on him, man must still exercise his will. There is fact, and there is hope. Certain theological and psychological benefits may be gained from accepting the way things are. But whatever his nature, man still lives in a defective world with other defective men, and mutual responsibilitiy involves more of man's energies than a statement of weary resignation. Picking up the pieces may not put together another king, but the reminder of human fragility may stimulate the survivors to cherish what virtues remain.

These thematic dichotomies associated with the factual and the hopeful are futher articulated by the metaphorical possibilities of *rest* and *motion.* The way things are, man's depravity, the familiar pattern of failure after great effort — all these suggest *rest,* the state of certainty, the problem solved, the contest won (or lost). The possibility of hope even in these terms, the perpetual testing of values, the willingness to risk becoming reconciled after grandly repudiating — all these suggest *motion,* the trying-out of grace, direction if not destination. The confident Burden is the cocky newspaperman who pursues the embarrassing deed out of the past to "make it stick," the cynical observer of the political animals at play, the Student of History who exchanges without undue upheaval his brass-bound Idealism for the scientific positivism of the Great Twitch (and is perfectly certain that in each case he has arrived at Truth, or at least truth). In one of his definitive gestures — the flight West — he says, "meaning is never in the event but in the motion through event." This "direction is all" attitude is confirmed in his theological parries with the Scholarly Attorney. "Life is motion," he repeats several times; "if the object which a man looks at changes constantly so that knowledge of it is constantly untrue and is therefore Non-Knowledge, then Eternal Motion is possible." But these statements of self-assurance come from the king's man; in the end, Burden affirms the truth of both rest and motion.

The famous final paragraph of the novel shows the rhetorical manipulation of these two patterns. With its emphasis on depleted energies, memory, and nostalgia, the emotional associations are with rest; but the syntax and diction suggest motion: *to walk*

down the Row, walk down the beach, diving floats lift gently,
footfall, we shall move, we shall go out, and go into. The substance of the final paragraph is that even nostalgia will have no
easy time of it; even that indulgence "will be a long time from
now. . . ." The price of seeing things as they are has been high.
Burden has seen his two friends, Stark and Stanton, "doomed,"
but, though doomed, they have been men of individual will. Thus
the burden of Jack Burden is what he learns to bear: man, though
he accepts inscrutable providence, cannot luxuriate in a paralysis
of action because of that surety. The tone of the later Burden
cannot be called optimistic. He no longer rests his case in firmly
bound, well-labeled file folders. Except for his acknowledgement
of man's situation "in the world in which we live from birth to
death," he comes to see all other judgments as tentative, judgments which therefore require retesting to be continually relevant.

If Burden achieves a victory, it is in recognizing the necessity
for submitting the self to motion, for acting upon the slender
"green hope" in the face of defeat, and for resisting the temptation toward a retreat into despair. But one of the achievements of
Burden's memoir is that it can reveal the victory while simultaneously celebrating the occasionally debilitating movements toward
it. While in the tentative rest of the final period the tone of the
narrator is less patronizing, less dogmatic, the basic thrust of his
rhetoric remains the same. Artist that he is, he never allows even
his guilt, rooted in the magnitude of recent events, to paralyze
his ability to narrate effectively, and although Burden reconstructs
his own past with as much detachment as he does the entire context of the Stark era, he still bears the personal marks of that
ordeal. His name, we can see now, suggests something of his vital
centrality in that general reconstruction. Thematically, he bears
his past with difficulty, heavy obligation, and great expense; and
even the future must be borne. Structurally, and here the musical
signification of *burden* is pertinent, his story carries the "ground"
for the more obvious pattern of Stark's story, the obligatory
measures of the entire novel. When Burden permits the learning
character to catch up with the narrator who has learned, he admits
how tempting it has been to try to shoulder the least painful parts
of his burden. He is denied, for instance, the "inexpensive satisfaction in virtue" when, upon trying to give what was left of Irwin's
estate to Miss Littlepaugh, he finds she has died.

At the end of *All the King's Men,* Burden is both his own

judge and his own accused who, deprived of many of the intellectual and emotional conditions which he formerly demanded, must
now accept his own burden of being man. He is like Bunyan's
Christian at the beginning of the journey; but for Jack Burden
that journey lies beyond the confines of the novel, beyond 1939,
in the "convulsion of the world" where, we may assume, his own
travail will be convulsive before his burden can be rolled away.

October 9, 1946

The great news of the young theatrical season was that Broadway was to see the first production in twelve years of a new full-length play by Eugene O'Neill — undisputedly America's greatest playwright — who had become an almost legendary figure since winning the Nobel Prize in 1936.

The Iceman Cometh has failed to become one of O'Neill's popular plays. Although closely related in theme and tone to much of his earlier work like *Mourning Becomes Electra, Anna Christie,* and *Beyond the Horizon,* it is a long and excessively talky play that shows little interest in the expressionistic experimentation that has made works like *The Emperor Jones, The Hairy Ape,* and *Strange Interlude* especially popular.

The play was greeted with respect rather than enthusiasm. During O'Neill's long absence from Broadway as the result of illness and pathetic domestic problems, a new audience had grown up. His only successful plays since the beginning of the depression had been visits back to the New England past, nostalgically in *Ah, Wilderness!* and condemnatorily in *Mourning Becomes Electra.* It was a long time since his work had electrified the Freud-struck audiences of the 20s.

O'Neill was yet to have perhaps his greatest moment in the theatre, in his posthumous return to New England, neither to mythologize nor sentimentalize, but to exorcise the spirits that haunted him, in *A Long Day's Journey into Night.* The solemnities of *The Iceman Cometh* were not, however, what the post-war audience was looking for. Its production served perhaps most importantly to make it clear that the theatre — like the novel and the poem — must have a rebirth in the United States.

WF

203

O'Neill's Legion of Losers
in The Iceman Cometh

by Sy Kahn

Written in 1939, produced in 1946, set in 1912, *The Iceman Cometh* evokes a turn-of-the-century world. Yet the play speaks to contemporary dilemmas and renders an intense and immediate point of view. Nostalgia purified of sentimentalism by a passion for truth characterizes not only this play but also Tennessee Williams' *The Glass Menagerie* (1944), and Arthur Miller's *Death of A Salesman* (1949). In these plays all three of our major playwrights evoke a pre-world-War II America, but their final comment and concern are pointed toward the American temper and tensions of the post-war world.

In the Williams' play the narrator, Tom Wingfield, projects on stage his memory of the depression years of the 1930's in Saint Louis, but reminds us at the end that "now the world is lit by lightning." In the closing scene he advises his sister Laura to blow out her candles which lit, for a brief time, her eccentric and gentle qualities, somehow associated with a world between wars. If that world for Americans had its economic disasters, social inequities and political innocence, it also had a tenderness and poetry, a humanity that the incinerations of the death camp and atom bomb made all the more valuable. Many of us who saw that magic play knew, however, that somewhere back in the 30's we had left and lost a Laura and some of the feeling that made it possible for us to value her. We could no longer hold a candle to the glare of the new lightning.

In Miller's Willy Loman, American audiences found a greater symbol than in Laura and Tom, because Willy was so painful an image of themselves. (And if not for oneself, who did not have an Uncle Willy through which he could translate image back into reality?) Aside from its obvious social crticism of a heartless capitalism, the play spoke to all who in their middle years lived with the nagging fear that they had made the wrong choice, followed a dream that proved tarnished and shoddy, and now, too late, saw death as the only way out. One might also feel that the death of this salesman could be the foreshadowing image of the death of a nation, not only because of the great international tensions of the post-war years but also, as D. H. Lawrence once observed of Americans, having made material success and social status rule and subordinate our intuitive, instinctive selves, we planted the seed of our own destruction.

Both Williams' and Miller's plays succeeded, I think, because they manipulated the past to reveal the moods and fears of post-war America. Recalling a longer span of time, creating a larger cast of characters and writing a play twice the length of the ordinary three-act drama, O'Neill made his play serve the same purpose. His was a dark, if not the darkest view. When interviewed in 1946 about the play, he commented, "I'm going on the theory that the United States, instead of being the most successful country in the world, is the greatest failure." In *The Iecman Cometh* one may discover why O'Neill made this judgment at a time when the military victory of World War II gave Americans a feeling of the country's great strength and encouraged a belief in its success. In part O'Neill's dark judgment springs from the man's characteristic brooding and tragic view of life; in part it springs from his reading of American culture.

Harry Hope's bar in lower Manhattan is the last haven for a legion of losers, a refuge for the social failure and the spiritually derelict. On this sleazy stage whiskey-soaked men play out the ragged ends of their lives and three female characters ply their ancient profession. Taken together, they shape a motley chorus of failure, but they are so down and out, so deep below the surface of American life that ordinarily a busy America would hardly know they were there, much less hear them. However, in their

various laments, ambivalent feelings and rationalizations one hears
the arguments, the self-delusions and guilts that pervade a society
and could account for its massive failure. By various routes and
from all levels of society, the characters have sunk to the "No
Chance Saloon, Bedrock Bar, The End of the Line Café, The
Bottom of the Sea Rathskeller," as Larry Slade, the "Old Foolosopher," characterizes it. As the play unfolds, the inmates of Harry's
make manifest that their besodden condition is not the cause but
the symptom of their individual defeats, their defections and dis-
affections from the mainstream of American life. As Larry comments later, "here they keep up the appearance of life with a few
harmless pipe dreams about their yesterdays and tomorrows. . . ."
In the bar's perpetual, dirty twilight they keep a moribund peace
together, as long as they accept and support each other's illusions
about how it was and how it might be. "The lie of a pipe dream
is what gives life to the whole misbegotten mad lot of us, drunk
or sober," Larry observes. Sardonically, he amplifies meaning when
he says, "It's a great game, the pursuit of happiness," a game, one
can conclude, in which there are only losers. It is not without
point that the bespectacled Hope is both hard of hearing and
short-sighted, though far less so than he pretends. The irony is
doubled when we learn that Hope also depends on his beggarly
customers to sustain his own illusions. So they lean together, group
and regroup, sustained by their illusions and Hope's nickle whiskey, an orchestration by O'Neill of the themes of defeat.

An event anticipated by this becalmed crew is the occasional
visit of Hickey (Theodore Hickman), a hardware salesman who
goes on periodic drinking sprees and invites the inmates of Hope's
bar to share his lavish revelry and ribaldry. The play opens on the
day before Hope's sixtieth birthday, raising the expectation that
Hickey will soon appear and stir them. He is an old-time drummer
of the hard-sell school, fat, jovial, ready with a joke and a drink.
In his early background is a Fundamentalist preacher for a father
and in the immediate background is a small-town, local girl sweetheart who became his abused but relentlessly forgiving wife. To
the forces generated by them and his hard-sell capitalistic culture,
Hickey responds with great energy. A desperate hilarity and vulgarity masks the guilt that drives him.

Among all O'Neill's examples of losers in the pursuit of happiness, Hickey is the most suggestive of the themes and implications of the play. A salesman, not unlike Willy Loman in many

ways, he represents, first of all, a frequent American type: profit-seeking, energetic, transient, optimistic, middle class; in short, a jovial huckster. Typically, neither can he remain faithful to his wife (he once contracted a venereal disease and passed it on to her), nor can he fulfill her idealization of him, which is perhaps more puritanic than romantic. His failures permit her to luxuriate in the role of forgiving martyr, retaining the hope, her "pipe dream," for Hickey's reform. In his turn Hickey fails to realize that his drinking bouts, his loveless sexual encounters, and his vulgar joke about his wife and the iceman are expressions of his accumulated hostility and unbearable guilt because his life and wife bring him neither happiness nor peace.

Further, Theodore Hickman's name, "Hickey," suggests that as a "country hick," he is psychologically naive and a buffoon. It is for this son of a preacher and his obliterating whiskey that the desperate congregation of Hope's bar wait. Theodore (which means "gift of God") is clearly meant to be an inverted and pathetic saviour whose strong waters help sink his friends deeper into their illusions. In Hope's bar we have an image of sheep and shepherd even further removed from insight and salvation than were the Fundamentalist preacher-father who sold, as Hickey saw it, "nothing for something" to his Indiana congregation.

The comic and ironic inversion of the saviour figure does not stop at this point. It is a new Hickey who this time appears in the lower depths; he has a gospel to sell that he feels has not only solved his old dilemmas but also will bring peace and happiness to his friends. No longer able to bear what he imagines has been his wife's terrible unhappiness because of his failure to reform, he has murdered Evelyn. He rationalizes this act as an ultimate expression of his love for her because it ended her suffering. Though he does not reveal the murder until the end of the play, he arrives at the bar convinced that by his act he has faced the truth, understood his motives, and attained a freedom and salvation that compels, even ordains, him to help his barroom friends. They have only to stop dreaming, explode their illusions, accept themselves and thus be free of both guilt and futile hope.

Most of the members of Hope's bar harbor the dream that "tomorrow," when they stop drinking, spruce up and present themselves to a world long deprived of and eargerly awaiting their talents, they will regain their former respectability. Typical is James Cameron, called "Jimmy Tomorrow," a former correspon-

dent but now a hopeless alcoholic and the "leader of the Tomorrow Movement," as the choral leader of the play Larry Slade observes. Hickey plans to urge Jimmy and all the other dreamers
of their "tomorrows" to translate hope into reality, each in his
own way. They do not understand that Hickey himself does
not believe they will succeed. His strategy is to encourage their
failure in order to free them of the delusion that they can change.
Consequently, they will accept themselves, finally absolved of guilt
and frustration. As for the prostitutes and their pimp, Rocky the
bartender, Hickey encourages that they face the fact of their true
relationships and that the girls cease euphemistically calling themselves "tarts" and that Rocky stop deluding himself that he is not
a pimp simply because he holds a job and does not beat up his
"stable." Similarly he encourages Harry Hope to take the walk
around the ward he has threatened for twenty years, and for Cora,
an older prostitute, and Chuck, the relief bartender, to consummate
the legal marriage they have contemplated for years while living
together, and for Larry to face the fact that he does not really want
the death he claims he courts.

As each character approaches the moment of commitment, he
experiences excruciating tension and terrifying fear that translate into hostility toward Hickey who magnanimously bears all
insult and rejection. Deadly earnest, now he is a comic and pitiful
psychiatrist attempting to impose a simple formula on complicated phychological dilemmas. Hickey's naivete makes the comedy
ironic and dangerous when we know that his theory is based upon
his own rationalization and delusion. Late in the play, during his
long confessional speech, his real motive for killing his wife spills
out. It was not to stop her misery and to bring her peace but
rather to express the insupportable humiliation and resentment
her dependable forgiveness engendered in him and that prevented
him from accepting himself. Recalling his feelings after the
murder, finally he blurts out:

> I remember I stood by the bed and suddenly I had
> to laugh. I couldn't help it, and I knew Evelyn
> would forgive me. I remember I heard myself
> speaking to her, as if it were something I'd always
> wanted to say: "Well, you know what you can do
> with your pipe dream now, you damned bitch!"

When Hickey stumbles onto his real feeling and motive, the

shock is so great that he can accept his statement only as evidence of his insanity. All his friends shrewdly seize upon Hickey's "insanity" as a way to justify their resentment of him and their own failures to translate their illusions about themselves into action; they can retreat to "the bottom of the sea" again and sentimentalize and pity the Hickey they hated. At the end of the play, Hickey removed by the police, they sing a cacophonous medley of songs, sentimental, political or lamenting, each according to his character and dilemma, making a wild, hilarious chorus as they return to their whiskey-laced illusions. Thus the play comes full circle.

In its comi-tragic way, the play warns that man is more comfortable encapsulated by his illusions than in the revealing light of self-knowledge. Of course, it may be argued that Hickey is an insufficient and crude agent for either salvation or psychological insight, guilt-ridden and pipe dreaming himself, driven by unrecognized resentment, but I think this is part of O'Neill's ironic joke, his jibe at and judgment of America. We want our illusion of success, no matter how hopelessly out of reach, while wisdom, salvation and insight, in the hands of a hard-sell salesman, turn into inept, bludgeoning instruments, particularly when wielded by one who lacks insight into himself. Seen this way, the play is a bitter and comic allegory about America; it is O'Neill's warning to a victorious country in 1946 that the inner dilemmas of man are not solved by materialism, martial victory, or simple formulas. In part Hickey symbolizes an American tendency to reduce human complexity and desperate need to simple solutions — one easy application, one swipe and wipe, and presto! — a repaired psyche.

Already a murderer when he arrives on the scene, Hickey is the "iceman" who brings death into the midst of hope, and the grim figure of his own joke about his wife "in the hay with the iceman." The "Cometh" of the title gives to Hickey as death figure an ancient and universal implication, as well. Indeed, he catalytically brings one character, Parritt, to suicide and the "Old Foolosopher" to a real acceptance of the death he has always feared more than desired. By implication, all that Hickey represents is touched by death. Early in the play one character says, "Let us join in prayer that Hickey, the Great Salesman, will soon arrive bringing the blessed bourgeoise long green! Would that Hickey or Death would come!" Such a speech announces O'Neill's theme and also associates death with "the bourgeoise long green," and "salesmanship."

Hugo voices all the characters feeling when he observes after Hickey's confession, "Yes, I am glad they take him to asylum. I don't feel I am dying now. He was selling death to me, that crazy salesman." To Parritt, the youthful suicide, Hickey is "something not human behind his damned grinning and kidding." Well-intentioned, well-heeled, rationalistic, Hickey is a parabolic figure for the American who threatens himself and perhaps all the world because of his shallow insight into the death that is instinct in all that he represents. In Hickey, guilt, hostility and resentment, engendered by moralistic simplicities and bourgeoise idealism, conspire to create a passion for destruction, masked and justified by altruistic motives. By comparison, the deluded dreamers of Hope's bar fare better than the self-righteous killer.

It will come as no surprise to readers of O'Neill's earlier plays to discover that women stand at the center of most of the characters' dilemmas. We have seen how crucial Evelyn is in shaping Hickey's problems, and we may consider her as pervasive a type as Hickey himself. Incrementally, most of the other characters reveal that they, too, are bedeviled by the women in their lives, making women a powerful motif in the play, though curiously only three prostitutes appear on the stage itself.

As crucial as Evelyn is to Hickey, young Don Parritt's mother is to him. His name indicates his function in the play; he is a reverberating echo to Hickey and Larry. The youngest and latest addition to Harry Hope's premises, he has run from the West Coast after informing the police that his mother is deeply involved in an Anarchist bomb plot. In New York he seeks and finds Larry Slade, his mother's old friend, cohort and lover, long withdrawn from "The Movement" and life. Despised instinctively by the group, despising himself even more, no character is more pitiable than Parritt. Posing as a fugitive from the police, he fastens himself upon Larry, seeking in him a father and a judge, a person both to condemn and to absolve him. Larry, however, repelled by Parritt, wishes neither to know him nor to help him expiate his guilt for having traduced his mother. Like Hickey, Parritt moves through a series of rationalizations for his action — patriotism, money — but his real motive proves to be his ambivalent love-hate for his mother who has neglected him for a series of lovers and who has made "The Movement" and her free style of life of greater moment than her son. Unable to accept her sequential liaisons, he is particularly hostile toward the prostitutes in that they represent to him the debasement he feels in his mother. Rejected by both Rosa Parritt and Larry, he is the most orphaned and alienated character in the play, and in leaping to his death makes manifest the self-destructive forces implicit in Larry and Hickey. Larry withdrew from Rosa for reasons that parallel Parritt's, and in finally condemning Parritt, plays out his own death-wish and resolves his old tensions.

Hickey and Parritt, who have little to do with each other, nevertheless define the hard line of a theme: both men take an ultimate revenge on the women they love because they resent and hate the humiliation women have made them feel — forces that destroy both the women and the men. O'Neill makes his strategy clear when Parritt parrots Hickey's confession with his own and makes the same explosive judgment of his mother that Hickey made of his wife. Parritt confesses that after trapping his mother he felt like saying to her, "You know what you can do with your freedom pipe dreams now, don't you, you damned old bitch!" Larry replies, "Go, for the love of Christ, you mad tortured bastard, for your own sake!"

In Harry Hope and his dead wife, Bessie, we find the theme of ambivalent feeling given further dimension. For twenty years Harry has sentimentalized Bessie, but under pressure from Hickey, he explodes. "Close that big clam of yours, Hickey. Bejees, you're a worse gabber than that nagging bitch, Bessie, was." These examples do not exhaust the point but are sufficient to illustrate the theme of life-long but repressed hostility toward the "good" women in the men's lives. Each is shocked when he confronts his feeling that the woman was a "bitch," and recoils, and in some cases destroys not only the women but also himself.

The three streetwalkers, Pearl, Maggie and Cora, comic and pathetic figures like many of the men, serve as foils to the off-stage women. Though they have their small illusions too — they are "tarts" not "whores" — they ironically remind the audience of certain virtues. If disreputable, they are often kind, generous, and unjudgmental toward the men; they have an acceptance of the flesh that is natural and without illusion. They neither forgive nor condemn men from some intimidating moral pedestal. They are the uninhibited whores one finds not only in O'Neill's other plays but also frequently in American literature: women with hearts of gold, human and natural. These literary whores may not often have their counterpart in life, but whether they do or not, they serve as an indictment against the sexually pure or correct women who drive their men to desperate ends, or to end desperately; they do express the outrage of American male writers against those women, and the codes and culture, that have exacted a punishing ordeal upon men.

The unmasking of real motives, especially the real motives of male-female relationships, always ambivalent, always dangerously destructive, is common to American literature of this century, and particularly in O'Neill's plays. Ultimately, there is an indictment of America here. As we have seen, both men and women are subject to "pipe dreams," to idealizing each other and life in general. Impossible goals make failure and guilt inevitable. The failed dream, when not buried under a desperate optimism, a busy and distracting materialism, or sodden alcoholism, can foment frustration to the point of violence, murder and suicide.

In *The Iceman Cometh* O'Neill catches the pattern of the America he experienced and which impelled his judgment that America was a failure. We have the perspective of almost a quarter of a century since the end of World War II and the production of the play to measure his statements. Read for its broad implications, the play suggests, I think, that victory and world-involvement, celebration, affluence and the pipe dream of peace can neither mask nor repress our emotional ambivalence and tensions, not if the off-stage ladies and the on-stage men are an index of reality. The play evokes the truth that man is easily trapped in a dream. If it is the wrong dream — and one might recall Biff's speeches at the graveside of Willy Loman, and Edward Albee's *The American Dream* — the dream becomes the trap that can kill us all.

February 19, 1947

Eugene O'Neill's *The Iceman Cometh* contained a message for post-war America, but not a message that a nation tired of austerity and flushed with transient victory wanted to hear. Another ill-timed work was Malcolm Lowry's *Under the Volcano,* a powerful study of the events of one day in November, 1938, "The Day of the Dead" in Mexico and the last day in the life of Geoffrey Firmin, British Consul in the Mexican town of Quauhnahuac, which Walter Allen calls "the finest and profoundest work of fiction written by an Englishman during the decade."

Allen's remark reminds us that Lowry's work is too rarely studied as part of American literature because he lived mostly in Canada. Even if twentieth-century Canadian literature in English can really be artificially separated from that produced south of the border, Lowry and his work were so intimately involved with the United States and Mexico that it is perhaps best to consider his major writings "hemispheric," so that they distinctly deserve consideration. He and Katherine Anne Porter may stand indeed as the first of a new breed of writers, not distinctively concerned with their own countries, but with the inter-relationships of American cultures.

Despite the enthusiasm of a small band of admirers, this grim tale of drink, decay, and death did not appeal to a public that was fed up with tragedy. As other novels of the period have been forgotten, however, *Under the Volcano* has remained a small but steady "underground" success. During the 60s — largely because of its almost clinical study of alienation — the novel has enjoyed a considerable revival, and Lowry is beginning to enjoy a reputation as one of the few artists with the talent and courage to develop a tragic vision to match the times.

WF

215

The Drunken Wheel: Malcolm Lowry and Under the Volcano

by ELEANOR WIDMER

The fascination with Malcolm Lowry, today as in the 40's, turns upon the unique fusion of the man with his work, in which auto-biography, cast as fiction, grows into compelling, universal symbol. Lowry's was a strange and isolated voice and his major work, *Under the Volcano,* which dealt with an alcoholic who meets death in a remote province of Mexico, seemed, from its early American success to derive its strength from its exoticism. But its reputation two decades later testifies to the broadness of its theme — the tenuous exaltation of man, cast from paradise into a harsh, alien, fragmented world that betrays him with unfulfilled promises. Though the particulars which inform the book are those of a self destructive alcoholic in a violent landscape, its infernal thrust extends beyond these confines. The forsaken man, Lowry recognized, could find hell everywhere in our irreligious world.

Under the Volcano was begun in Mexico in 1936, underwent four different versions before its completion a decade later, and after its rejection by a dozen publishers, was finally published, both in the U.S. and England, in 1947. The second World War, which swept away American literary provincialism in an irreversible tide, confirmed the artistic imagination based on nomadism and internationalism. In this regard, Malcolm Lowry had few peers. Born into comfortable middle class surroundings in England, he went to sea at a youthful age, returned to Cambridge where he read in the modern tripos, and, uncertain of his future, drifted first to Paris, then to New York, finally to Mexico. Impoverished, racked by alcoholism and bad health, he became a squatter on the outskirts of Vancouver, living in a shack he and his wife built. When the story of his life became known, as it inevitably did, it fired the sympathies of the deracinated everywhere. Momentarily, Lowry became a double hero, as artist-in-penury struggling to produce the classic masterpiece that would transcend his mundane miseries, as the actual character in his book, the Consul, who had experienced the journey into dread. Creator and created, flesh and blood as well as fictitious hero, Lowry exemplified the man of sensibility — because of and in spite of alcoholism — as poetic conscience of a denuded world.

Moreover, the rise of existential philosophy, which posed such compelling questions about the absurdity of modern existence and the paltry ways available to meet death heroically, helped vindicate the Consul of *Under the Volcano* as a universal, rather than a particularized spirit, and released its author from the stigma of peculiarity. Drunk, the Consul might very well be, but his quest, and his descent into hell, had claims prior to disease and anterior to mere clinical observation. How can we save ourselves from Hell? Lowry asked, and the answer had nothing to do with Alcoholics Anonymous.

There was no denying that Lowry drank to excess and that ultimately he paid for it with his life. He also had long and extended periods of sobriety during which he wrote twelve to sixteen hours a day. Still, bad health, unrelated to alcoholism though intimately connected to his volatile personality, hounded him, while ironic, ceaseless bad luck pursued him to his grave. This bitter awareness combined with the richest panoply of hope provided Lowry's distinguishing quality.

His astonishing letters (*Selected Letters of Malcolm Lowry*, ed. by Harvey Breit and Margerie Lowry, 1965) testify to the unflagging humor, if not detachment, with which he viewed his misery. At one period or another, Lowry suffered from the Bends, streptococcic glandular fever, osteomyletis due to an absessed tooth, ear infection resulting from ear canal spiraling in the wrong direction, suspected T.B. and failing eyesight. He underwent several operations. In a series of compelling accidents to which he seemed especially prone, Lowry managed to break nearly every bone in his body; once, he fell off the pier in front of his house and broke his back; another time he smashed his leg in a trap in the forest; he severed an artery in his forehead while rescuing a pigeon from an apartment air vent. Like his fictitious other self, the Consul, Lowry began to feel that no matter how he chose — for good or evil, with or without alcohol — ill fated destiny was closing in on him. In a letter to his editor Lowry wrote, ". . . maybe I am the chap chosen of God or the devil to elucidate the Law of Series," such law being predicated on the notion that destiny resides in some magical or mystical accounting system over which man has no power.

Lowry, like the Consul, hoped to transcend the spectre of death by magic — the corruscating if demonic visions of alcohol, belief in the Cabalistic notions of special numbers — 7 and 12 ranked high in Lowry's system — and the obsessive, overwhelming concern with language. To evoke or deny either deity or devil, Lowry resorted to the incantatory word. It took him as long as six years to rewrite several chapters of *Volcano* and he kept as many as twenty versions of a single paragraph going at the same time. He believed that the proper word, the perfect chapter, the unflawed major novel could flatten or destroy the walls of the abyss. He read omnivorously, he wrote diligently; when, after heartbreaking disappointments, *Under the Volcano* was accepted by an American and British publisher on the exact day, he cheered the efficacy of his magic and his total commitment to incantatory art.

But the fated series continued. His wife and fellow writer was threatened with prospects of brain tumor and infections of every kind. On the very day that her husband crushed his leg in the forest, she was attacked by a husky dog as she ran towards the town for help, and was so badly mauled that she was hospitalized in peril of her life. In spite of the magic of words and his faith in the Buddhistic wheel of eternity, a fire destroyed the Lowrys' shack and with it years of writing, some of it never recovered. Twice, the Lowrys were evicted from their property, the last time necessitating their fatal move back to England. The long awaited inheritance that would have saved them from penury muddled through years of legalities while he and his wife lived on ninety dollars a month. Resort to words, to hard work, to alcohol or sobriety, to hope in the Cabala, to ancient philosophy, modern literature, or all the powers of all the multiples he could come by, everything failed. The publication of *Volcano* brought immediate success and some fame. The book was translated into several European languages, appeared, for a brief period, on the American best seller list. But this magical victory was transitory at best. In exile from Canada, and with works promised to publishers that ill-health and ill-luck prevented from completion, Lowry, like his alter-ego the Consul, stood isolated and alone, doomed the more he perceived and hoped.

Though he knew better and referred to barbiturates as "my faithful enemy, treacherous to the last," he took a dose following a heavy bout of drinking and was found dead in the morning, in his cottage in England, in June, 1957, exactly a decade after the appearance of *Under the Volcano*. Essentially then, in spite of an early novel, *Ultramarine* (1933), and a volume of short stories, *Hear Us O Lord From Heaven Thy Dwelling Place* (published posthumously 1961), *Under the Volcano* remains Lowry's only, exotic yet literal, monument.

Seen against the background of his own life, *Under the Volcano* becomes a self-fulfilling prophecy, a statement of man's alienation from himself and his surroundings, an alcoholic nightmare, and a bitter, cultivated reflection on a life fully threatened with, and encompassed by, meaninglessness. It is also a dazzling display of everything Lowry knew or had read, believed, doubted, praised, or could evoke. It is thus a doomsday book, a catechism, a performer of magic and a prayer.

Although the alcoholic sensibility was quite fashionable in the 40's — Charles Jackson's *The Lost Week End* and *Under the Volcano** captured the popular as well as intellectual interest of the

---

* Editor's Note: Since Mrs. Widmer completed her essay there has appeared, *Dark as the Grave Wherein My Friend is Laid,* an intensely autobiographical "novel" about the publication of *Under the Volcano,* assembled by Douglas Day and Margerie Lowry from Lowry's fragmentary manuscripts. The work, in which Lowry's alter-ego is named Sigbjorn Wilderness, should add, I regret to say, little to Lowry's reputation; but it is particularly interesting as evidence that Lowry had tremendous fears that the publication of *The Lost Weekend* — which Lowry retitles *Drunkard's Rigadoon* — might destroy the commercial potential of the work that he had labored over so long.

time — the condition of alcoholism is but one factor in the downfall of the Consul. Intrinsically, he is immobilized, living in a state of dread, a ubiquitous if shadowy figure whose alienation is reenforced by the place in which he lives.

No one who has ever stayed in Mexico can forget the radiant blue of the immense sky, the lushness of the almost obscene flora, the proliferation of all that flies and stings and bites and crawls. Nor its palpable, unforgivable inequities — its poverty, lavish corruption and brutality — juxtaposed against a searing landscape of unrelenting sun. Amidst this beauty and decay the Consul, deteriorated gentleman and would-be scholar, whose duties as a consul are purely metaphoric, must grapple with his soul.

Under the Volcano is divided into 12 chapters (following the Cabalistic number 12); its central action occurs within 12 hours of the day; its story opens in retrospect, exactly 12 months after the death of the Consul. And so much did Lowry believe in this number that he refused at any point to tamper with the structure of the book lest the number 12 be compromised. Wisdom was multiplication — numbers, series, words, awareness. Lowry conceived of modern man as fragmented, torn by multiple desires, and prevented by fate, bad luck, or the malignancy in the universe from achieving wholeness.

Lowry had been a sailor, song writer, movie scenarist, a poet, pioneer in Vancouver, a man riddled by guilt, a man obsessed. Every one of these roles or guises appear in *Volcano,* heavily burdened with the theme of the *doppelgänger* or double, without which, Lowry felt, the pitiable state of man could not be elucidated.

In consequence, the Consul has a series of doubles who at every point reflect and mirror his own inadequacy and doom. His most immediate double is his half-brother, Hugh, a sailor, song writer and petty journalist, on verge of boarding a cargo ship for embattled Spain. Hugh, the personification of Lowry's as well as the Consul's youth, accompanies the Consul and his wife on their fatal trip to Parián. Later, while the Consul and Yvonne passively watch a bull fight, Hugh jumps into the ring and by sheer dint of will subdues the bull. This impulse defines his primary success. Hugh fails to come to grips with his feelings for the Consul's wife, he fails to comprehend his own worth or future, and most significant, he fails to discover the whereabouts of the Consul, who has drifted off by himself, and thus cannot save him. We last see Hugh, drunk, singing revolutionary songs in a dark forest, at the very moment that his brother, or other self, is being murdered. Youthful verve and political idealism, Lowry argues, are insufficient to avert disaster.

Jacques Laruelle, the avant-garde French movie director and boyhood friend of the Consul, who by odd coincidence also lives in this remote Mexican province, represents yet another aspect of the Consul. Sensitive, learned, down on his luck, he plans a film on Faust which he never completes. Laruelle mirrors not only Lowry's concern with the cinema and the Faust theme, but provides a glimpse of the Consul released into partial creative activity. Were the Consul diverted from alcohol and anxiety, he would be no better or worse than Laruelle. In Lowry's essential vision, man, whether energetic and youthful, diseased and ineffective, or creating and questing, must fail. This is underscored by the fact that all three men are in love with, and have made love to, Yvonne, the Consul's wife. Neither of the three men can break through the labyrinthine circumstances and feelings surrounding him; neither can claim Yvonne for his own.

Like the Consul, Yvonne is drawn larger than life. A former child movie star, an accomplished horsewoman who performed her own stunts in films, a beauty in tune with nature's beauty, she appears as the stricken love goddess, destroyed by the imperfectibility of love. At the book's opening, Yvonne, divorced from the Consul the year before, returns to him at 7 a.m. on the Day of the Dead, in hope of reclaiming their life together. Though she dreams of their escape from sultry Mexico to cool Vancouver, from the Consul's alcohol inspired visions to sober work, the Consul, who has prayed for her return and the reassertion of his powers to love, fails to meet her simple demands. Impotent at every level, he drags his wife and brother through a ridiculous journey to another town, where, confused by alcohol and mescal, he is shot at 7 p.m. by the secret fascist police, and Yvonne is killed by a frightened horse that the Consul misguidedly set free. Yvonne meets death because the Consul has wilfully separated himself from her, thereby releasing the most brutal elements in nature.

This infernal journey exfoliates still another set of doubles. Not only does the Consul represent several aspects of tormented civilization in the modern world, he is equally the naïve, simple Indian whom they see from the bus, dying in the roadside. According to Mexican law, anyone found touching a dying man is considered an accomplice. The Consul and his brother refrain from moving the Indian who dies a pariah, uttering the word *compañero* which no one heeds. This foreshadows the Consul's own death a few hours later, when he too, hears *compañero* as the last word. The Consul thus becomes the mute, stricken pariah (like Lowry, sick and adrift in Vancouver), whom no one can save.

At the Indian's death, a *pelado,* or literally "peeled one," a man so stripped of honor that he will prey on the poor, steals the Indian's money. Dressed garishly in two hats — a bowler over a sombrero — the *pelado* acts so swiftly that not until he brazenly pays his bus fare with the dead man's legacy does the Consul grow aware of the theft. Just before his own murder, the military police accuse the mescal sotted Consul of being "an espider," (spy) and a *pelado.* The last the Consul does not deny, for he sees himself as "the pilferer of meaningless muddled ideas out of which his rejection of his life had grown, who had worn his two or three bowler hats, his disguises over his abstractions. . . ." In addition to his other roles, the Consul identifies himself as the thief who has robbed life of its basic meaning.

In any or all of his guises, the Consul is doomed. Confronted with choices, he either abnegates his option or chooses by default. Though his wife begs him to flee with her alone, he muddles the decision until his energetic brother shows up to take the question out of his hands. Given the opportunity to travel to Guanajuato, where presumably he might assert life, he saunters towards the sinister town of Parián, noted for its secret police. He promises to refain from mescal, only to order doubles when offered by a bartender. Similarly, he vows to assert his love for his wife, but does not, and when separated from her during their brief journey, he copulates with a whore. As death closes in on him in the bar which he thinks of as "the paradise of his despair," he twice has warnings to escape. He does not and cannot.

Although incapable of reversing his destiny, the Consul recognizes his own absurdity. He tells himself, "There is no explanation of my life." He prays for the return of his "purity," he longs for "simplicity." He sees his struggle as "my battle for the human consciousness." Knowing what crucial questions hang in the balance, he nevertheless takes joy from his immobilization, realizing that "out of an ultimate contamination he had derived strength." Unlike Camus' Merseault, who awaits with pleasure the howling execrations of the crowd, the Consul's insights at the point of death is that he will miss "the burning draughts of loneliness" as "the happiest things his life had known."

Had Lowry stopped there, with fragmented man crushed by an illogical and irreversible fate, in a world as besotted as its suffering hero, the vision of misery would have been too unalleviated to contemplate. Surely, few books are as ominous and fearsome as *Under the Volcano* with its cries of human despair and its evocation of death on every page. Nature, for all of her brilliance, spews forth the scaly armadillo, sundry emaciated and hidious pariah dogs, vultures, and even ironically, a horse with a magical number 7 stamped on its saddle that becomes an instrument of death. The grotesque natives the Consul either imagines or sees are death-like, one, "apparently the devil himself," another, badly lamed, carrying an older, more decrepit Indian on his twisted back. "*Es inevitable la Muerte del Papa*," a newspaper headline screams. " 'A corpse will be transported by express,' " sings a disembodied voice. And the very last words of the book, "Somebody threw a dead dog after him down the ravine." Omniscient death grants few reprieves under Lowry's destructive volcano.

But two other themes, played in muted counterpoint, direct us to Lowry's final resting place. Early in the story, the Consul sees written on a wall, "*¿Le Gusta Este Jardin? ¡Evite Que Sus Hijos Lo Destruyan!*" (Do you like this garden? Those who destroy it are evicted!) The garden is the literal garden which Yvonne carefully tended and which the Consul let deteriorate during her absence; it is the lush garden of Mexico spoiled by its politics; it is the promising garden of the world stricken by the second World War. Most obviously, it is the Biblical garden from which the first man was dispossessed.

How can mankind, so evicted, achieve grace? asks Lowry. An alternate sign on a whitewashed wall reads, "*No se puede vivar sin amar.*" (It is not possible to live without love.) Repeatedly, throughout his journey, these words flash into the Consul's mind, and after he has been shot they occur again, as a revelation. "*No se puede vivar sin amar*" . . . which would explain everything . . . How could he have thought so evil of the world when succor was at hand all the time?" The hands that lift him are those of his enemies, ready to cast him, like a dead dog, into the ravine. The Consul believes that they are Yvonne's and Hugh's coming to rescue him, but they cannot because he has lovelessly failed them. Ultimately, what the Consul discovers is that the inability to love is the greatest sin against mankind and for this failure he pays with his life.

Under the Volcano constantly reechos the theme of the double: as a prophesy of doom and as a plea for love, as a tormented alcoholic vision and a sober statement of faith. Shifting from past to present, from despair to hope, its ornate style propels it, like any work of magic, to reveal wonders within wonders. For after all, as he exercised his own devils, praying to his personal magicians for salvation, Lowry, after a decade of labor, did offer up this novel as a gift of love. And what a stunning gift it is!

Take the first chapter, for example. The scene is the Cafe de la Selva which alludes to Dante's inferno and to the woods where Yvonne is killed. It is the Day of the Dead. The local movie shows *Los Manos de Orlac,* the same film that had played exactly a year ago on the day of the Consul's death. The picture of the man with the bloody hands symbolizes the guilt of mankind, the guilt of the Consul and his double, the failed cinema artist, Laruelle, the blood of the murdered Indian, and the blood of the hands of the *pelado* or thief. On his way home, Laruelle sees the drunken horseman who may be viewed as the symbolic appearance of the Consul, or of mankind. The horse foreshadows the death of the Indian and Yvonne. Before Laruelle enters his house, he notes the Ferris wheel in the square, moving backward. This may be seen as the Buddha's wheel of the law, as eternity, or as the flashback itself, the wheel or film or journey reversed. Thus each theme of this elaborately structured book is sounded in the first chapter and explored, like an oriental puzzle, convolution upon convolution until the last.

And herein lies one of the major defects of *Volcano.* It is eclectic, it contains too many disparate elements. Obsessive, it lets no motif or metaphor go, attempting to weld into cohesiveness ornate occultism with an analytic statement on modern man, the belief in the eternal wheel with the transitory Mexican journey of one lonely soul. In attempting to provide us with his gift of love, Malcolm Lowry was too lavish, his prayer, not too encompassing, but made up of too many bits and pieces which could not be totally assimilated. The desire overly to enrich the texture of the novel coupled with his preoccupation with death resulted, not merely in majesty, as Lowry had hoped, but in oppressiveness as well.

No work should be faulted for attempting too much, and surely

Lowry can be forgiven for imperfection based on excess. But the intense moment of encompassing poetic vision both creates and restricts this novel, allowing small possibilities for irony or the capriciousness of chance.

Describing the flora of Mexico, Lowry wrote, ". . . the tall exotic plants, livid and crepuscular . . . [were] perishing on every hand of unnecessary thirst, staggering, it almost appeared against one another, yet struggling like dying voluptuaries in a vision to maintain some final attitude of potency, or of a collective, desolate fecundity. . . ."

The image of the dying voluptuary sums up nature as well as man, and Malcolm Lowry as well as the Consul. And the intoxicated wheeling poetry of *Under the Volcano* also achieves a deathly potency, the desolate fecundity that its author exalted and to which he heroically committed himself.

May 5, 1947

In recent years there have been increasingly frequent objections to the creative works selected for Pulitzer Prize awards, but there were none in 1947. Although no award was made in drama, those in fiction and poetry were among the most satisfying of the decade. Indeed W. J. Stuckey flatly asserts in *The Pulitzer Prize Novels* that Robert Penn Warren's *All the King's Men* (already analyzed in James Justus' essay) "is the best novel ever to be awarded a Pulitzer prize."

Few would make the same statement about Robert Lowell's *Lord Weary's Castle;* indeed Robert Frost, Stephen Vincent Benet, Karl Shapiro, W. H. Auden and Peter Viereck were among other winners of the poetry prize during the decade. The importance of the award, however, was that the usually cautious committee did decide to honor a fresh, young talent. Lowell's first book, *Land of Unlikeness* had appeared in 1944, although he had been contributing to magazines five years earlier, when he was only 22. Although his second book had received high critical praise when it had appeared in November, 1946, it received little more attention than collections of poetry by little-known young men usually do, even though this young man was a great-grand-nephew of James Russell Lowell. His book is discussed in connection with his reception of the Pulitzer Prize, because it was this award that first attracted widespread attention to the man and his work and started him on his way to being one of the most respected and often one of the most controversial poetic spokesman of post-war America. His shifting political and religious enthusiasms have made him perhaps the most conspicuously representative figure of the recent American literary establishment.

WF

The View from
Lord Weary's Castle

by KENNETH JOHNSON

In the years 1941-45, a new generation of American poets emerged. Some, such as John Berryman and J. V. Cunningham, did not gain much critical attention at this time. Others, including Karl Shapiro, Peter Viereck, and Randall Jarrell, won immediate acclaim. However, the poet of this generation who caused the biggest stir in the literary scene during these years — and has continued to do so — was Robert Lowell.

Lowell's first collection of verse, *Land of Unlikeness,* was published in 1944. Quite dissatisfied with it, he spent the next two years revising many of the poems as well as writing new ones. The results of this effort appeared in his second book, *Lord Weary's Castle.* Published in 1946, this book received enthusiastic critical attention and won that year's Pulitzer Prize.

But the plaudits given this volume proved to be a mixed blessing. For one thing, several later critics, examining Lowell's accumulated canon, read this first much-praised major volume and thought that it was just not all they had been led to believe it would be. In their disappointment, they tended to dismiss it as "minor" and to save their enthusiasm for later volumes. Equally serious was the confusion surrounding Lowell's literary position in relation to his generation of poets. Because of the critical excitement he evoked, many readers automatically assumed Lowell was the leading pioneer in the new generation's literary explorations. Thus, the first point to be made concerning *Lord Weary's Castle* is that the book did not signify the debut of a poet proclaiming the beginning of any new literary movement. Instead, the book clearly illustrates the all-encompassing influence of the preceding generation's poets and critics. In form and content, *Lord Weary's Castle* is replete with echoes of many of the poets emphasized in *Understanding Literature,* a textbook reflecting the taste of Lowell's predecessors.

In point of fact, Lowell has never been a literary trailblazer. For, even later in his career, his dramatic change of style and content in *Life Studies* follows the lead of others. Lowell himself has stated this. His contributions to "Confessional Poetry" resulted, at least in part, from W. D. Snodgrass' approach to subject matter. In style, he reacted to the stimulus of a variety of poets, from Allen Ginsberg to Elizabeth Bishop. The most famous poem in *Life Studies,* "Skunk Hour," was modeled closely on Miss Bishop's "The Armadillo."

The importance of *Lord Weary's Castle,* then, is that it presented the first finished products of a talented, sensitive young poet whose works must be studied "simply" because he is so talented. The reader wants to see what this gifted poet achieves when he utilizes other poets' experiments in order to express his own thoughts and emotions. Thus, the two most important aspects of *Lord Weary's Castle* to be studied are: Lowell's delineation of himself and of our world as revealed in the poems and as compared with his later work and the quality of the collection as a whole.

Such a study soon reveals that the poet, a convert to Catholicism at the age of twenty-three, is on a spiritual quest. Intensely aware of man's spiritual failings, he seeks the path that can lead him — and all mankind — to salvation. In this search, he analyzes the effects of war and the processes of decay and corruption. He also investigates the spiritual meanings contained in the past, both Europe's and America's. Finally, he evaluates our present-day world and predicts its future course.

The first poem in the collection, "The Exile's Return," presents Lowell's basic concern. Commenting on the end of World War II, it states that this moment is not really the end of anything but, rather, the beginning. For there now exists both the possibility of a sterile engulfing corruption or the possibility of a fertile moral resurgence. The final outcome is up to us — "the unseasoned liberators." If we want to bring about the latter possibility, we must undertake a spiritual quest.

"Winter in Dunbarton" and "The Crucifix" focus directly on decay and corruption. However, the best poem on this theme is "Colloquy at Black Rock." In his poem, Lowell comes to the conclusion that "All discussion" — all of man's ideas and actions — "End in the mud-flat detritus of death." But, later, the narrator remembers that human flesh, though in one sense mortal, is also the "House of our Saviour who was hanged till death." He then realizes that man can defeat mortality through Christ; and is granted a vision of Christ.

Although war is referred to, this poem is not primarily concerned with war. Rather, Lowell is concerned with surmounting all the phases of decay and death which threaten mankind. Other poems, such as "France" and "The North Sea Undertaker's Complaint," return to the subject of World War II as a force of brutality and corruption. But Lowell does not confine his thought to the Second World War. In "Napoleon Crosses the Berezina," he describes Napoleon but also evokes "Charlemagne's stunted shadow" and, by implication, Hitler. All three generals — and so *all* generals — lead their men not to glory but into "snow" which "Blazes its carrion-miles to Purgatory." In other poems, however, Lowell emphasizes that it is not just generals who are to blame for this recurring catastrophe. All mankind is to blame — as the victims in "The Dead in Europe," who exclaim in spiritual terms "we fell down," have comprehended.

The realization that man must comprehend his world if he is to improve it and to give his own life a moral direction leads Lowell, quite logically, to a further realization: to comprehend one's present world, one must also understand the past. That Lowell acted upon this realization is made abundantly clear in such later works as his version of *Prometheus Bound, The Old Glory,* and his later collections of poetry, especally *Life Studies.* Yet all of these later works are merely a continuation of the probing detailed in many poems in *Lord Weary's Castle.* Some of these poems, including "Charles the Fifth and the Peasant," "The Fens," and "Dea Roma," center on Europe. However, Lowell's primary concern is with the New England past. "Salem" and "Concord" decry the now lost grandeur and religious fervor of the early New

Englanders. But Lowell, by no means, simply contrasts the corrupt present to some sort of imagined pristine past. Instead, he seeks to discover the flaws in the New England past that led to both its downfall and ours. And he finds in "Children of Light" and "At the Indian Killer's Grave" that the Puritan religion itself was responsible for its own decline. For one thing, the Puritans sinfully justified their self-aggrandizement, even when it involved murdering Indians. So, too, they were "unhoused" by their creed's insistence on man's depravity.

Lowell also condemns the Puritans for falling away from their best ideals and pursuing materialistic wealth — and he blames later Protestant generations for continuing the process. One might ask: Why single out just the Puritans? or just the Protestants? Did not Catholic-dominated societies also become preoccupied with materialism? In *Poetry and the Age*, Randall Jarrell suggests that Lowell, in reply, might cite Max Weber's theory that Protestantism, unlike Catholicism, encouraged the pursuit of materialistic wealth. Yet even if one concedes this vulnerable point, the fact remains that, actually, we are dealing here with a human truth, independent of any creed. For, whether given religious sanction or not, how often has any cluster of people not yielded to worldly temptation when environmental hardships decreased and materialistic prosperity became possible? My point here is that Lowell's sweeping condemnations reveal that he is still young and, so, both oversimplifies and is too critical of man's moral shortcomings. Thus, his insistence that man maintain a spiritual purity that is beyond man's capacity to sustain is ultimately unrealistic and so, too, intolerant. I will return to this point later.

Other poems concentrate on the stultifying bleakness of the Puritan world-view. In "Mr. Edwards and the Spider," a dramatic monologue, the speaker is Jonathan Edwards. As Laurence Perrine (in *100 American Poems of the Twentieth Century*) has stated: "Edwards' Calvinistic theology — his belief in original sin, in predestination, in the littleness of man, and in the absolute sovereignty of God — is clearly seen in this poem." In "After the Surprising Conversions," which, like the previous poem, incorporates phrases from Edwards' own writings, Edwards reports that after one of his sermons, one listener "showed concernment for his soul" and ultimately "cut his throat." His suicide, in turn, touched off a series of suicides — all of which Edwards blames not on Puritanism, but on Satan, who, with God's approval, "seemed more let loose amongst us."

There is, I think, one particular reason for the power contained in these two poems, namely, that Lowell has much the same temperament as Edwards. Thus, in these poems, Lowell is doing more than criticizing Puritanism; he is also, consciously or subconsciously, trying to purge himself of all Puritan strains. That he fails in this attempt is proven by the fact that in later poem-collections and in *The Old Glory* Lowell felt compelled to return to the subject of Puritanism again and again. He can never wholly free himself of Puritanism because it is a quintessential part of his being; he can only — brilliantly — study it and try to balance or offset it with other elements in his make up.

Also in this regard, Jerome Mazzaro, in *The Poetic Themes of Robert Lowell,* has pointed out that "Napoleon Crosses the Berezina" is based on a cyclical world-view of history, a world-view that is deterministic, that undermines the concept of man's Free Will, and that is Greek, not Catholic. I would suggest that the influence here is not Greek, but Puritan; that Lowell, here again, gives unintentional proof that his Catholicism is only super-imposed upon his basically Puritanical nature.

The poem that sums up Lowell's views on New England, past and present, and does so by employing his own family history is "In Memory of Arthur Winslow," written about Lowell's grandfather. That Winslow's life, and the "life" of modern New England society, has been a failure is indicated in Part One by the juxtaposition of awesome religious possibilities with the actual drabness and narrowness of both Winslow and Boston. Part Two declares that the life of New England's early settlers was better, richer. However, their "day is done." In Part Three, Lowell states that Winslow, in a pathetically misguided effort, was trying to match the grandeur of his ancestors' achievements and that although these ancestors were also tainted by the desire for material wealth, they were still not such thoroughgoing materialists as Winslow and other modern men. In the fourth and final section, Lowell again criticizes Puritanism for encouraging man's desire for material wealth and implores the Virgin Mary to cleanse our present world's prevailing moral corruption.

Lowell's severe condemnation of mankind, of which I spoke earlier, bears directly on his attitude toward his relatives. Lowell is quite harsh on his grandfather because he does not see Winslow as a human being, but as a symbol of degenerate Puritanism. Later in his career, he will describe particular objects and particular people and only imply their symbolic significance. But this stylistic shift is paralleled — if not preceded — by a change within Lowell himself. He will shift his primary concern from man's moral wickedness to man's suffering. As he does so, his prevailing mood shifts from intolerance to compassion. Thus, in *Life Studies,* he re-evaluates his relatives and presents them with understanding and sympathy. A similar shift occurs concerning himself: later, he will continue to present his flawed self, but he will try to accept, not "remodel" himself.

The persona in the later poems, then, is that of a human being living among other human beings. However, in *Lord Weary's Castle,* the major persona is that of the prophet. In "Colloquy at Black Rock," the narrator, like the prophets of old, is granted a vision. Other facets of this role that Lowell assumes include the prophet as someone who sees the essential meanings in quotidian reality and who predicts, hopes for, or fears world destruction. In "To Peter Taylor on the Feast of the Epiphany," Lowell declares his belief that world destruction must occur before man can purge himself of moral corruption, a view repeated in "As a Plane Tree by the Water" and "Where the Rainbow Ends." In the latter, the poet is "a red arrow on this graph/Of Revelations."

Unfortunately, Lowell as Young Prophet is rarely convincing. If he sometimes succeeds in attaining an effect, we are usually still aware of the effort involved. Another problem is that because Lowell was moving toward a climax in his own spiritual crisis, he believed that the whole western world was — or should be — nearing an apocalyptic cataclysm. That this event did not in fact take place undercuts the authority of the poems which state its imminence. Thus, only if studied as depictions of the subjective reality of a soul in turmoil do these poems contain any degree of power. This is especially true of "The Quaker Graveyard in Nantucket."

In his excellent analysis of this poem in *Robert Lowell: The First Two Decades,* Hugh B. Staples summarizes the poem as an elaboration of Lowell's "most urgent preoccupations: the nature of God, the possibility of salvation, the destructive effects of spiritual alienation, the Heraclitian flux of warring elements in the phenomenal world, and man's ultimate impotence in the grip of natural forces and the hands of the great God." In Part One, the corpse of a "drowned sailor" is taken on board a warship where sailors "weight the body, close/Its eyes and heave it seaward whence it came." These sailors, who — instead of learning anything from "this portent" — continue to fight in the war, will also soon die. Part Two states that only those already dead, those in the Quaker graveyard, realize the moral decay that the world war reveals. However, in Part Three, Lowell points out that the Quaker sailors, when alive, also forsook God and suffered in consequence. In Part Four, Lowell again foresees the world's total destruction. Part Five asks: When Christianity has been completely corrupted by corrupt Christians, will man be able to save himself or will he — as the phrasing indicates —complete his self-corruption by engaging in war? Knowing the answer, the poet asks that Christ, once again, lead us to salvation, which, Part Six tells us, can only occur if man seeks salvation and strives to reach the purely spiritual realm. In the seventh and concluding part, the poet, having learned of man's nature, can now accept the war — for the war led him to this knowledge. Moreover, he is calmed by the fact that God has a cosmic design and is everlasting.

Part Six of this poem reveals one further problem concerning Lowell-as-prophet: its advice to mankind — to live the contemplative life — is too impractical. But Lowell will eventually forsake this role. And there are poems in the collection which indicate that Lowell, on his own, was already moving toward the type of poem that, later, the writings of other poets stimulated him to achieve. For instance, "In the Cage" depicts life in prison as Lowell (a conscientious objector) experienced it, a subject he described more graphically in "Memories of West Street and Lepke," in *Life Studies*. Also in that later volume, he will utilize the same directly autobiographical material from his childhood presented in "Buttercups." This poem, which always focuses on richly connotative concrete objects, foreshadows the technique used in many poems in *Life Studies*. (Still later, in *For the Union Dead* and *Near the Ocean*, Lowell will continue to emphasize concrete details; but, as was not generally the case in *Life Studies*, he will also succeed in capturing the emotional intensity permeating many poems in *Lord Weary's Castle*.) Lastly, two other poems, "Between the Porch and the Altar" and "The Death of the Sheriff," employ a type of dramatic monologue which prepares for the excellent "Mother Marie Therese," from *The Mills of the Kava-*

naughs, while the "Katherine's Dream section of "Between the Porch and the Altar" anticipates the intensity of the female voice in "To Speak of Woe That is in Marriage," in *Life Studies.*

Before concluding, one must face the question of the book's overall quality. Certainly recent critics are correct in claiming that the book, originally, was over-praised. It contains far too many failures to justify the initial acclaim. Still, it cannot be dismissed because any collection that contains poems as brilliant as "Mr. Edwards and the Spider" and "After the Surprising Conversions" must always be singled out for special attention. Nor can one brush aside the flawed but powerful "Colloquy at Black Rock" and the even greater heights reached in sections of "The Quaker Graveyard in Nantucket." Then, too, there is the very moving "Katherine's Dream" and the small-scale perfection of "Buttercups." Thus, my evaluation would, very undramatically, lie between the extremities of both critical positions; although not among the best single volumes of American poetry, *Lord Weary's Castle* is clearly too good to be labeled "minor."

October 12, 1947

In view of this country's deep-seated and widespread anti-intellectualism, it is not surprising that the intellectual novel (or poem or play) has not flourished in this country. To borrow Hemingway's term, the United States has produced principally a "gut" literature, and it is hard to think of an American writer of any stature, except Henry Adams, who is distinguished for the rigorousness of his thought. (Emerson, Thoreau and Whitman had lots of "ideas," but their arguments were visionary and inspirational. Wallace Stevens ranked the imagination above the intellect.)

Beginning in the 30s, however, one group stood out firmly against this American tendency. Settled mostly at Columbia University and involved largely in the effort to create in the *Partisan Review* (founded 1934) an influential outlet for creative intellectuals, the group has made an enormous amount of noise, but probably has not been much listened to outside of New York City — despite its efforts to spread its message to the hinterland through a succession of book clubs.

Leader and most articulate and opinionated of the group is Jacques Barzun — a Columbia administrator who has probably wrung his hands over the state of contemporary culture more continually and publicly than any other man; by far the most successful literary product of the group during the 40s (and later) has been Lionel Trilling's novel *The Middle of the Journey.* Trilling is better known as an unusually subtle and perceptive literary critic and short story writer; his novel, however, is a forlorn effort to press fiction into the service of the continuing assessment of liberal ideologies that have preoccupied this group. Chester Eisinger, in *Fiction of the Forties,* calls *The Middle of the Journey,* "the most distinguished contribution to the new liberalism"; and the novel has been kept alive by a small band of dogged admirers. The novel's failure to win a wide audience, however, may not be attributable so much to Americans' distaste for ideas as to — as William Freedman suggests — its being the most impressive failure in the finally impossible effort to fuse art and ideology.

WF

The Middle of the Journey:
Lionel Trilling and the Novel of Ideas

The Middle of the Journey, Lionel Trilling's novel of the liberal's crisis of reorientation, reads at times as though it were first serialized in *PMLA*. Now this is not intended to be an entirely negative judgment. Much intelligence is discoverable between the covers of that most academic of literary journals, and intelligence is the novel's most conspicuous and most impressive characteristic. It is there, first of all, in the consistent acuteness of Trilling's understanding of middle-class manners, the small, often unnoticed gestures, expressions, signals, and hypocrisies that make up a more important part of our daily conduct and experience than the more striking insights or experiences we are so much more likely to remember.

Intelligence also characterizes the structure of this novel. Trilling replaces straight chronology with an intricate network of artfully scheduled flashbacks and a consistent development for his "hero" John Laskell with a weave that presents us with the same pieces of information viewed from a variety of vantage points, some filtered, some direct, and requires both Laskell and the reader repeatedly to reexamine and reassess. The function of these temporal and spatial manipulations is not merely to delineate the development of Laskell's thought from an old naive liberalism to a new, more chastened one, but to embody, to serve as icon, for the liberal mind. The novel's patterns of motion — flashbacks and the perception of identical facts from various points of view — reflect the involutions and weaving of a groping mind, a mind that tries to see from all sides, that tries to tolerate, face, and accept, and a mind that tries to relate experiences — past perceptions and attitudes with those of the present — all in the attempt to arrive at a new moral, political, and psychological point of departure.

But the novel's intelligence is probably most gratifying and most obvious in the many discussions of political ideology, psychologcal motivation, and ethics that make this book what it unmistakably is, a novel of ideas in the tradition of *The Magic Mountain* and *Howard's End*. There is no condescending to the presentation of ideas in *The Middle of the Journey,* none of the feeling that we've been here before or might just as well have never come, for two of the characters at least — Laskell and Gifford Maxim, the Communist turned reactionary Christian — are far cleverer than we. With hardly a flinch they parry shots that send us lunging, our rackets flying from sweaty palms. Like the brightest people in the fiction of Henry James, they understand more than we do, they understand more quickly, and they are far more adroit than we at knowing what to do with what they know. The result is that these ideological discussions, usually almost guaranteed to be boring, are often dramatic and rarely tire or disappoint us.

It is a good thing that they are dramatic, though, for it is the great flaw of the novel that little else is. There are only two "events" in the traditional sense of that term, a love scene and a death scene, and the former is more accurately a non-event. Trilling is not interested in action here; he is interested in perception, and while that is certainly a legitimate interest for a novelist, Trilling is sometimes carried away by his own acuity and seems more interested in producing the effects we tend to associate with essays than those of a work of fiction. Too little, in other words, is left to our imaginations and emotions. Just as we are beginning to respond to a presentation or to mutter to ourselves, "Say, I know what that stands for," there is John Laskell responding for us and assuring us that we were right if not quite thorough enough.

Laskell (who, significantly, is 33 as it seems is nearly everyone else in recent American fiction) is too often an interpreter of symbols, a literary critic. Nothing passes him by; everything is subject to immediate analysis and interpretation that draws an intellectual ring around its object, blocking out the suggestiveness and emotive implication that separates fiction from the essay.

The preoccupation with ideas and the intellect is most profound, though, in its effect on characterization. However much Trilling may be reacting against the aesthetic and ideological clichés of the Marxist and "old liberal" writers like Fast, Sinclair, and Steinbeck, he does not escape their respective commitment to "typed" characters. Nancy Crooms is the naive, childlike, optimistic "old liberal" or fellow traveler, a representative, in Laskell's early, as yet unmodified, view of the life force itself, the future of America. Arthur Crooms is an even more clearly defined political type than his wife. "He was the man in whom the drive for power did not destroy intelligence and character . . . the kind of man [Laskell thought] who was going to dominate the near future. . . ."

At the time prior to the opening of the novel, Gifford Maxim, the other principal figure, has been "the revolutionary," not merely a member of the Communist Party to which Laskell and the Crooms contributed only their sympathies and some tangential assistance, but a secret agent. But Maxim has defected, and being a man of absolutes (of maxims), a man of will with a strong instinct for power and a sense of where it resides, he has swung with a vengeance — to reactionism and an almost fanatical Christian devotion. Maxim, too, is as much if not more an element in the dialectic of history and this novel than he is a breathing being.

John Laskell, of course, is the man in the middle, the man searching for a persuasion, or perhaps more accurately a life-style, somewhere between the extremes of the old left, with its denial of personal guilt and human imperfection and its naive faith in reason, the future, and the nobility of the working man, on the one hand, and the new right, with its denial of reason in favor of faith, innocence in favor of a Christian sense of original sin, and the working man in favor of a ruling elite, on the other. As Chester Eisinger observes, the Crooms represent the thesis, Maxim the antithesis, and Laskell the new synthesis, the enlightened new liberal who has shed his innocence.

The minor characters are no less classifiable and no more reluctantly classified for instant recognition. Duck Caldwell, the

Crooms' handyman, is the efficient, visceral, vulgar proletarian, the thinly covered manhole into which the old liberalism, its eye on the utopian future, summarily plops. His wife Emily is the anachronistic remnant of an equally unsatisfactory past, the shallow, self-conscious individualist, the quaint tea-room, *"Carpe diem"* bohemian of a dead era.

Something is a little too neat about all this. People do not live, they *mean,* a point Nancy emphasizes when she responds to Laskell's distaste for Duck with the observation, "He's a very important *kind* of person . . . even if you don't consider him personally" (p. 113).

Ideas, then, not people and not emotions, are Trilling's main concern, and it is in his handling of ideas that he most nearly succeeds. For Trilling, unlike most of his contemporaries, manages to transform the political questions raised by his novel into several more fundamental and less time-bound questions of psychology, ethics, and human nature. Perhaps it is more accurate to put the emphasis the other way, to say that politics in this novel is primarily an outlet for more basic metaphysical questions.

In *The Middle of the Journey* the questions about reality resolve into three closely related problems besetting man at every stage of his history: the problem of human imperfection and its moral and political implications; the problem of free will and personal responsibility as opposed to determinism and social or metaphysical rather than private guilt; and the problem of how to deal with ugliness, evil, and mortality. All three are integrally related not only to one another, but to the overt focus of the novel, the conflict between liberalism and dogma, John Laskell's political disillusionment and reorientation. All three present also a dialectic of complexity and oversimplification. In each instance, the Crooms on one side and Maxim on the other reduce to simplicity and dogma questions that defy reduction from their inherent complexity. Oversimplification is a recurrent bugaboo in Trilling's *The Liberal Imagination;* he finds it the failure, among others, of Dreiser and Sherwood Anderson. And Trilling is careful to avoid it ideologically as well as aesthetically in *The Middle of the Journey.* What distinguishes the liberal from the extremist is, perhaps above all else, a recognition and tolerance of complexity and uncertainty.

When the novel opens, Laskell has just recovered from a nearly fatal bout with scarlet fever and is on his way to a Connecticut farm to convalesce in the company of his revered friends and political idols, Nancy and Arthur Crooms. Laskell's illness can be understood in three complementary ways. It is, first of all of course, a dangerous illness which demands a period of convalescence during which he learns to his surprise just how far he has drifted from his friends. But the illness is also a kind of metaphorical trip to the underworld during which Laskell has been compelled to confront and recognize death and, worse for someone intellectually committed to social reform, his own capacity for self-indulgence, even a desire for extinction, the ultimate evasion of responsibility. And finally, scarlet fever can be read as a pun for red fever, a love affair with Communism which he is now over but from which he has not yet fully recovered. Laskell, placed in his historical context, is acting out the plight of thousands of left-wing 1940s liberals disenchanted by the disclosure of Russia's tainted role in the Spanish Civil War, the Moscow trials, and most shockingly the Russian-German Pact of 1939.

What Laskell learned is that he has not been alone in his longing for abdication, for evasion of painful realities. On the contrary, virtually everyone in the novel is in flight in one form or another, though unlike himself they misconstrue evasion for confrontation. Most important to Laskell's process of disillusionment and discovery is the evasiveness of the Crooms, particularly Nancy, who simply cannot face up to the fact of death. Whenever Laskell raises the subject of his illness she blanches white and nervously changes the subject. What Trilling is showing us here is the self-delusiveness of the old liberalism, the naive utopianism that simply cannot or will not cope with mortality, not only in its most literal form, but in the general stink of human flesh. "O, let me kiss that hand!" cries Gloucester. "Let me wipe it first," replies the wiser Lear, "it smells of mortality." The Crooms' persistence of belief despite the unmistakeable signs of blood on the hands of revolution and the Party is but one manifestation of a more deeply rooted malady, the escape into wilfully blind idealism.

Nor is Nancy alone in her refusal to confront directly the uncertainty and wretchedness of the times and of the human condition. If the Crooms retreat into a stubborn idealism, Maxim hides behind Christian dogma; Emily Caldwell protects herself with a flimsy and outdated individualism, Duck with alcohol, cultivated irresponsibility, and mindless vulgarity. Recognizing the inadequacy of both the Crooms' and Maxim's solutions, recognizing that they are in fact escapes and not solutions at all, Laskell "had an image of the world's misery, of what was to be faced, and he did not know who was strong enough to face it." Mark Schorer, Chester Eisinger, and Morton Dauwen Zabel have all taken different views on the question of the "central theme" of *The Middle of the Journey,* and I will not enter this outsized company; surely, though, this is a statement of one of the book's central concerns, and what hope there remains for the future rests with the pessimistic realism of the John Laskells, a realism that accepts the responsibility not to "cease from mental fight," in the words of the Blake poem, but to resist, with a tolerant and chastened view of realities and possibilities, the waves of absolutism flooding in at both gates. The promise of the future depends on what one does with the present, and the promise of the present depends in turn on a kind of negative capability, an ability to endure with intelligence in a world of contradictions.

The recognition of realities includes as one of its chief components the recognition not merely of the fact of evil where we had thought lay only good, death where we saw only life, but the intransigent fallibility and imperfectibility of man. Here again the novel's rejection of a political idea is but part of a rejection of a more comprehensive and more basic attitude toward human nature. For in the Marxist view all evil is social evil, the product not of human will or failure, but of institutions, specifically the institutions of capitalism. It is the failure of Duck, the man of tool and soil, who in a fit of drunken rage accidentally kills his own daughter, that enacts for us the inadequacy of Nancy Crooms' idealized view of mankind and his future, for it is on his "kind" of person that she has built her hopes. But Maxim, riding the pendulum to the other side of the clock, has an equally oversimplified hence equally inadequate world-view. If for the Crooms man is inherently good and by his nature perfectible, for Maxim, in his embracement of a characteristically rationalized form of Calvinism, we are all bearers of the curse of Adam, redeemable only because of the infinite mercy of God. Once again Laskell forms the synthesis. "It seems to me," he observes to Maxim, "that you have lost your sense of community with men in their suffering and goodness and found it only in their cruelty and evil" (p. 229). Though he does not say so here, Laskell's view is clearly between the two, and the attitude he evolves is not the product of mere abstraction; it is the consequence of perception, for the novel bears persistent witness to the complexity of human nature: its capacity for escapism, stubbornness, willfulness, vulgarity, stupidity, and cruelty on the one hand, and its balancing potential for tolerance, flexibility, sensitivity, forgiveness, and love on the other. Whereas tragedy arises out of the awesome combination of human dignity and imperfection, political novels often define themselves by their emphasis on one or the other of these sets of attributes of man. Those that press for or sympathize with revolution or sweeping social reform — novels like *Man's Fate, The Grapes of Wrath,* and *The Fixer* — characteristically do so on the basis of an underlying faith in human nature and human dignity. Anti-revolutionary or anti-reformist novels, such as *The Possessed* and *Darkness at Noon,* habitually betray a greater skepticism about the possibilities of the human will and its capacity to resist corruption. Trilling, though insisting on the dignity of the liberal mind, puts his energies into a critique of man's weaknesses and places himself squarely in the latter camp.

The question of good and evil in man's nature inevitably raises the twin problem of free will and responsibility as against determinism and innocence. Again political ideologies serve as channels through which deeper commitments publicize themselves. Since Marxism denies the imperfectibility of man, refusing to acknowledge that evil may be as much private as social, as much inherent as external, it consequently denies that man is responsible for what evil he does. In an attempt to explain why Nancy insists that what Duck has done is not Duck's fault (though he cannot explain why she refuses to let him in her sight any more than either of them can explain Marx's hatred for the ruling class), Arthur enunciates the social determinist's position:

> "Nancy means," Arthur said when Nancy did not immediately speak, "that social causes, environment, education or lack of education, economic pressure, the character-pattern imposed by society, in this case a disorganized society, all go to explain and account for any given individual's actions" (p. 307).

Maxim's is, as always, the antithetical view. For him, man, the perpetrator and product of Original Sin, is evil. "His will is a bad one," and he is "wholly responsible" for his acts. "Wholly. And for eternity, for everlasting." But while Nancy, despite her protestations of Duck's metaphysical innocence, will not tolerate his presence, Maxim can forgive him "because I believe God can forgive him. . . . For you — no responsibility for the individual, but no forgiveness. For me — ultimate, absolute responsibility for the individual, but mercy" (p. 309). In keeping with the dialectal pattern of the novel and with the identification of politics with metaphysics, Laskell rejects both the left and the right, seeing both as oversimplifications and evasions. If the Crooms escape into the comfort of universal innocence and perfectibility, Maxim offers nothing better; his view, for all its seeming harshness, is not the less an escape from the torment of his own guilt into the soothing reassurance of universal guilt. If everyone is guilty then no one is truly guilty, and Laskell, penetrating both forms of retreat, rejects them both. He cannot deny the profound formative influences of the world, society, God, his parents and nature, but neither can he define himself solely in their terms. There is also the free and responsible will to be acknowledged:

> An absolute freedom from responsibility — that much of
> a child none of us can be. An absolute responsibility —
> that much of a divine or metaphysical essence none of us is
> (p. 310).

Laskell's model is no longer the Crooms. It is, as Maxim perceives, "the human being in maturity, at once responsible and conditioned."

Precisely what kind of man is this new liberal John Laskell and where does his liberalism take us? And what, finally, are the implications of the answers to these questions for *The Middle of the Journey* as a novel and for the "new liberalism" of the 1940s?

Laskell, it must be admitted, is a man virtually without feeling or passion. A love scene with Emily Caldwell is given the before-and-after treatment, one feels, not merely because sex is no vital part of this novel, but because Laskell is virtually unimaginable as a lover. His emotions no less than his body suggest the enervation of the convalescent; they are forever at rest, resisting an overexcitement they seem disinclined to. And this lassitude seems to envelope his political and intellectual life hardly less than do his muscles and passions. For a political novel to succeed, it seems to me, the political attitudes accepted or adopted by the principal figure (or figures) must have a significant impact either on others or upon himself. If he is a political activist in the process of withdrawal or reaffirmation, his decisions are bound to affect his "movement," its adherents, and perhaps his world. If he is not (as is often the case in political novels of ideas rather than action), one expects compensatory impact on the man himself. His political conclusions, replete with all their metaphysical and ethical implications, may not profoundly affect others or influence the course of history, but they will, we expect, have an important effect on him. With Laskell, however, neither seems to be the case. He is not, by his own admission, a "political man," and his association with the Communist Party and related political causes has always been relatively tangential. But when we look for the alternative psychological or emotional effects we are disappointed. When he has at last convinced himself that the Crooms are not the models he once imagined them, when he recognizes that his severance from the Movement is total, he feels only a vacancy.

Trilling knows what he is doing. The void left by the Party in the lives of disillusioned liberals, is, among other things, what he wishes us to see. But one never feels that it matters much, that the void is filled even partially either by the pain of loss or a subsequent commitment. Laskell strikes us as a man who is quite simply effete and we soon tire of his tiredness. Trilling is again his own best critic, though this time perhaps inadvertently. Speaking of Kermit Simpson, a liberal editor with more money than mind, more conscience than commitment, he writes,

> Kermit was all too bland. There was no roughness in him. He never followed passion where it led, nor did necessity ever constrain him to resistance. The blandness was fatal to his character (p. 217).

The same, I am afraid, goes for Laskell.

Laskell, then, is but half a human being — mind without passion or the penchant for action. But *The Middle of the Journey* is basically a novel of ideas, not of character, and a failure of character is not necessarily fatal to the book. If the ideas live, the character may die with hardly time out for a funeral. But do they? In one sense. The "new liberalism" Laskell espouses is presented with subtlety, insight, and attention to complexities. It is also in many ways convincing, and, most important, in the climactic death scene, it grows flesh. Yet somehow it does not quite come alive as a viable political alternative to the dogmas it seeks to replace. It may be sounder than they, it may ring truer when tapped, but it lacks (only partly because Laskell lacks) strength of conviction or a commitment to action. In fact this brand of liberalism is, as R. W. B. Lewis shrewdly observes in "Lionel Trilling and the New Stoicism," "not a program for creative action at all, but a device for shoring up defenses. It is a plan for holding one's own. It cannot conduce in what Mr. Trilling looks for: the renovation of the will for the benefit of art and life, though it may preserve the will a little longer." The trouble with Laskell's reoriented position is that it is by definition untranslatable into significant action. It commits him to nothing more than an occasional ten-dollar contribution to the Urban League, and that, as the past quarter century of American history testifies and as daily events make painfully clear, simply has not done and will not do. One envisions Mr. Laskell huddling with his fellow cerebral battlers somewhere in the middle of the road reciting in measured phrases "*I will not cease* from mental fight," as the twin diesels of revolution and reaction bear down from either side. Perhaps this is precisely the picture Trilling wants to leave us with, but if it is, he should also leave us with a sense of just how pathetic the John Laskells truly are, just how inadequate, however reasonable, their defenses, and this he does not do. There is little distance between author and protagonist here, and one senses that he is expected to regard the Laskells of the world with admiration and anticipation. If so, in *The Middle of the Journey* Lionel Trilling may have revealed more about the liberalism of postwar America than even he intended.

December 3, 1947

Tennessee Williams was not a newcomer to Broadway when *A Streetcar Named Desire* began the long run that would carry it around the world (long after the actual streetcar had disappeared from New Orleans.) He had already scored a large success with *The Glass Menagerie* in 1944. The two plays have always been rivals in popularity, and indeed many would argue that it is the earlier around which this essay should be built so that it would mark the revelation of the prolific talent that was to succeed Eugene O'Neill as the dominant force in the American theatre.

Whatever one may think personally, however, of the two plays, one cannot escape the emblematic significance of *Streetcar* for the post-war American theatre. Although it has shocked, it has never been denounced and boycotted as *Death of a Salesman* has been. Although not everyone likes it, everyone who knows anything about American theatre knows it and employs it as the benchmark for judging other works. Clearly more than any other serious work of the decade — more than any other serious play between *Strange Interlude* and *Who's Afraid of Virginia Woolf?*, it gave the theatre-going public what it wanted.

Careful analysis of the play is particularly important then not so much to reveal its garishly obvious qualities as an autonomous work of art, but to enable us to understand the expectations and obsessions of the post-war audience. Under its baroque trappings, *Streetcar* repeats the ageless myth of the decay of former grandeur and its brute conquest by the irresistible force. It is the fall of the Roman Empire reenacted in the Mississippi moonlight. We learn about ourselves as we learn about the play and its author as seen through the eyes of a perceptive young British critic of the American scene.

WF

Tennessee Williams: Streetcar to Glory

by C. W. E. BIGSBY

The theatre has long been the poor relation of the American arts and Eugene O'Neill's Nobel Prize (like Sinclair Lewis's and Pearl Buck's) was a gesture having more political than cultural significance. For all the interest of Kingsley, Odets and Hellman, indeed, American drama is largely a post-war phenomenon and its new and enhanced prestige owes a great deal to a man who started his working life in a warehouse, writing poems on shoe boxes.

Thomas Lanier Williams was born on March 26, 1914. His parents were a travelling salesman and the daughter of the local minister — which may account for the strange mixture of prurience and puritanism in his work. His first play was written in 1935 and he scored a moderate local success in St. Louis with a series of plays written for a little theatre group called *The Mummers*.

The forties, however, opened somewhat inauspiciously. His first play intended for Broadway production, *Battle of Angels*, was withdrawn after its Boston try-out. Nevertheless in the course of the following two decades he emerged as a major dramatist and attained the two-fold distinction of being awarded a Pulitizer Prize and being banned from the public stage in Britain, surviving both experiences reasonably intact. Always controversial, his plays were welcomed not only for their unique vision but also for the frankness and vitality which they brought to a theatre all too often starved of those qualities.

Critics have often been at pains to draw a distinction between Tennessee Williams and Arthur Miller on the basis that the former is concerned with personal fears and frustrations while the latter is concerned with social issues. Yet Williams, too, has his roots in the social theatre of the 30's while, like Miller's *All My Sons* and *Death of a Salesman,* most of his work is concerned with the plight of the individual in the modern world. *The Mummers* itself was a radical group and the plays which he produced for it were largely protest dramas.

The atmosphere of hysteria and violence in his work is, therefore, not merely an expression of personal neurosis. It is also a legacy which he has inherited from a theatre in which emotionalism, sentimentality and violent action were seen as legitimate substitutes for dramatic tension. Like Miller, too, he has inherited not merely the over-simplifications of agit-prop drama but also a suspicion of wealth itself. In common with Brick, in *Cat on a Hot Tin Roof,* he is in fact something of an "ass aching Puritan." Thus the division betweeen rich and poor in his work is, for the most part, also a division between brutality and compassion, sterility and vitality. He is enough of an old-fashioned moralist, indeed, to see bodily disease as the fruit of sin. Thus the rich are frequently pictured as being eaten away from within: Boss Finley (*Sweet Bird of Youth*) apparently by tuberculosis, his daughter by syphilis, Mrs. Venable (*Suddenly Last Summer*) by madness, Jabe Torrence (*Orpheus Descending*) and even the rich but attractive Big Daddy (*Cat on a Hot Tin Roof*) by cancer. Perhaps this is why Williams, a man who sold the film rights of one of his plays for half a million dollars, is so concerned about his own health.

On the other side of the coin are the pure in heart; the poets, romantics, bohemians, and, of course, playwrights. For he has hardly written a single play which is not obliquely concerned with his own plight as a writer in a world which values only material things. When Cervantes was asked whom he intended to represent through the figure of Don Quixote he is said to have replied, "Myself." Williams might well give the same reply with regard to any of a dozen characters. So it is that in the persons of Laura Wingfield, Blanche DuBois, Alma Winemiller, we have a series of portraits of those characters for whom Williams has the greatest sympathy; those who, like himself, have been unable fully to adjust to a world in which honor, sexual passion, integrity and compassion no longer have a place.

Williams' first Broadway success came with *The Glass Menagerie* in 1945. This play, which won the New York Drama Critics' Award, exhibits a delicacy and control frequently lacking from his later work. Perhaps this derives, in part at least, from its biographical nature, for it is an enactment of his own relationship with his mother and sister — the latter having been committed to an asylum in 1937. In the play she appears as Laura Wingfield, a crippled girl who has apparently withdrawn from a world which seems to offer her nothing but pain and humiliation. Alienated from society in general she creates her own world with her collection of glass animals.

Her mother, Amanda, is equally ill-at-ease in the real world and compensates for her drab surroundings by recalling memories of her youth in the old South. She is sufficiently alive to the economic realities of life, however, to wish that Laura would get married and to this end she encourages her son, Tom, to bring home one of his workmates. When he does so Laura is for a brief while drawn out of her private world only to be brutally thrust back into it again when the boy, a young man concerned only with the glittering world of the American Dream, confesses that he is already engaged. The play ends as Tom, a poet with a job in a shoe warehouse, finally leaves and Amanda tries to comfort her daughter.

Obviously the play has a special meaning for the playwright who had himself lived the nightmare which he describes but it also functions as an image of the world as Williams sees it. For he has said that "for me the dominating premise has always been the need for understanding and tenderness and fortitude among individuals trapped by circumstances." Clearly the play's setting — "the Wingfield apartment is . . . one of those vast hive-like conglomerations of cellular living units" — is, therefore, concerned with emphasizing not merely the physical oppressiveness of life lived in a materialistic society but also the destruction of the human spirit which seems, to Williams, a natural corollary of modern living.

Moreover Laura herself is not merely a disturbingly accurate picture of his own sister. She stands also as an image of Williams' central theme; the destructive impact of society on the sensitive individual. Like the glass unicorn which is smashed by her unthinking "gentleman caller," she, and the delicate humanity which she represents, is, in Williams' words, virtually "extinct" in a modern world founded not on tenderness and understanding but on the dynamic cycle, *"knowledge —* zzzzpppp! Money — Zzzzppp! POWER! Wham!"* Looking for compassion she is brought face to face with the brutality of a world in which there is an apparently unbridgeable gulf between aspiration and fulfillment. This is a lesson, too, which has to be learnt both by Blanche DuBois, in Williams' second Broadway success of the 40's, *A Streetcar Named Desire,* and by Alma Winemiller, in *Summer and Smoke,* writen before *Streetcar* but not performed until the following year.

Williams' world, for the most part, has the simplicity and directness of moral allegory. Good is opposed to evil, spirituality to sensuality and the romantic to the brutally realistic. Indeed his characters are all too often simply manipulated in order to fulfill their functional roles in his modern parables. Alma Winemiller and John Buchanan, in *Summer and Smoke,* are supreme examples of this moral puppetry. Alma, we are pointedly reminded, is Spanish for "soul" and lest we miss the symbolic significance of this she is also made the daughter of the local minister. John Buchanan, on the other hand, stands for the body and predictably, therefore, must become a doctor, complete with an anatomical chart with which to preach his Lawrentian sermon on the dominance of the physical over the spiritual. This simplistic approach to symbolism even extends to the play's setting which, in dividing the stage between the doctor's house and the rectory (body and soul), projects the Manichean naiveté of the plot onto a visual plane. This misuse of symbolism has over the years become one of Williams' less fortunate trade-marks, at its worst in *Camino Real* and *Night of the Iguana.* Yet in his best work Williams avoids this tendency to "write too much on the nose." Indeed in an interview which he gave in 1961 he confessed that if you "write a character that isn't ambiguous you are writing a false character, not a true one." With this remark he was in fact indicting creations of his own such as Alma, Boss Finley and Mrs. Venable. Yet with his next play, *Streetcar,* which won both the New York Drama Critics' Award and the Pulitzer Prize, he showed that he was fully alive to the complexity of human nature and to the danger of facile moralising.

The mood of *A Streetcar Named Desire* is effectively summed up by the opening paragraph of a book which Williams greatly admired, *Lady Chatterley's Lover.* Here Lawrence had expressed his view of man's situation in the modern world: "Ours is essentially a tragic age, so we refuse to take it tragically. The cataclysm has happened, we are among the ruins, we start to build up new little habitats, to have new little hopes. It is rather hard work: there is now no smooth road into the future: but we go round or scramble over the obstacles. We've got to live, no matter how many skies have fallen." Williams' play is concerned with just such an attempt to discover a means and a purpose for life in surroundings which seem to offer little grounds for hope. As one of the characters says, "Life has got to go on. No matter what happens, you've got to keep on going."

Lawrence's influence on Williams has been plotted before but is especially important with regard to the work which he produced during the 40's and to *Streetcar* in particular. In 1939 he had gone to Taos, New Mexico, to interview Frieda Lawrence. He had long been planning a play about Lawrence's death and this now finally took some kind of shape. Significantly he described the theme of this play, *I Rise in Flame, Cried the Phoenix,* as "a man's . . . pilgrimage through times inimical to human beings." As such it clearly anticipates not only *Streetcar* but also much of Williams' later work. In 1945 he once again turned to Lawrence, this time adapting one of his short stories but it was not until *Streetcar* that he managed fully to digest his Lawrentian lessons and incorporate them into his own perception of an America caught in transition from genteel sterility to brutal indifference.

Blanche DuBois is a thirty-year-old woman who, when young, had made a disastrous marriage. Her husband had turned out to be a homosexual and in forcing him to face this fact she had provoked his suicide. Unable to admit to what she had done or to accept the loneliness which stretches out ahead of her, she turns, like Alma in *Summer and Smoke,* to a series of casual intimacies with strangers and is finally run out of town when she seduces a sixteen year old boy.

At the beginning of the play she arrives in New Orleans to stay with her sister, Stella, fully aware that she no longer has anywhere else to run. The two sisters had been brought up on a Southern plantation but Stella has abandoned the aristocratic pretensions to which Blanche clings so desperately. She has married Stanley Kowalsky, a Polish immigrant worker, and, much to Blanche's disgust, appears to revel both in her husband's brutality and his sensuality.

Hope suddenly appears for Blanche, however, in the person of Mitch, a lumbering mother's boy. He is attracted to her and she realizes that marriage will provide a kind of answer to her problems. But she reckons without Stanley. There is an instinctual animosity between these two. Blanche responds to him with a pathetic mixture of aristocratic contempt and unsubtle flirtation, while Stanley sees in her only a threat to his own way of life. When he discovers the truth about her past, therefore, he warns Mitch off and completes her destruction by raping her as his own wife is in a hospital having his baby. The play ends as Blanche, now mentally unhinged, is led away from the apartment by a doctor and nurse, her contact with reality finally severed.

We are offered, it seems, a hopeless choice between decadence and brutality and, like Williams himself, have to pick our way through the personal treacheries and frustrations in an attempt to find something worthwhile endorsing. For if Williams rebels against the cruelty of the modern age he clearly recognizes too the irrelevance of Blanche's posturing. Yet for all that, she — and the Southern tradition which she represents — obviously holds an attraction for Williams which goes beyond a romantic regret for past glory. He values the Southern past, in fact, not because he has any illusions as to the nature of its justice or the quality of its life but simply because, to his mind, it represents order. Here the anarchic power of sexuality was masked behind a cultivated manner and the naked pursuit of wealth cloaked by the whole cavalier tradition of the South. Like Joseph Conrad he felt that we are saved from chaos only by the "sovereign power enthroned in a fixed standard of conduct." The ordered nature of society in turn suggested a cosmic order and purpose. Now, in the modern age, the veneer has been stripped away and the structure of society has disintegrated. The individual is forced to admit to the reality of flux, to what one of Williams' characters describes as "the terrible — fast — dark — rush of events." It is this new, impersonal, world "sick with neon," which terrifies Williams and his protagonists. For, with order destroyed, the individual falls victim to what he sees as the blind illogic of much of human activity.

Williams' personal reaction is the predictable response of the artist. By the act of writing he tries to re-impose a sense of order. The creative act itself thus becomes an act of defiance, or, in another light, a form of escapism. This, indeed, is how one of his characters, significantly called simply, The Writer, justifies himself in a one act play called "The Lady of Larkspur Lotion" — a play which in many ways anticipates *Streetcar*: "Suppose that I, to make this nightmare bearable for as long as I must continue to be the helpless protagonist of it — suppose that I ornament, illuminate — glorify it! With dreams and fancies! . . . suppose that I live in this world of pitiful fiction! What satisfaction can it give [anyone] to tear it to pieces, to crush it — call it a *lie?*. . . . There are no lies but the lies that are stuffed in the mouth by the hard knuckled hand of need, the cold fist of necessity." The same is true of his other protagonists. Some, like Tom Wingfield, Sebastian Venable, and Chris Flanders, are writers themselves; others, like Laura Wingfield, Alma Winemiller and Blanche DuBois, are simply content to retreat into a world of illusion. Blanche, for example, invents a lover who will come and rescue her and by an act of will tranforms her harsh surroundings, placing a paper lantern over the electric light and filling the place with pastel shades. But the final futility of this response is amply demonstrated in *Streetcar* when Blanche's desperate pretence is shattered by a man "as coarse and direct and powerful as the primary colors." For illusion is only effective so long as others are prepared to tolerate it. Hence there is a sad truth to the popular song which Blanche sings as a counterpoint to Stanley's revelations of her debauchery: "It's a Barnum and Bailey world. Just as phony as it can be. But it wouldn't be make believe if you believed in me."

The real hero of the play, therefore, is Stella, for she alone is prepared to offer the necessary comfort and understanding. Like Connie Chatterley she discovers a genuine fulfillment based on sexuality but, more significantly, she thereby stumbles on the urgent need for that tenderness and compassion which, to both Williams and Lawrence, is the key to the human predicament. If she emerges also as the weakest character in the play this is because, however much he feels committed to seeking out some positive response to the modern world, Williams' sympathies are always with the weak and defeated while his admiration is always with those who manage to survive in and even dominate contemporary society. These latter — men like John Buchanan and Stanley Kowalsky — are described by Williams as Promethean figures "brilliantly alive in a stagnant society." Yet for all their vitality these "Prometheans" are too much a product of the modern world to offer any real hope. John Buchanan, before his somewhat incredible *volte face,* lacks true compassion and sympathy while

Stanley Kowalsky's brutality towards Blanche finally disqualifies his mindless sensuality as a viable alternative. Nevertheless, despite this inhumanity there are moments of tenderness between Stella and Stanley which clearly offer some slight hope for the future. For Williams, in surveying the post-war world, has said that "the only satisfactory thing we are left with in this life is the relations —if they're sincere — between people," love being "the closest we've come" to such a satisfying relationship. Where the modern European theatre stresses the impossibility of communication he continues to insist that some kind of contact is possible. But like Arthur Miller, in *After the Fall*, he is prepared to confess that this contact is imperfect and the love which it engenders an incomplete answer to the human condition. This, indeed, is the sense of the Hart Crane poem which Williams uses as an epigraph to *Streetcar*. For this is a poem which describes not only the desperate situation of Blanche DuBois and her fellow romantics but also the plight of a dramatist who from *Battle of Angels* onwards committed himself to a cause which perhaps seemed lost from the very beginning:

> And so it was that I entered the broken world
> To trace the visionary company of love, its voice
> An instant in the wind (I know not whither hurled)
> But not for long to hold each desperate choice.

January 18, 1948

The first two years after World War II saw the production of some memorable American fiction, poetry, and drama. *All the King's Men, Lord Weary's Castle, A Streetcar Named Desire,* at least, will probably long hold their places in anthologies of the best and most significant American literature.

By 1948, however, a strain set in. The continued unsettled conditions throughout the world disillusioned people who had sustained themselves through the black years with the hope of victory and peace. The major literary energies pent up during the war years had apparently exhausted themselves. Warren and Williams continued to write, but the new works failed to measure up to the earlier. The surviving writers of the 20s and 30s failed to add to their reputations.

Television, too, was unquestionably beginning to draw people away from both books and the theatre. Panicky publishers became distrustful of sound but unsensational books, began to hunt for flashy works that could be promoted by "gimmicks." Ominously, 1948 began with the launching of a first novel by a new writer with one of the most lavish and unliterary publicity campaigns that had ever been engineered, even by the business's arch-showman Bennett Cerf of Random House.

Other Voices, Other Rooms was promoted mainly on the strength of the publicity photographs that presented the young author as an affected voluptuary. Even if no one knew what the novel was about, everyone knew what Truman Capote looked like.

The surprising thing, in view of the mode in which the book was presented, is that *Other Voices, Other Rooms* was one of the best novels of the year and that its author developed into one of the more important writers of the post-war decade. One would never have expected it of a book that was peddled like a deodorant or a breakfast food or of an author whose penchant for sensationalism was to reach its apogee with the publication of "the non-fiction novel" *In Cold Blood* after he had been kept continually in the public eye for nearly two decades.

WF

Truman Capote:
The Novelist as Commodity

by GENE W. RUOFF

> No man had the art of displaying, with more advantage
> as a writer, whatever literary acquisitions he made.
>   *James Boswell on Oliver Goldsmith*

The most predictable literary event of 1968 should have been
the appearance of a twentieth anniversary edition of Truman
Capote's *Other Voices, Other Rooms,* with a new, nostalgic preface
by the author. Not that the edition was needed, for the book
has never been out of print; not that Random House has a special
weakness for commemorative editions, for it does not; simply that
Capote's first novel has always been so inseparable from its merchandising that an edition designed expressly for the cocktail tables
of America harmonizes neatly with its history. The only genuine
surprise of the new edition is that the author did not himself
prepare a series of woodcuts to embellish it. So that the anniversary
might be even more complete, Capote published his new preface
in *Harper's* well in advance of the edition, recalling his early
personal appearance in *Life,* equally in advance of the first publication of the novel.

Whenever *Life* runs short of serious starlets, humane warriors,
and hoodlum priests, it revives its quest for the Great American

Novel (or more properly, Novelist). The effects of this search on the state of the art have been profound, as John Updike has attested in a stirring pronouncement of the new sense of purpose it helped him to discover:

> I'm going to write a novel, hey,
>   I'll write it as per *Life*:
> I'm going to say, "What a lovely day"
>   And "How I love my wife"

For their June 2, 1947, issue, the editors called in John Chamberlain, as a grand old man of fiction reviewing, to cast a knowledgeable glance at the country's most recent crop of writers. He considered eleven of them, including three who have proved relatively durable: Capote, Gore Vidal, and Jean Stafford. Among the residue were Thomas Heggen, whose name has almost been lost in the fame of his *Mister Roberts;* and Calder Willingham, whose notoriety is insured by *Eternal Fire,* the reigning outer limit of the subliterature of Southern decadence. The remaining writers in the group — Elizabeth Fenwick, Peggy Goodin, Ann Chidester, Peggy Bennett, and Nancy and Benedict Freedman — have hardly fulfilled the promise we were told lay in them. Chamberlain's verdict on the generation was measured but optimistic, and exceedingly dull: none of the youngsters had approached in vision or craft the mature works of Hemingway, Fitzgerald, or Dos Passos, but their beginning efforts held hopes for the future, and so forth.

The most intriguing aspect of the article is the visual prominence it gave to Capote. His full-page photograph led off the piece: legs crossed, cigarette in hand, he sat primly on a full circular couch with ornately carved arms and back. He wore his characteristic checked waistcoat and artistic expression, mouth sullen and eyebrows ever so slightly arched. Despite the Victorian bric-a-brac that cluttered the background, Capote's eyes dominated the picture, refusing to reveal whether he loathed his onlookers or only found them vaguely amusing. No other writer commanded more than a small, pedestrian snapshot. Paradoxically, Capote was the only one of the group who had not yet published a novel. His handful of short stories had received some critical attention, but certainly not enough to justify his upstaging Jean Stafford, who had by that time published *Boston Adventure* and *The Mountain Lion,* and was married to the newly Pulitzered poet, Robert Lowell. In all probability the photograph itself gave Capote precedence: give *Life* its picture, as any schoolboy knows, and it will *create* the story. The young author's impending renown was carried back to England by Cyril Connally, who came to this country on a cultural souvenir hunt for *Horizon,* and went back to report that the New York publishing houses echoed with a single cry: "Get Truman Capote."

When *Other Voices, Other Rooms* finally appeared in January of 1948, its advertisements gleefully stressed its premature fame: "It happens rarely, perhaps once in a decade, but every now and then an author appears who has that magical quality that fires discussion months before his book is published. This was true of William Saroyan. It is especially true of Truman Capote." Considering the massive publicity coup demonstrated in creating "that magical quality," this particular praise suggests once more that for advertising, self-congratulation is the sincerest form of flattery. The public image of Capote — the portrait of the artist as a delicate, decadent young man — showed further refinement in the famous photograph taken for the ads and dust jacket. On yet another Victorian sofa, Capote reclines this time, still sullen, with reflected light expertly accenting his penetrating gaze. He is the child who is older than we will ever be, the unlined youth who seems incredibly weary of life: a potential victim, perhaps, of the hyperaesthesia that was later to do in James Purdy's Malcolm.

The popular magazines seemed to react to the build-up; they took the book seriously and reviewed it widely, no mean achievement for a first novel. The reviewers seemed particularly solicitous of Capote's future, apparently sensing from his photographs that he might not last the night. In the *New Republic* (Jan. 26, 1948) John Farrelly suggested that the young man was a victim of his advertising: "Capote's present reputation is the sort concocted from fashionable ballyhoo which is too likely to exploit the 'glamorous' elements of his talents at the risk of his future development." When Capote's early stories were collected in *A Tree of Night,* the reviewer for *Time* (Mar. 14, 1949) joined in the protest, chastising Random House for "selecting rather tender jacket photographs with which to publicize him." His publishers could help, *Time* urged, "by respecting his youth instead of exploiting it." The notion of Truman Capote — host of the Great Party of 1966, sponsor for the acting career of Lee Radziwill — *exploited* by publicity, has a faintly ironic charm.

Other Voices, Other Rooms may have profited as much from

the condemnation as from the praise of its early reviews. Writing for *The Nation* (Jan. 31, 1948), Diana Trilling lauded Capote's writing ability; but a writer's "style," as such, is seldom a stimulus to his sales. Mrs. Trilling went on, though, to attack the book's moral vision. Too sophisticated to be disturbed, as *Time* was, by the mere presence of the homosexuality "dripping like Spanish moss" from the tale, she took exception to the author's attitude toward his material. She saw the novel as a study of the nurturing of homosexuality in its youthful hero, Joel Knox, and found his final accession to perversion unbearably deterministic. She was flustered by Capote's apparent implication that Joel had to turn to his transvestite cousin, Randolph, because love had been denied him in normal society. Such environmental justification of perversion, she objected, is "surely a very dangerous social attitude." Then as now a high priestess of artistic and intellectual responsibility, Mrs. Trilling ended her review with a call for today's novelists to return to the time-honored foundations of their form: "to base its artistic stature on its moral stature." Although one might not buy a novel because of its author's "ability to bend language to his poetic moods, his ear for dialect and for the varied rhythms of speech," his moral irresponsibility just might be tempting.

Any moral irresponsibility detected in the novel was certainly compounded by the blatant attempt of the publicity surrounding it to identify Capote with his fictional perverted child. Set beside the photographs of the author, the novel's early description of Joel seems conclusive proof for an autobiographical imputation: "He was too pretty, too delicate and fair skinned; each of his features was shaped with a sensitive accuracy, and a girlish tenderness softened his eyes, which were brown and very large. . . . A kind of tired, imploring expression masked his thin face, and there was an unyouthful sag about his shoulders." The details of Capote's life revealed in interviews seemed to support at least a spiritual identification between created and creator. Capote's biography received national currency in *Saturday Review* (Feb. 12, 1949), an issue devoted to the young novelists of the preceding year. Interviewed by Rochelle Girson, he said that he had lived as a child "with a posse of cousins and elder kin in 'this terribly isolated place' near New Orleans, a locale not unlike that in 'Other Voices, Other Rooms.' " By ten he was "madly in love" with Willa Cather, Flaubert, and Proust, and before coming to the *New Yorker* at fifteen, he had been a tap-dancer on a riverboat,

painter of imaginary flowers on glass, and a protege of a lady fortune teller, where "he developed a marvellous intuition — a kind
of secret knowledge." Even his experience on the *New Yorker,* a
respectable enough employer, was out of the ordinary: hired into
the accounting department, he confessed his mathematical inepti-
tude and was transferred to the art department. Whether Capote's
account of his life is factual or fanciful is beside the point; his
selection of the details serves to enhance the fundamental eccentricity and otherness of the boy genius. His skill in presenting his
image gains when it is compared to that of the other writers
interviewed: Norman Mailer spoke of the place of obscenity in
fiction, but his tentativeness and embarrassment made him fall
disappointingly short of his present fervor and eloquence on the
subject; Gore Vidal seemed spiritless, hardly likely to run for
Congress or expose the Kennedy family. Only the sketch of Ross
Lockridge was more spectacular than Capote's: Lockridge had followed the enormous success of *Raintree County* with suicide.

Given more time to digest the novel, reviewers for the intellectual quarterlies tried not to fall for the manufactured image
of the novelist. Their pervasive objection to *Other Voices, Other
Rooms* was its derivative nature. In the *Kenyon Review* (Summer,
1948) Leslie Fiedler characterized the novel as "an accomplished
anthology of all southern literature: Poe is there first of all in the
ambivalent image, half fairy-tale, half psychopathic revelation;
Faulkner does the décor; the young girls are by Carson McCullers,
the freaks by Eudora Welty — ontology recapitulates ontogeny!"
From the more severe forum of *Partisan Review* (March, 1948) ,
Elizabeth Hardwick called the novel the inevitable parody that
rang "a tinkling funeral bell for some of our recent Southern
fiction." Capote, she claimed, "shows us that in literature, too, you
can reach the equivalent of those sophisticated painters who seem
miraculously to have been born with precisely the same imagination as Paul Klee. In that sense, *Other Voices, Other Rooms*
already has a quaint historical significance."

The novel's most severe notice came in the *Sewanee Review*
(Summer, 1948) , where Henry Rago directly attacked its style,
the one aspect of the work that had been relatively unscathed
elsewhere. Rago saw little point in allowing that "Mr. Capote is
capable of writing some beautiful sentences here and there and
perhaps a paragraph or two. He cannot sustain these accidental
successes because he has neither taste nor judgment; and he is a

prodigy in the sense that one can predict, even at this early stage of Mr. Capote's career, that he will never have the artistic and intellectual prerequisites to either of these qualities." Rago's severity, however, is counterbalanced by the fulsome praise of Marguerite Young, whose views competed directly with Fielder's in the same issue of *Kenyon Review*. Miss Young's approach prefigures that of such later critics as Irving Malin, who probes the novel's psychological structure in his *New American Gothic* (Carbondale, 1962). Miss Young found that Capote's primary concern is with "the extra-marginal, the symbols interloping among otherwise unintelligible experiences, the dreams, memories, perceptions, the fleeting peculiarities of human nature as revelatory of the psychic underworld which we all inhabit in daylight." If both Rago's censure of Miss Young's praise seem somehow disproportionate, one may well trace the source for this back to the merchandising of the book. Its publicity roused expectations that might, or might not, be satisfield. If a reviewer for a quarterly were ordinarily to find a novel as worthless as Rago found Capote's, his logical response would be to disregard it. But the hoopla surrounding *Other Voices, Other Rooms* made it impossible to ignore; Rago seems to have bridled under this compulsion. If a reviewer were, conversely, to deem the novel worthy, his praise must be sufficiently elevated to justify the work's fame. Because the volume's publicity was not at all conducive to critical detachment, it is little wonder that even the best of the reviewers failed to grasp just what *Other Voices, Other Rooms* is.

Of course it is a Gothic novel, but not in the broad sense of the designation with which Malin embraces those recent writings that seem darkly introspective and symbolic: any term which can be used to describe the writing of Capote, Purdy, McCullers, J. D. Salinger, Flannery O'Connor, and John Hawkes has lost all discriminative usefulness. *Other Voices, Other Rooms* does not even derive from the widely accepted Southern antecedents suggested by Fiedler. Its form goes back to the beginnings of fashionable Gothicism, where its two distinctive stances were established. From Horace Walpole's *The Castle of Otranto* we get the Gothicism that takes its mysterious trappings seriously, either as materials for sensationalism, in the case of Walpole himself, or as symbolic extensions of some hidden, inner evil, in subsequent works like Emily Brontë's *Wuthering Heights*. From Ann Radcliffe's romances, such as *The Mysteries of Udolpho,* we get the Gothicism in which the mysteries turn out to be demonstrably false; "super-natural" events are rationally explained, often as the products of a specifically human malevolence. An early twist on this form is supplied by Jane Austen in *Northanger Abbey,* in which the "evil" explained and expunged at the end existed nowhere except within the overactive imagination of Catherine Morland. (There are several adequate accounts of early Gothicism; for a particularly spirited approach see Fiedler's *Love and Death in the American Novel.*)

Regardless of the actual sources proposed for *Other Voices, Other Rooms,* its basic pattern is fully in the tradition of Mrs. Radcliffe. The primary requirement for this form is a protagonist with a sufficiently delicate sensibility to convey the full shock of the horrors it is exposed to: innocence, accuteness, and inquisitiveness are necessities. Capote's first playful inversion of his tradition is to fill this, obviously the feminine lead, with an effeminate boy. Called to the remote, decaying mansion at Skully's Landing to meet the father he has never seen, Joel is immersed in an atmosphere of mystery. When he asks about his father, his mindless step-mother and Wildely gay cousin seem deaf; Zoo, the colored servant with a striking scar from a youthful throat-slitting, seems frightened when the boy asks about his father: "Don't ever ax me nothin about Mister Sansom. Miss Amy the one take care of him. Ax her. Ax Mister Randolph. I ain't in noways messed up with Mister Sansom." As Joel wanders around the ruined porch on his first afternoon at the house, he looks up to see a strange lady peering at him from an upper window: "She was holding aside the curtains of the left corner window, and smiling and nodding at him, as if in greeting or approval; but she was no one Joel had ever known: the hazy substance of her face, the suffused marshmallow features, brought to mind his own vaporish reflection in the wavy chamber mirror." While he is talking of the lady to Amy and Cousin Randolph, who seem never to have heard of her, Joel hears a mysterious sound: "like the thump of an oversized raindrop, it drum-drummed down the stairsteps. . . . The thumping stopped, an instant of quiet, then an ordinary red tennis ball rolled silently through the archway." This red tennis ball, which infuriated Mrs. Trilling, is at the heart of the novel. Given the pitch of Joel's emotions, only a severed head rolling into the room would have satisfied his fearful anticipation. His response is mixed: "He wanted to laugh. Only it wasn't funny. He couldn't believe in the way things were turning out: the difference between this happening and what had been expected was too great." Capote is parodying his Gothic materials; still, the fact that the sound is made only by a tennis ball makes its appearance no less mysterious.

One by one the mysteries are brushed away: not by Joel, the former treasurer and Official Historian of "the St. Deval Street Secret Nine, a neighborhood detective club"; but by simple explanations. He has been kept from his father not by the malevolence of his step-mother and cousin, but because his father, having been accidentally shot by Randolph, is a mental and physical paralytic, able to move only the hand with which he brushes tennis balls from the bed whenever he needs attention. The lady in the window is no ghost, only Cousin Randolph dressed as a countess, reminiscing about the Mardi Gras night when he waltzed with his lost love, the boxer Pepe Alvarez. The slight catch in these revelations is that they are more horrible than the mysteries they explain away. A father secreted from his son is preferable to one who is hopelessly paralyzed; a ghost is at least as tolerable as a cousin in drag.

True to the tradition of Mrs. Radcliffe's heroines, Joel chooses the rational over the mysterious. Tempted to flee with the tomboy Idabel, he becomes frightened of the fascination she seems to feel for the carnival midget, Miss Wisteria, and returns to Skully's Landing and Cousin Randolph. Perhaps the novel is ultimately about the human proclivity to prefer the known present, however disagreeable, to the unpredictable future. Even such slight symbolic extension may violate the novel, however; for it is thoroughly literary. When it looks outside its private world, it looks to the tradition in which it exists. *Other Voices, Other Rooms* is an uncomfortable example of art as serious play. As such it does not approach the perfection of Vladimir Nabokov's *Pale Fire,* but it is far superior to the productions of the recent camp vogue led by Susan Sontag.

Other Voices, Other Rooms could not be marketed for what it was; that its Gothic vehicle fitted the temper of the late 40s, though, is evidenced on the literary level by the contemporaneous popularity of McCullers and the rediscovery of darkest Faulkner. In the popular arts the decade was the heyday for remakes of the classic horror films, and the squeaking door of "Inner Sanctum" haunted the airwaves. Although there may be no particular time at which Gothic novels are written, they seem to come into widespread favor at times when sheer physical violence, national or international, has become so commonplace as to be banal. Whatever the serious artist intends through his choice of this convention, I am not convinced that it provides its larger audience with anything more profound than a sense of relief that a world can be imagined more terrible than its own. With rows of paperback "Gothic Libraries" filling the book sections of supermarkets today, the twentieth anniversary edition of *Other Voices, Other Rooms* may harmonize not only with its history, but with ours as well.

February 10, 1949

The last great theatrical event — really the last great literary event — of the decade was the production of Arthur Miller's *Death of a Salesman*. Like Tennessee Williams at the time *A Streetcar Named Desire* was produced, Miller was not a newcomer to Broadway. He had already enjoyed a substantial success with the hard-hitting social problem play, *All My Sons* (1947). With Miller, there is no doubt, however, which is the more important play. *All My Sons* still lives fitfully as a skillfully constructed presentation of a moral dilemma, but *Death of a Salesman* has transcended the limitations of its period and has come to be regarded throughout the world as the dramatic embodiment of the death of the American dream.

Streetcar and *Death of a Salesman* have often been linked, especially by those intrigued by the question of whether it is possible to write a true tragedy of the contemporary world. Clearly if tragedy must meet the classic prescription of dealing with "gods, kings, and heroes," it is not. The gods are dead; the kings are mostly playboys, and "heroes" — in the supernatural sense of the term — are unacceptable to today's earthbound audiences. But if "tragedy" can deal with the destruction of a vision, *Death of a Salesman* qualifies, for Willy Loman's importance lies not in himself — as his son Biff says, he is "a dime a dozen" — but in his embodiment of the man who is thoughtlessly encouraged to dream beyond his capacities in order to achieve some meretricious end. *Death of a Salesman* reveals that the trouble with the American dream is not that it was too shoddily manufactured, but that it was priced too low and attracted too many bargain seekers.

The play brings to an end with complete symbolic appropriateness a decade in which a mammoth successful effort to win a war was followed by an intellectually and emotionally paralyzing failure to win a peace.

WF

271

Death of a Salesman: An Appreciation

by LOIS GORDON

Willy Loman, the salesman who sacrifices himself upon the altar of the American dream, has become as much of an American culture hero as Huck Finn. Like Twain's boy, Willy has met with enormous public success and is capable of moving the middle-brow audience as well as the intellectual sophisticate. The latter, however, has belabored *Death of a Salesman* to no end with two questions: Is the play primarily a socio-political criticism of American culture, or, does Willy Loman fall far enough to be a tragic figure?

While these issues are continually provocative, they, as Miller points out in his famous Introduction to the *Collected Plays*, have been explored ad nauseum and to the point of meaninglessness. Perhaps Miller's stand arises from his awareness that either conclusion is too simple and too pat, each utterly destroying the other's possibility. Certainly a play cannot be both tragic and social, as Eric Bentley notes, for the two forms conflict in purpose. Social drama treats the little man as victim and arouses pity but no terror (for man is too little and passive to be the tragic figure), whereas tragedy destroys the possibility of social drama, since the tragic catharsis "reconciles us to, or persuades us to disregard pre-

273

cisely those material conditions which the social drama calls our attention to and protests against."

It seems to me that the brilliance of *Death of a Salesman* lies precisely in its reconciliation of these apparent contrarieties, that Arthur Miller has created a sort of narrative poem whose overall purpose can be understood only by a consideration of its poetic as well as narrative elements. *Death of a Salesman*, the major American drama of the 1940s, remains unequalled in its brilliant and original fusion of realistic and poetic techniques, its richness of visual and verbal texture, and its wide range of emotional impact.

The drama of the 30s (including Miller's first plays at the University of Michigan and even his later *All My Sons*) leaned too heavily upon the depiction of social forces that were not emotionally recognizable. The emotional, or if you will, the poetic realization of man's totality was lost in the oversimplification of conflicting social and moral ideologies. The plays were external and linear; they moved to a single climax. The central issue of *All My Sons*, for example — man's responsibility to his society — was just too clearcut, and its protagonist's realization of this had too much of a lightningbolt quality. Although its social issues were meaningful and competently portrayed, Miller gained no sense of inner reality, of his hero's emotional struggle for truth, self-realization and self-understanding.

The drama of the 50s and 60s, generally speaking, lies at the other end of the spectrum, for this theater relies upon emotion without perceivable social or psychological context. The term "total theater," Artaud's original concept of a theater that would hit to the heart of its audience's emotion, has been very popular as a theory since the early 50s. Nevertheless, most of its embodiments have been in mad, free form, or perhaps formless, orgiastic rituals, where audience and actor rollick together somewhere across the footlights. Those who feel that there is a point beyond which form cannot bend without breaking and the art object ceasing to exist, while applauding the "experimental," find the emotion of revulsion more powerful than those presumably being communicated. But these plays are said to reflect the times, the anguish of an age where meaning has been destroyed, personality fragmented, and man alienated from man. The use of visual poetry, the stage as metaphor, existential anguish as a central theme, fragmentation of logic in time and space — all these are said to help us in evolving a new awareness of ourselves. But somewhere, when we watch all this, although we may be moved, we have the feeling that life, in the terms that we know it, of the daily questions of how to get along with one's father or sons or boss, or how to find, in rather ordinary terms, an ideal by which to live, are lost. The events that go on on stage — really poetic attempts to involve us emotionally — are, in a sense, too abstract. We want meaning in a play or any literary form, but we also want to recognize our own lives.

Miller succeeds, where so many of his 30s and 60s contemporaries fail, in fusing all of these disparate elements. He presents a sort of total theater and, in a sense, is the transitional genius of the American stage, 1930-68. As Eliot might say, on the one hand he represents the turning point of the literary current, for he continues the human values and forms of the past in the terms of the present. He concentrates upon human endeavor and heroism with the contemporary, fragmented, anguished (in existential terms) world of the middle class citizen. But on the other hand, considering once again the drama preceding and following *Death of a Salesman,* he recreates a total theater by harmonizing subjective and objective realism, or in theatrical jargon, expressionism and realism.

As Miller notes in his Introductory essay, the fundamental problem in a play is to create within the framework of a realistic statement symbolic significance which arises organically from that realistic frame. The central issue, it would seem, is action as metaphor. The meaning of life, or an understanding of life, as seen in a protagonist's commitment to social, psychological, and metaphysical (tragic) issues, must be inherent in the dramatic situation. Intellectual understanding, or meaning in a discursive sense, must be, much as Eliot has noted, wedded to emotional perception.

In a sense, to consider whether Miller's work is solely social or tragic is to split this unified sensibility. It is to deny that Miller's drama builds upon, to borrow another of Eliot's phrases, the objective correlative to gain its richness and complexity of texture. One recalls Eliot's famous dictum:

The only way of expressing emotion in the form of art is by finding an "objective correlative"; in other words, a set of objects, a situation, a chain of events which shall be the formula of that *particular* emotion; such that when the

276

external facts, which must terminate in sensory experience, are given, the emotion is immediately evoked.

That Miller's concern is with this sort of total effect is apparent in his comment:

The metaphor is everything, the symbolized action, the action which is much greater than itself and is yet concrete is what we're after, I think. I think the structure of a play should be its essential poem — what it leaves out. And what it follows to a real climax. Before there can be the other poetry, there must be that.

Death of a Salesman succeeds by Eliot's and Miller's standards. Miller finds the appropriate concrete symbols for the social realities of his time and place. He achieves through a series of emotional confrontations among the members of a single family an emotionally valid psychological statement about the particular conflicts of the American family, as well as the universal psychological family struggle. And by placing all of these events within the context of one man's thoughts, rambling over his past and present life, he achieves an internal drama of a man's epic journey to self-knowledge through experience. The entire play is, in this last sense, a recognition scene.

On the social level, Willy is a victim of the American dream, personified in all its confusion by three different figures. First, there is Ben, Willy's brother, the self-made man who went into the (capitalist) jungle and came out rich, the totally self-assured man who knew what he wanted and would brook no ethical interference with his designs for material success. "Never fight fair with a stranger" is Ben's motto. For him, ruggedness, rather than personality or personal integrity, is the key to success: "Who ever liked J. P. Morgan?"

But the dream is also symbolized by Dave Singleman, the salesman who lived on trains and in strange cities, and who, by virtue of some incandescent, irresistible personal loveableness, built his fame and fortune. Finally, the dream is symbolized, in perhaps its most noble embodiment, by Willy's father, who not only ventured into a pioneer's wilderness with no security or assurance of success, but who was also a creator, a man whose avocation was as well his vocation, a man who made flutes and high music.

Willy, as victim of this inexorable social system which drives its men to frantic, all-consuming dreams of success, is doomed not only by their grandiosity but also by their inherent contradictoriness. And as social victim, he is given his elegy in the last scene by his friend Charley, who, ironically, by a kind of indifference and lack of dream, has succeeded within the American system. Charley points out that a salesman must dream of great things if he is to travel the territory "way out there in the blue," but that he is also a man who really has no trade like the carpenter, lawyer, or doctor, and when the brilliant smile that has brought his success begins to pale, he must fall, though "there is no rock bottom."

Because this portrait rings true, the play seems to indict a system that promises and indeed demands total commitment to success without regard to human values, a system that, as Willy says to Howard, will "eat the orange and throw the peel away." Miller, in this sense, does attack the society that says "business is business," where the cruel inhuman son can replace his kindly father and say to a longtime employee, who gave him his Christian name, "Look, kid, I'm busy this morning."

It is a system symbolized ultimately in the play by the car, that strange, uniquely American obsession, which Willy and his sons (in Willy's glorious recollection scene in the first act) polish, love and cherish as a manifestation of their manly glory. But the car is something that wears out and breaks down, and soon enough, unless one can afford an ever-shinier, newer one, he is driving an old Studebaker, smashed up many times, with a broken carburetor. He is driving the symbol of an outlived usefulness.

The road is also part of this symbol. The road his father travelled in a covered wagon, by sheer ruggedness, individuality and courage, becomes early in Willy's lifetime the road to territories not ever opened, but it ultimately becomes the hellish road beside which the woods burn, and it no longer leads anywhere. In the end, the road, which had idealistic as well as realistic meaning for his father, is merely a journey devoid of significance. Meaning in Willy's life lies in the scenery beside the road — in the beautiful elms and the hills, in the creative sense of a spiritualized nature.

If it appears that Willy's dilemma is purely social, Miller cautions against this final interpretation. Charley, he reminds us, is Willy's counterbalance, and he is a man of humanity. His loyalty to Willy has a sincere, saintly quality. Though he gets furious at Willy, calls him stupid, proud, and childish, he remains faithful to a man for whom he has affection. Despite his material success, which undoubtedly pleases him, he has never been corrupted by the myth of success, nor has he ever lost the sense of human relatedness.

Even more than this social theme, it is undeniably Miller's psychological drama — his story of a family with its multiple loves and antagonisms, its conflicting aims and yet total involvement — that drives his audience to tears shortly after the play's beginning. Miller's psychological setting is particularly American, for we are largely a second and third generation country.

The first generation (Willy's father) has been forced, in order to make a living, to break up the family. But, while Willy's father achieved and was creative, he left behind him a wife, a young son-become-fatherless, and an older son driven to find success at the expense of love.

Willy, the second generation, is his father's victim. While he wants to love and "do right" by his sons, (His poignant "Was I right?" echoes throughout his lifetime), he is driven to use them as heirs to the kingdom that he believes must be built. Thus, he must pass on to them not only love but the doomed dream. He cannot relent even now, in the present time of the play, with his son thirty-four years old, a boy obviously not destined to achieve the greatness Willy wanted for him. Willy must still, at the expense of endless quarrels and his son's hatred and contempt, give Biff minute instructions in big business morality: "Tell him you were in the business in the West. Not farm work." "And if anything falls off the desk . . . don't you pick it up. They have office boys for that." "And don't undersell yourself. No less than fifteen thousand dollars." Willy must perpetuate that now hollow ideal that is his father's legacy.

Yet because Willy did remain at home with his mother and receive more in the way of love and human affection, he has come to know their value. For this reason he stays in New York with his wife Linda, whom he loves, rather than go to the New Continent; he looks forward to being with his boys more than travelling; and, at the play's end, he finally knows an exultant peace in a momentary spiritual communion with his son.

In recalling his father, Willy says to Ben in pride: "Please tell about Dad. I want my boys to hear. I want them to know the kind of stock they spring from." But his comment is filled with an anguish that permeates and gives richness to Willy as a man: "Dad left when I was such a baby and I never had a chance to talk to him and I still feel — kind of temporary about myself." Willy has searched for a father's approval throughout his life, through living out his fantasy of what his father was and would have wanted. So too, Willy's sons are trapped by their father's fantasy, even more hollow for them, and its fulfillment remains their means to gain his love.

A revealing example of this is both Biff's thievery and Willy's approval, virtually a logical extension of the same "You can get away with it" fantasy that is Willy's: if you are beautiful enough, you can steal and the coach will approve. Biff, even before his disillusionment in the final scene, chronologically in his life at age seventeen, has been destroyed by his acceptance of Willy's dream. Biff has always felt that to gain his father's love, he had to be The Best — the most beautiful and most popular boy, the football hero and All-American. Yet somewhere he has known that his father loved him and that this love did not solely depend on appearance. All the same, because so much of their relationship has hinged on Biff's being special, a kind of "Adonis" in Willy's eyes, so too Willy has had to be godlike in Biff's eyes. Rather than enjoying and appreciating the emotion they share, they have had to relate through the medium of their common fantasy. But with the episode in Boston, Biff's immaculate father fantasy has broken once and for all time, and Biff has spent the next seventeen years of his life living in a twilight world somewhere between the sunshine and trees, the free life that his father also loves which, as Biff says at the end of the play, "was the best part of him," and the nightmare of stockrooms, empty roads, continual smiles, and phony charm that he has absorbed from his father as necessary to both success and parental love.

Biff is the third generation, a representative of the sons of the middle class for whom the middle class dream has failed but for whom the only alternatives are various, all-embracing idealisms totally free from social structure. He is the beatnik, the hippie, and the radical, in whom one cannot help but see that the potent part of idealism is rebellion against the father and the father's way of life but in whom a desperate longing for father-love remains.

Hap, the younger son, less favored by nature and his father, perhaps as Willy was in comparison with Ben, has escaped the closeness with his father that destroys Biff in social terms. Thus worshipping his father from afar, Hap has never fully come to realize that phony part of his father and his father's dreams. He does have longings to be outdoors and to get away from the crippling fifty-weeks-of-work-a-year routine, but because he has never seen his father's feet of clay, he has more fully than Biff accepted his father's dream. He is not a social rebel, and he will carry on with the life of a salesman, and, one suspects, go on to the death of a salesman. He will violate the boss' wife out of some lonely desperation, as Willy sought support and solace in his Boston woman. He will also prove his manliness with fast cars and fancy talk, but again like Willy, he will never really believe in his own manliness in any mature way. Just as Willy is called a kid throughout, and referred to as the diminutive Willy by everyone except Ben, ("Willy, when are you going to grow up?" asks Charley more than once), Happy has been trapped by the infantile American *Playboy* magazine vision of the male.

Linda, as the eternal wife and mother, the fixed point of affection both given and received, the woman who suffers and endures, is, in many ways, the earth mother who embodies the play's ultimate moral value — love. But in the beautiful, ironic complexity of her creation, she is also Willy's and their sons' destroyer. In her love Linda has accepted Willy's greatness and his dream, but while in her admiration for Willy her love is powerful and moving, in her admiration for his dreams, it is lethal. She encourages Willy's dream, yet she will not let him leave her for the New Continent, the only realm where the dream can be fulfilled. She wants to reconcile father and son, but she attempts this in the context of Willy's false values: She cannot allow her sons to achieve that selfhood that involves denial of these values.

While these are the basic social and psychological themes of the play, they subserve its central theme.

Miller notes in his comments on *Death of a Salesman* that he initially intended to write a monodrama — a play called *The Inside of his Head* — which would re-create a man's entire life in terms of past and present, by means of his recollections at a particular point of self-reevaluation late in life. This is really the play Miller has written. *Death of a Salesman* is a drama of a man's journey into himself; it is a man's emotional recapitulation of the experiences that have shaped him and his values, a man's confession of the dreams to which he has been committed; and it is also a man's attempt to confront, in what is ultimately a metaphysical sense, the meaning of his life and the nature of his universe.

The play has been criticized because there is no recognition scene in the traditional sense. There is a notable absence, it has been said, of the classic, tragic, articulated awareness of self-delusion and final understanding. But, in emotional terms, the entire play is really a long recognition scene. Willy's heroism and stature derive not from an intellectual grandeur but from the fact that, in an emotional way, he confronts himself and his world. As Lear in madness comes to truth, so does Willy Loman. Miller has pointed out that social laws have replaced fate as man's inexorable enemy, and we might add as their helpmate, psychological determinism.

The play begins at what is basically that moment of anguish that Camus has talked of in *The Myth of Sisyphus,* that moment where the order of things fragments, where the ordinary social realities and values, in Willy's case the American success dream, are no longer adequate. The road and Willy's car, for all their social and psychological significance, have metaphysical meaning. Willy's soul can no longer travel the road; it has broken down because the road has lost meaning. That multiplicity within himself, his creative yearnings, and that part of himself which sees creativity as a moral value, now intrudes on consciousness. The woods burn, and he is thrown into a hell of disorder and conflicting value within himself. The two bags which are his salesgoods, his emblems of material success, the two bags which his sons would carry into the capitals of New England and so carry on the tradition of his dream, are now too heavy. His sons will never bear them for him, and the values which they represent are now the overwhelming burden of his existence.

The refrigerator and the house, though paid for, will never house the totality of his yearnings. They will never be the monuments to his existence that he has sought to make them. His sons, who would also have been the immortality of his dreams, his mark on the world, have failed him. As the play progresses and Willy's sons finally leave him kneeling in a bathroom to take their chippies, in consonance with the manliness they have learned from him, they leave him alone to face the void within his soul.

In the play Willy has no traditional religion; his religion has been the American Dream; his gods have been Dave Singleman, Ben, and his father, but they are now all dead — to the world and as meaningful values for himself. When Willy goes to Howard to demand his just due and winds up confronting a babbling recording machine, which he cannot turn off, he is confronting the impersonal technologic society which metes out its own impersonal justice. But he is also confronting a world without justice, a world where final truth is a babble. Ironically, the capitals which elsewhere function as symbols of the pioneer spirit and Willy's pride in his own travels, are now controlled by a child, and Willy's own sword of battle is turned against him.

The play is about *the death* of a salesman. The wares which Willy has sold, as well as being symbolic of his role in a capitalistic society, are, as Miller has said, "himself." In the final analysis, it does not matter what he sold, or in objective terms, how well he succeeded.

The particulars concerning Willy's situation also have universal significance. Willy has lived passionately for values to which he is committed, and he comes to find that they are false and inadequate. He has loved his sons with a passion which wanted for them that which would destroy them. He has grown old and he will soon vanish without a trace, and he discovers really the vanity of all human endeavor, save perhaps love. His foolishness is really no greater than Othello's raving jealousy or Lear's appreciation of the insincere, outward appearance of love. A pension would not help him, nor, had he come to be J. P. Morgan would it have helped. Linda says, "A small man can be just as exhausted as a great man," and she cries out "Attention must be paid." Inevitably, no matter what material heights a man succeeds to, his life is finite and his comprehension finite, while the universe remains infinite and incomprehensible. Willy comes to face, if you will, the absurdity of life, and it is for this reason that attention must be paid.

The vehicle for his realization is the play, which is the poem of his life. As in a poem, intensity is built through images of multiple meaning, through rhythmic repetition, through a logic of association, through an evocation of emotional intensities, through a time sequence which is subjective, and, appropriate for a poem of the theater, through visual and auditory imagery and leit-motifs handled as metaphors.

The flute music is his father's flute, the music of his father's life and the music of Willy's dream. The entire stage setting is transparent with objective and subjective experience occupying the same space, much as if they are equivalent to and intermingle inextricably in a man's life. Lighting is used to echo Willy's emotional states. Images — car, road, refrigerator, valises, silk stockings, a woman's laughter — through their rhythmic reappearance in the past and present, in different contexts, grow into symbols of his entire life. This is the poetry of the play. That the language itself is not traditionally poetic is only to say that it is no less so than Yeats' description of his heart as a rag and bone shop, the form no more traditionally poetic than the fragments of *The Waste Land*. The imagery is drawn from the hard cold facts of the life of a particular man — Willy Loman, the salesman for the Wagner Company, who lives in a house in Brooklyn. It grows in meaning by association and juxtaposition to metaphysical significance. Willy's death is not just his driving a car to a suicide which will bring some much needed money to his family. It is Willy's soul in triumphant revenge upon the dream that has broken him. It is a final act of will in defiance of a chaos which he cannot end, and it is made possible by his realization of a human value, his son's love, which he cannot live by, because the world is too complex, but which he can die for. If it is ironic, it is because fate, social law, psychological law, and the illusions of life are necessary, inevitable and always, of course, victorious over the individual man in the end.

February 19, 1949

As a political decade, the 40s began with terror, despair, and threat of Armageddon; they ended pettishly in disillusionment and mutual recrimination. The American literary history of the decade followed precisely the same pattern. The period began with Carson McCuller's first poignant tale of the terror, despair and self-destruction of a man boxed off from the world: it ended pettishly in probably the worst display of disillusionment and mutual recrimination the American literary world has witnessed — not even over a published work, but over a pretentious prize.

The private Bolligen Foundation — publisher of the writings of Carl Jung and many more exotic volumes — had prevailed upon the Library of Congress to give an air of official sanction to its annual award of a substantial prize for distinguished poetic achievement.

This award attracted little notice until on February 19, 1949, it was announced that a distinguished panel of poet-jurors had awarded the inaugural prize to Ezra Pound for his *Pisan Cantos*. Pound at the time of the award was incarcerated in St. Elizabeths Hospital in Washington, D. C., with the threat hanging over him of being tried for treason against the United States if he were ever declared sane.

Pound had gotten himself into this awkward situation by making a number of broadcasts from Rome during the War, denouncing American involvement on the side of the Allies and especially President Roosevelt and his Jewish advisors. He was extremely unpopular with most of his countrymen, and the announcement of the award was greeted with cries of outrage.

Whether the award was a honest tribute or an act of spite, we shall probably never know. Many of the poets professed to admire Pound's later poetry — though most readers found it incomprehensible — and many of them had substantial personal and professional obligations to this man who had always encouraged talented young experimenters. On the other hand, by 1949, most serious poets were hopelessly alienated from their society. They were practically unanimous in denouncing the smug, mechanical, middle-class culture of the United States; and the granting of an award to Pound did provide what would certainly be an irresistible opportunity to strike back at one's tormentors.

Whatever the jurors' reasons, they were intentionally or unintentionally successful in provoking such a controversy as poetry had not before in this century. The decade ended with angry voices still hurling accusations at each other. Robert A. Corrigan rounds out the story of the literary 40s by taking us on a guided tour of the Pound fuss.

WF

Ezra Pound and the Bollingen Prize Controversy

by ROBERT A. CORRIGAN

The background to the story of Ezra Pound and the writing of *The Pisan Cantos* is too well known to develop in any detail at this time. It is enough to recall that the famed expatriate American poet was captured by the United States Army in Italy after the fall of Mussolini and charged with treason for having broadcast over Radio Rome for the Fascists. Pound, however, never stood trial on the treason charge because a trio of government psychiatrists pronounced him insane and he was locked up in a mental institution until his release in 1958.

Before going to the United States to stand trial, however, Ezra Pound was imprisoned outside of Pisa, Italy for a period of six months. It was at this time that he began to write the eleven cantos (74 to 84) which make up the 118 pages of *The Pisan Cantos*. These poems were published in 1948, while Pound, certified insane, was in St. Elizabeths Hospital in Washington, D. C. For the most part, the *Cantos* were greeted with praise and a certain amount of grudging respect throughout the literary world. Many poets owed a great deal to Pound and an increasing number — led by T. S. Eliot and Archibald MacLeish — were anxious to see him removed from the Hospital's insane ward and sent back to his home of two decades — Rapallo, Italy.

What caused the comment was *not* the publication of the poems, but the award that was given to them in 1949 by the Library of Congress Fellows in American Literature; a panel of 14 respected writers and scholars* who had been empowered to select the best volume of verse published by an American poet in 1949 and award to it the first annual Bollingen Prize in Poetry of $1000.00. There had been a number of nominations, but on the final ballot, 10 of the 12 voting jurists selected *The Pisan Cantos*. The jurists fully expected to be criticized for their choice, but they had no reason to assume the violence of the controversy. It began with an attack in *Senior Scholastic* (March 2, 1949), followed by a vicious harangue in *Masses and Mainstream* (April, 1949). It reached a high level of scholarly debate in *Partisan Review*.** But by far, the most interesting phase of the controversy took place in the pages of the *Saturday Review of Literature* and it is with that debate that I should like to deal at this time.

All the while that the *Partisan Review* controversy was being waged on the relatively high level that usually characterizes scholarly disagreement, *Saturday Review* patiently awaited its own opportunity to enter the fray. The editors — Harrison Smith and Norman Cousins — had quietly commissioned Pulitzer-Prize-Winning-Poets Robert Hillyer and Peter Viereck to write three articles on the merits of the Prize itself and on the undue influence exercised by T. S. Eliot and the New Critics on American poetry.

Hillyer's first article, "Treason's Strange Fruit: The Case of Ezra Pound and the Bollingen Prize," was published in the June

---

*Leonie Adams, Conrad Aiken, W. H. Auden, Louise Bogan, Katherine Garrison Chapin, T. S. Eliot, Paul Green, Robert Lowell, Katherine Anne Porter, Karl Shapiro, Allen Tate, Willard Thorp and Robert Penn Warren. Theodore Spencer died before the final vote was taken; Archibald MacLeish and William Carlos Williams were not appointed until after the decision had been reached.

**William Barrett, "A Prize for Ezra Pound," *Partisan Review*, XVI (April, 1949) and responses by W. H. Auden, Robert Gorham Davis, Clement Greenberg, Irving Howe, George Orwell, Karl Shapiro, Allen Tate, and William Barrett (May, 1949), 512-522.

11 issue, accompanied by an editorial note declaring the board stood squarely behind Hillyer and inviting legal action if he or the board were guilty of libel or misrepresentation. The editors accused Pound of having "voluntarily served the cause of the greatest anti-humanitarian and anti-cultural crusade known to history" as an "official of considerable standing and an intimate of Mussolini, to boot" and even suggested that the award to Pound might be a calculated attempt on the part of the "super" snobs like W. H. Auden and T. S. Eliot to bring about the release of the traitorous mad poet. Arguing that "art cannot be separated from life and attain true greatness" the editors refused to accept the "anti-humanitarian ravings of an insane man, the incoherent medley of wild ideas, of symbols that reflect nothing but obscurity, as a work of genius."

Robert Hillyer, if anything, was even more honestly outraged than editors Cousins and Smith as he dismissed *The Pisan Cantos* abruptly as a "vehicle of contempt for America" and as a "ruthless mockery of our Christian war dead." The jury had "defied all critical standards" by choosing the *Cantos* for the Prize. And in an involved argument linking the Mellon family (donators of the money) with Carl Jung (an accused Nazi), Hillyer demonstrated to his own satisfaction that the Bollingen Foundation (named by Mellon for Jung's summer home in Switzerland) and the Library of Congress Fellows were linked together in a fascist-like conspiracy to strangle native American verse.

In the second installment of his two-part attack, "Poetry's New Priesthood" (*SRL*, June 18, 1949), Hillyer announced that if the *Cantos* were a poetic achievement, then "everything we have known of poetry in the English language from Chaucer to Frost is *not* poetic achievement." He condemned Eliot as a Jew-hater and suggested that his philosophy of literature was undermining the teaching of literature in the schools and colleges of the nation. The panel members were but the dupes of Eliot since half their number, at least, were "disciples" of him and Pound. Finally, he linked the so-called new aesthetic with totalitarianism and pictured the award of the Bollingen Prize to Ezra Pound as a symbol of that unholy union.

On July 2, the editors gave over the editorial page of the magazine to Luther Evans, the Librarian of Congress, who admitted that he personally regarded the choice of Pound's *Cantos* as unfortunate, since from his "poetically ignorant point of view Mr.

Pound's book is hardly poetry at all." But Evans refused to admit to the demands of some that poetry be politically sound to be good since "a political test for art and poetry" must be regarded as a sign of a "dictatorial, illiberal, undemocratic approach to matters of the mind." *SRL*'s editors responded to Mr. Evans' letter in a more temperate manner than that of their original statement. They agreed with him that it was indeed necessary to divorce politics from art but wondered if it were not quite another matter to use the word politics as "a substitute for values." "We do not believe that a poet can shatter ethics and values and still be a good poet," argued Harrison Smith, nor do we believe that poetry can convert "words into maggots that eat at human dignity and still be good poetry." He concluded with the observation that this "Congressional Award," as he termed it, might well have gone to Mark Van Doren, Archibald MacLeish, or Peter Viereck.

Peter Viereck, who won his Pulitzer in 1948, had already been chosen by *SRL* to launch the second round of the attack on Pound, Eliot, and modern poetry in a self-conscious analysis of "My Kind of Poetry" in the August 27th issue. Viereck's theory of art can be summed up in his own maxim "Be Thou Clear" and he is proud to admit to having sinned against the orthodoxy of the higher criticism. As Viereck viewed his own poetry, it was guilty of having content, that is, he has something to say "about the profane world" the new critics scorn and not "only form" which makes him an "impure poet" in their eyes. His other sin is of trying to "communicate to the qualified layman also, instead of only to fellow poets and critics." As for the Pound *Cantos,* declared Viereck, just so much "ugly gibberish;" but the Bollingen judges were not guilty of a fascist conspiracy in his opinion. Rather, the choice represents "an untenable doctrinaire attempt to separate form from content and to separate poetry from its inextricable moral and historical context."

The second half of Viereck's attack on Pound and modern poetry in the *Atlantic Monthly* (Oct., 1949) began disarmingly enough with praise for the verse of Edith Sitwell with its "legitimate and ultimately rewarding difficulty of a deep pool rather than the meaningless obscurity of a shallow and muddy puddle." As for Ezra Pound's poetry, he continued, it cannot be aesthetically attractive because "beauty is banished by the moral ugliness basic to the contents"; thus, the Bollingen Prize reflects the new critic's "irresponsible qualmlessness about immorality and about unclarity," the result of ideas originally "liberating and refreshing," but by now exerting a despotism of their own through the second generation of new critics who, like all second generations, are "earnest, sterile, (and) pedantic." The Bollingen Prize, therefore reflects the triumph of two critical attitudes: first that of "detailed textual criticism for its own sake" and second, the Eliot maxim that modern poetry must be "complex" — a maxim that has been pushed so far as to make critics afraid to "object to obscurity lest they be called insensitive middle-brows."

In the eyes of many, however, the *Saturday Review of Literature* had already succumbed to the pressure of the middle-brows and neglected its obligations to first-rate writers and their work. It was left to *Poetry* magazine to reassert the values of freedom of artistic expression. The editorial staff of *Poetry* felt that it had been badly treated by *SRL* and resented Mr. Hillyer's implication that it had been taken over lock, stock, and theory by the "obscurist" poets and New Critics. *Poetry* had first responded to the announcement of the Bollingen Prize to Pound somewhat tongue in cheek. By the time of the June issue, however, the critical stakes had become too high and editor Hayden Carruth felt obligated to defend his position.

By August, Carruth was so angered by *SRL* and by Hillyer, that he proposed that the worst enemy of poetry may be "the poet himself since he can't reach the heights of the great poet." Admitting that good poets have always violated tradition, he conceded that Pound was "very likely a traitor" and that it was difficult to defend him on "any but the narrow grounds of service to his craft" but there was still not "a single poet whose whole work does not suffer from serious deficiencies, deplorable lapses." Because the values that poetry concerns itself with cannot die, Carruth saw greater danger in the critic's attempt to restrict the domain of the poet and called upon all poets to exert their genius to honor poetry and "maintain its integrity." He challenged Hillyer's assumption that there was a party line operating in modern criticism by scoffing that it was ridiculous to conceive of critics such as Burke, Blackmur, Winters, Ransom, Richards, and Leavis as maintaining a party line, let alone subscribing to one.

The same month that *Poetry* attacked the *Saturday Review of Literature,* the Committee of the Fellows of the Library of Congress in American Literature, chaired by Leonie Adams and including Louise Bogan, Karl Shapiro, and Willard Thorp, issued a detailed mimeographed statement defending itself against the charges raised in *SRL*. Among others they rejected the accusation that Pound was handpicked by T. S. Eliot by demonstrating that Pound had been originally nominated by six different jurors, none of whom was Eliot, and that Eliot had never spoken up in favor of *The Pisan Cantos* in their discussions. The statement was mailed special delivery to the *Saturday Review of Literature* whose editors refused to print it.

On October 3, Malcolm Cowley joined the fray via an article in the *New Republic*, in which he rejected the notion of a conspiracy and asserted his belief that in the past too many second-rate authors had been rewarded for expressing the right opinions. He considered, however, that *The Pisan Cantos* was the weakest of Ezra Pound's many books and inferior, in fact, to several other volumes of poetry published in 1948. He maintained, though, that Robert Hillyer had "misled the public about the nature of an argument among poets and critics" and had "gone over to the enemy, like Pound in another war" because he had been "worsted in a struggle among his colleagues and compatriots" forcing him to appeal over their heads and "under false colors to the great hostile empire of the Philistines."

By the Fall of 1949, so many men of letters were angered and frustrated by the stand taken in *Saturday Review* that John Berryman circulated a letter for their signatures to be printed in *Saturday Review* as a protest to the Hillyer articles. This letter signed by 84 writers and critics was returned to Berryman after three weeks by the editors of the magazine with the lame objection that it was a petition rather than a letter and as such it was necessary to list the names of all those writers who had refused to sign it. Angered by this response, Berryman published the letter in the December 17th issue of *The Nation,* instead, along with a heated covering statement from Margaret Marshall. This letter condemned the *Saturday Review of Literature* for publishing "under pretense of attacking the award . . . a prepared attack on modern poetry and criticism, impugning not only the literary reputation but the personal character of some of the foremost writers."

Poetry magazine continued its attack on the *Saturday Review* by publishing, along with its usual November issue, a special edition devoted almost entirely to reprinting the response of the Library of Congress Fellows to the charges hurled against them. To this response, originally circulated in mimeographed form, were added reprints of several previously published articles and six hitherto unpublished letters of protest from eminent scholarly figures. Two of these letters, from Archibald MacLeish and Mark Van Doren, had actually been written prior to the publication of the Hillyer articles at the request of Harrison Smith who sent the manuscripts to a dozen or more literary figures to read prior to actual publication. MacLeish's original comments had caused Smith to urge certain changes in the articles, but MacLeish was still unhappy about the final results and asked how "a responsible publisher can offer his pages to personal aspersions as little supported by evidence as those Mr. Hillyer has committed to paper." Van Doren remarked to Smith that he did not "care for Pound's *Cantos,* early or late," and he agreed with much of "what Mr. Hillyer says about contemporary criticism, New or otherwise." But he could not countenance an attack based on such flimsy evidence.

The second two letters, by William Meredith and William Van O'Connor, were written in response to the publication of the Hillyer articles, but *SRL* declined to publish them. William Van O'Connor had originally reviewed *The Pisan Cantos* for the *Saturday Review of Literature* (Sept. 4, 1948) and thought that he deserved to be heard on the Bollingen issue, but the editors arbitrarily rejected his letter in which he attacked Robert Hillyer as a man who has "for many years been writing poetry as though he had been living in a little hamlet in Maine without benefit of radio, telephone, or any but a local weekly newspaper."

Although the *Saturday Review of Literature* had refused to print the letters of such eminent men of letters as Yvor Winters, William Van O'Connor, Mark Van Doren, and Archibald MacLeish — to say nothing of a letter carrying the signatures of 84 of the most important writers in America — it did open its weekly letter columns for six months to the charges and counter-charges of its general readership. All told, in 1949, *Saturday Review* published 106 letters on the controversy with the editors maintaining from the beginning that the letters were almost seven to one in favor of the magazine's position — although they promised to give equal space to the opposition. But a detailed examination of the 106 letters published indicates the following to be true: 56 letters were openly in favor of Hillyer's position (most of them enthusiastically so) ; 24 letters were opposed to his stand — but not one of these came out in favor of the award to Pound; 12 letters were written in defense of Carl Jung; thirteen can only be classed as middle-of-the-road or incidental to the main issues (people who asked that the government get out of the arts or who queried what all the fuss was about since poetry was so unimportant anyway); and one lone letter can be construed to have been completely and unequivocably pro-Pound. In other words, out of 106 letters published in 1949 by the editors of the *Saturday Review of Literature* on the Bollingen Prize controversy, only one was written to support the choice of *The Pisan Cantos*.

It is worth noting in passing, perhaps, that at least three of the correspondents offered financial assistance to the magazine should it be sued for libel or defamation of character and that at least three poetry societies came out as opposed to modern poetry and Pound and Eliot, including The Poetry Society of Texas and the Los Angeles Chapter of Poets of the Pacific. Finally, and most interesting, three of the writers identified themselves as college teachers and a fourth as a prep school teacher; they were enthusiastic in their support of Hillyer and vehement in their denunciation of the Higher Critics.

It is enlightening to discover that the only letter writers actually identifying themselves as college teachers should come out in opposition to the award and in praise of Robert Hillyer as these did. For although the Pound-Bollingen controversy is provocative on a number of levels, perhaps the most intriguing aspect is how quickly Pound himself was pushed into the background and the emphasis shifted to T. S. Eliot, the new poetry, and the Higher Criticism.

The Library of Congress Fellows in American Literature had steeled themselves for the hostile reaction of the public, but they could hardly have been prepared for the type of onslaught their judgment precipitated. They had fully expected the verdict of *Senior Scholastic* that *The Pisan Cantos* were fit reading for only Pound's psychiatrist or, even, the *Masses and Mainstream* suggestion that it was all an anti-communist plot to embarass Lenin. They seem even to have been aware of the likelihood of serious and profound debate over the anti-semitic quality of the poetry, a debate which, indeed, did take place in the pages of *Partisan Review*. But it appears more likely, judging by their statement of February 20th, that these objections were conceived of in terms of the well-known fact that Ezra Pound was an accused traitor and a convicted lunatic. It would seem that the irrational, intemperate, and often inaccurate attack launched on the award by the *Saturday Review of Literature* and the two Pulitzer-Prize-winning poets had little to do with Pound's actual physical or mental state or even with the quality of his verse.

The layman objecting to *The Pisan Cantos* would return time and again to the seven lines of vicious anti-semitism in the poems and would question, often in a bewildered tone, how *good* poetry could be a vehicle for such reprehensible ideas. But the *Saturday Review of Literature* knew how it was that *good* verse could be expressive of bad ideology and laid the blame at the door of the New Criticism. Indications are that for some years previous, in fact, the editors of *SRL* had been receiving more and more perplexed letters from intelligent readers about the nature of modern poetry. Judging by the letters published from teachers in small colleges throughout the nation, even the so-called professional was bothered. This is to say nothing of the poetry lovers — the myraid readers and writers of verse — who make up the membership of such organizations as the Los Angeles Chapter of Poets of the Pacific.

This is not the place to chart the history of the rise and fall of formalistic criticism, but it is tempting to suggest that the award of the Bollingen Prize to Ezra Pound in 1949 must mark some sort of high point for its dominance of American letters; moreover the controversy engendered by Hillyer and Viereck over this award may also reflect the degree to which the reaction against the new orthodoxy had already set in.

Indeed, what more ironic footnote to the whole proceedings can be offered than a brief reminder that it was not T. S. Eliot, Ernest Hemingway, or Archibald MacLeish who succeeded finally in obtaining the release of Ezra Pound from St. Elizabeths Hospital in 1958. It was Robert Frost, beloved national poet of the American people (and friend of Sherman Adams) who succeeded where all others had failed. It might well be that no other poet could have accomplished what he did. But with Robert Frost to vouch for him, to lend him some of the dignity and respect that had become attached to his name and position over the years, Ezra Pound gained his freedom and a controversial era came to an official end.

September 11, 1949

The literary history of the American 40s really does end with the controversy over Ezra Pound and the Bollingen Prize. This final essay is really a kind of after-piece that looks both back behind the 40s and beyond them.

Nelson Algren began publishing fiction back in 1935 with *Somebody with Boots,* but his novel got lost in the flood of proletarian/tough-guy stories that were appearing during the decade. It was not really until after World War II in 1947 that Algren first won considerable attention for his short stories published under the title *The Neon Wilderness.*

His first really smashing success — and the high point of his career to date — was, however, *The Man with the Golden Arm,* one of the early novels of the 1949 fall season. It brought the dope addict into serious American fiction as Malcolm Lowry had earlier brought the alcoholic.

The novel, however, seems to belong more to the 50s than the 40s in two ways. First, the subject of dope addiction that Algren had hit upon was to become much more of an issue in the 50s and even the 60s than it had been in earlier decades. Late in 1949, Algren opened up a new vein for fictional exploitation rather than rounding off the treatment of a well-established subject.

Second, Chester Eisinger makes the point in *Fiction of the Forties* that Algren's "distinction is that he is a naturalist who cares about style." Just as his naturalism and concern for social criticism links him to the 30s, his sense of alienation and his concern for style links Algren to the 50s, to writers like Salinger and Bellow and James Purdy. With *The Man with the Golden Arm,* we do not close the story of the 40s; we begin the story of the 50s.

WF

Nelson Algren and the Whole Truth

by Sheldon Norman Grebstein

Nelson Algren evokes little attention these days. Although he has published nine books, his last work of fiction, *A Walk on the Wild Side,* appeared in 1956, and the journalistic writing he has done in recent years hardly warrants our concern. It seems understandable, then, that Algren should be ignored by serious critics. In searching the critical literature I have found only a few treatments of Algren of any substance, and nothing more recent than that by Chester Eisinger in his fine book *Fiction of the Forties,* published in 1963.

But upon reflection, such neglect is hardy justified. Far less able writers are winning far more attention. Indeed, a generation ago Nelson Algren was considered among our most promising writers. Although Algren's earliest writing originated in the '30s, no writer who matured during the war decade had a better claim to the recognition Algren received when his 1949 novel *The Man with the Golden Arm* was chosen for the National Book Award. The current critical neglect lends credence to Algren's own claim that he has of late refused to make the total commitment serious art requires because the economics of publishing and the vagaries of critical taste together prohibit his kind of work from earning any sort of just appreciation. In the candid *Conversations with*

Algren, recorded by H. E. F. Donohue, Algren defends his somewhat cynical practice of quasi-literary journalism by arguing that
it is an activity forced upon him rather than chosen. As he told
his interviewer: "The only way I can really write is to go all out
and I no longer see any reason for going all out. . . . Now the
scene is changed. There is no feeling of this being wanted. . . .
There is no feeling, that I can sense, of any kind of spiritual need."

The need that Algren speaks of is the need for truth, truth that
he himself can conceive only in the most extreme and bitter terms.
For Algren there are neither partial truths nor soft truths, but only
the whole and hard truth. It is the compulsion to tell the whole,
hard truth as a contradiction to our national lies that constitutes
the basic impulse and moving spirit behind Algren's serious writing. Simone de Beauvoir shrewdly identifies this essential quality
in her depiction of Algren (as Lewis Brogan) in her autobiographical novel *The Mandarins*:

> At first, I had found it amusing meeting in the flesh
> that classic American species: self-made-leftist-writer. Now,
> I began taking an interest in Brogan. Through his stories,
> you got the feeling that he claimed no rights on life and
> that nevertheless he had always had a passionate desire to
> live. I liked that mixture of modesty and eagerness.
>
> "Whatever made you start writing?" I asked.
>
> "I always liked printed paper. When I was a kid, I used
> to make up newspapers by pasting press clippings in note-
> books."
>
> "There must have been other reasons."
>
> He reflected. "I know a lot of different kinds of people;
> what I want is to show each of them how the others really
> are. You hear so many lies!" He fell silent for a moment.
> "When I was twenty, I realized that everyone was lying to
> me, and it made me mad. I think that's why I started writ-
> ing and why I'm still writing."

Algren's whole truth, to name it in the terms he used in *Conversations with Algren,* is that there is a world whose existence the
middle-class American denies, "that there are people who have no
alternative, that there are people who live in horror, that there
are people whose lives are nightmares."

Such is the nature of Algren's world. Whatever its universal
human implications — and I intend to argue that Algren's world

conveys such implications — Algren's fiction depicts but three milieux: life on the road or in the jails of the Southwest in the 1930s; life in the slums, bars, and whorehouses of New Orleans of the '30s; life in the poorer working-class neighborhoods, especially the Polish, in the Chicago of the 1930s and '40s. Similarly, the population of Algren's world consists of hobos, prostitutes, criminals, fighters, drug addicts, cops, drunks, losers, cripples, down-and-outers, and innocent boys from small towns soon mutilated by life. Nowhere in Algren are there people vibrantly healthy, free of guilt, clean, fulfilled, content. Their existence — *our* existence, we would prefer to say — is suggested only in the abstract: as the faceless and faintly hostile crowds through which Algren's underground men travel, or as the invisible but potent force behind the police who are the nemesis of Algren's characters. The whole truth for Algren could also be described in vivid dramatic metaphors, especially in the scenes of violence so graphically depicted as to be nearly unbearable, and once viewed, unforgettable: a man in a jail cell dying of gunshot wounds, too far gone in shock to give the assent (required by law) to perform the surgery that might save his life; a legless man smashing to a pulp what had been the face of a handsome youth, in a fight over a prostitute.

Algren's first novel *Somebody in Boots* (1935) was in part a picaresque and in part a proletarian novel; it contained in episode, theme, and character the germ cells for some of Algren's later work, particularly a number of the stories in *The Neon Wilderness* (1949) and much of *A Walk on the Wild Side.* The theme of *Somebody in Boots* can be stated simplistically in Marxist terms: poverty corrupts. Men are driven to violence and crime by it; women are driven to prostitution by it; both men and women are degraded and dehumanized by it. Indeed, the novel's last two sections are prefaced with quotations from the Communist Manifesto. But there is much in the novel that drives from Algren's peculiar and consistent *weltanschauung,* rather than the social philosophy of Marxism which he was soon to abandon. The novel's protagonist has those qualities native to all of Algren's heroes; he is fundamentally innocent and well-intentioned, and he yearns most of all to love and be loved. His badness comes not from inherent viciousness but from the conditioning imposed by the jungle environment he inhabits. Although he commits crimes and boasts about his toughness, inwardly he remains fearful, even childlike, and never attains to the real savagery and evil of some of those around him. Together with what are for Algren's work prototypical descriptions of filth, brutality, poverty, hunger, the novel also advances Algren's prototypical assertion of the possibility of romantic love among even the criminal, the downtrodden, and the supposedly lost.

However, Algren's best work remains neither his first novel nor his last, but the two novels of the 1940s: *Never Come Morning*, 1942, and *The Man with the Golden Arm*, 1949. These books focus on the Chicago milieu which is the true center of Algren's world. They incorporate and integrate a number of the best stories published in *The Neon Wilderness*. They are largely free of the self-consciously florid writing that mars both Algren's earliest and most recent works. Their strongest effects come from keenly visualized dramatic scenes rather than from editorializing. They are of Algren's work the most fully realized in action, character, and structure.

Both novels belong in that important tradition or mode of American fiction which begins with Crane's *Maggie* and is continued in the best of Dreiser, ancestors Algren proudly claims, a tradition we might call symbolic realism or lyrical naturalism. This is a richer tradition than that of documentary realism and naturalism, wherein I would place such writers as Farrell. Like the best work in that richer tradition, *Never Come Morning* and *The Man with the Golden Arm* are distinguished by great verisimilitude and authenticity of setting and language, given emotional force by the artist's profound involvement in the lives of his doomed characters, sharpened by irony, supported upon a carefully designed structure, and made resonant by symbolic undertones. The pattern of action of both novels is identical: the essentially innocent and potentially noble protagonists, though besmirched by crime and fallen into vice, seek and temporarily find fulfillment and expiation through love, and even momentarily attain a kind of success, only to be trapped by their earlier misdeeds at the very moment of their greatest triumph and happiness.

If these protagonists, Lefty Bicek and Frankie Machine, are already lost when we first meet them, or soon after, if, naturalistic heroes that they are, their fates have already been determined, they nevertheless remain within the range of our sympathies because they are brought to life as neither subhuman brutes nor noble savages. Each is a victim of his environment, but each is also among the aristocrats of that environment. Lefty has a splen-

did body and ability as a fighter; Frankie has quick hands and a
nimble brain. More important, though their sensibilities have
been coarsened to the point where they can be casually cruel, both
have the ability to give love and the capacity to receive it. Despite
their surface toughness, both retain and respond to conscience.
Each has a lofty dream: Lefty to be a prizefighting champion;
Frankie to play the drums with a big-name band, but, in fact,
each would gladly settle for a pathetically modest reality: Lefty
to get enough money to marry his girl; Frankie to get the monkey
off his back. In short, despite the narrowness of their world and
its distance from ours, despite the fact that Algren's protagonists
both become murderers, we see them as men and we realize that
their suffering is meaningful.

The central theme of *Never Come Morning,* its whole truth,
so to speak, is the refutation of what has been among the hallowed
official truths of American society, a truth which Algren considers
the blackest lie: the belief that the individual retains the power of
choice, of deciding between alternatives, in plotting his destiny.
The novel's hero, Lefty Bicek, has no alternatives. The police
captain who arrests him, first for a mugging, and at the end of the
novel for murder, keeps this legend on the wall of his office: I
HAVE ONLY MYSELF TO BLAME FOR MY FALL. Yet, ironic-
ally, only after Lefty has already fallen, only after his doom is already sealed, does he assume the strength and wisdom to consider
alternatives. The fall itself is totally the product of what his
environment has made him. On the same night that Lefty has
taken his girl, Steffi, to an amusement park and has promised to go
to church with her, on the very night when he begins to realize
that he loves her — although the code of his environment would
never permit the utterance of the sentiment itself — on that
night he surrenders her to the savage pleasures of his "friends."
His motivation is basic and one conditioned by what he has lived,
fear born of self-preservation, fear both of losing the respect of
his comrades, and the physical fear of the knife one of them
carries. Then, driven by the anguish of his treachery, he point-
lessly kills a youth who has come to join the line of those awaiting
their turn with Steffi. From this episode derives his moral awareness.

Thus, working against its harsh surface naturalism and brutality, which includes such horrendous scenes as the mass rape,
there is a complex interaction of themes. The themes of the novel

are depicted as dualisms: love and betrayal, freedom and confinement, guilt and expiation, victory and defeat. In Book I of the novel Steffi's love and trust of Lefty moves her to give herself to him; he then betrays her love and gives her to others. In the last Book Steffi enters into a plot to betray Lefty to his former friends. But just as Lefty redeems himself to Steffi by confessing his shame to her and pledging himself to fight for her and marry her, so she reveals the plot to Lefty and fights for him.

From the moment Steffi surrenders her virginity to Lefty, neither is free. Ironically, the bond between them is permanently fixed when Lefty pretends to freedom by turning Steffi over to his gang. But the betrayal that is in part supposed to free Lefty from the sentiment of love and the obligations of sexual conquest produces slavery instead, slavery for both protagonists. Lefty falls slave to his conscience; Steffi to the whorehouse which is her only shelter after being used by the neighborhood toughs. Lefty must suffer the merciless inquisition of his thoughts; Steffi must suffer the entrance of any man who has her price. Each, too, has become a criminal in the same episode of betrayal, and thus permanently enslaved to the whims of the police and the machinations of the law.

Lefty's imprisonment for the mugging has the ironic effect of rehabilitating him not for society, but for Steffi; prison gives his life purpose. He emerges with the determination to free Steffi from her bondage. Both as a stage in his expiation and as a part of his newfound purpose, he takes the loathesome job of bouncer and pimp for the whorehouse. Here he can both participate in the suffering and degradation he has brought upon her and also stand watch over her. For Steffi the very sight of him is both a bitter reminder of their beginning and the faint promise of what might be.

Although Algren's fiction is more notable for its mood, its rendition of milieu, and its individually powerful scenes than for completely integrated and symmetrical structure, the novel's architecture does support its themes, in corollary or analogous form. It is organized around three motifs: fight, prison, dream, each of which is also crucial to Algren's work at large.

Never Comes Morning opens and closes with fight scenes, and there are other fights which occupy important intervals in the novel as well. The vital conflicts are those at the end of Book I and Book IV. Book I closes with Lefty's murder of the Greek, but his victory is in fact a disaster. At the end of Book IV, as the novel concludes, he is called to account for this killing, just after he has been victorious in the fight which would buy Steffi's freedom and make possible their marriage.

Prison scenes dominate the novel's middle sections, prison scenes of two kinds. In Book II the prison is the actual jail where Lefty is confined for his robbery of the drunken old man. In Book III the prison is that Steffi inhabits because of her life as a prostitute. In both cases the "prisoners" are at the mercy of their jailors, and in both, as I have suggested, a form of rehabilitation takes place.

Dreams, too, play an important part in the novel. Lefty's dreams of glory or at least of winning the respect of his neighborhood pals is an important element in his motivation, just as Steffi's dreams of romance are crucial to hers. More specifically, Lefty's dream in Book II of the championship fight against the tough and wily Jew presages his actual fight in Book IV against the tough and wily Negro. Lefty's dreams are paralleled by those of Steffi in Book III, who has nightmares of herself as a hunted creature, as a wanderer down endless corridors, and as the attendant to Lefty's dead body. Again, the dreams are a distorted but fundamentally accurate prediction of actuality.

As I have suggested, *Never Come Morning* demands a prominent place in an important American literary mode, which, contrary to a current critical cliché, is far from dead. But good as it is, *The Man with the Golden Arm* excels it. Not only is Algren's novel the first serious treatment in our literature of the drug addict, it is also a profoundly felt and profoundly moving book. This novel marks the culmination of Algren's identification with characters the "normal" man might think beneath or beyond his sympathies, yet such is Algren's craft that he extends the norm. I know no more powerful scene of its kind in any literature than that in which Frankie takes a shot of morphine from the peddler, Louie. This is a scene in which Algren makes us participate, regardless of our range of experience.

We participate because the novel is morally pertinent. As in Algren's other serious work the themes of love, freedom, and guilt are central to *The Man with the Golden Arm,* although expressed in different dramatic terms than in *Never Come Morning*. The particular conflict here is that between self-sacrifice and self-preservation, a conflict knotted into the relationship between

Frankie Machine and his wife Sophie, his friend Sparrow, and his girl Molly. These are dynamic relationships which fluctuate with the condition of the participants. Such is Algren's version of the whole truth that his people tend to prey on one another, whether in friendship or in love. There are no relationships in Algren's world in which each receives as much as he gives. Thus Frankie gives to his wife, gives and takes simultaneously in his friendship, and receives from Molly.

Before the accident which produces her psychosomatic paralysis, Sophie gives Frankie more than she gets. He marries her because he good-naturedly assents to her need of him, not because he loves or needs her. Her later dependence upon him, the intolerable and incessant tongue-lashings, her exploitation of his sense of guilt, are a form of vengeance for his earlier superiority over her. It is another version of the freedom-slavery complex, in which sex, love, and guilt are inextricably intertwined. Frankie's reliance upon drugs is largely the product of his attempt to find some surcease from what he must endure at "home." Yet an important measure of Frankie's moral stamina is his willingness to abide his wife, to stay with her, to accept the punishment she inflicts. After the accident he gives her as much as any man could.

Frankie's relationship with his friend Sparrow is even more delicate and variable. As the novel opens Frankie bestows his friendship on the somewhat pathetic and ludicrous Sparrow as a master might bestow a favor on his slave. But Sparrow also pays Frankie the vital reward of believing in him. Later, when Frankie is jailed for his part in the theft Sparrow has organized, he sacrifices himself for his friend by not revealing Sparrow's role. But when Frankie is released only to rebuff Sparrow's love and impugn his loyalty, we perceive Frankie's decline in moral stature, and that he has sacrificed his friend to his own pride. Sparrow grows in our moral esteem by remaining loyal to Frankie, by continuing to love him; later, he becomes almost heroic by resisting for so long the pressure applied by the police to betray Frankie.

The relationship with Molly is the simplest and the least variable. Briefly, Molly from beginning to end gives Frankie far more than she gets. His need for a woman to love him provides sufficient justification for her. His only gift to her is that of gentleness, a gift she has never known before, and for her that is enough.

In this way the novel establishes a general pattern of self-preservation and self-sacrifice. But such is the harshness and fatalism of Algren's world view, that the pattern of give and take does not result in anything like justice or equality. Just as betrayal, slavery, and guilt dominated *Never Come Morning* and determined the fates of its characters, so the major characters in *The Man with the Golden Arm* suffer cruel destinies, regardless of what their self-preservation or self-sacrifice would seem to earn them in an equitable universe: Frankie dies a suicide, Sophie is committed to an asylum, Sparrow and Molly face long prison terms.

Although I have stressed the tragic aspects of Algren's work, I should also point out that his books are not comprised of total gloom and unrelieved misery. There is considerable gusto and comedy throughout his work, especially in *The Neon Wilderness* and *The Man with the Golden Arm*. Indeed, the alternation between comic and tragic episodes is perhaps the most distinctive structural principle of *The Man with the Golden Arm*.

The opening scene of Frankie and Sparrow in jail, despite the scene's function as a dire prediction of later events, is essentially comic, with the emphasis on Sparrow's bravado and on his rich slang idiom. This episode is juxtaposed against that of Frankie's return home, replete with Algren's sharp insights into the ugly realities of Frankie's marriage. Sparrow's role as a comic foil to Frankie is further emphasized by his romantic escapades. In fact, the whole range of Sparrow's tempestuous affair with the passionate Violet, as well as the portrayal of Frankie's tender romance with Molly, serve as comic and ironic counterpoints to the relationship of Frankie and Sophie.

After Frankie has killed the drug peddler and thus determined the fate eventually to overtake him, Algren illuminates and re-lieves the mood of gathering doom by providing a hilarious episode which combines bedroom farce and comedy of errors, involving Sparrow, Violet, Violet's husband, and an officious, stupid police-man. As the outcome of the episode and as the result of the policeman's misunderstanding, the husband is hauled off to jail while the lover remains to enjoy the eager favors of the wife.

Another admixture of comedy and tragedy occurs at the New Year's Eve party which concludes the first half of the novel. All the neighborhood folk collect in Antek's bar for an evening of boisterous merrymaking; then, as the revels wane, Frankie learns from a friendly policeman that he is suspected of the murder of the drug peddler, but that no arrest can be made until evidence is collected. For Frankie what began as an evening of merriment becomes an occasion of disaster.

There is one other instance of Algren's technique, the only such instance in the second half of the novel, which is starkly tragic. During his incarceration for petty theft Frankie kicks his drug habit. But after his release he learns that Molly has disappeared and he deludes himself that he can no longer trust Sparrow. With his main sources of psychological support gone, Frankie finds that he is unable to function as a card dealer, that he has lost the magic in his "golden arm." Frankie's slide downhill is played off against the wryly comic episode in which Violet rids herself of Sparrow, who has become a liability to her. Pragmatist that she is, she increases her already voracious sexual demands on him until he reaches the point of utter exhaustion and almost begs to be released. Sparrow, too, undergoes a sort of decline, which Algren portrays in incongruous juxtaposition to Frankie's. Both men fail in the very powers that have provided both their sustenance and the source of their manly pride. Meanwhile, Violet has taken pleasure from the methods that accomplish her purpose.

Violet is only one of dozens of vivid characters who populate Algren's pages. I have focused on a few of the major figures to the exclusion of such admirably realized minor ones as Violet and the nauseating though totally credible Piggy of *The Man with the Golden Arm,* and the Barber of *Never Come Morning.* But they, too, document what Algren meant when he gave H. E. F. Donohue this definition of American literature: "American literature is the woman in the courtroom who, finding herself undefended on a charge, asked, 'Isn't anybody on my side?' It's also the phrase I used that was once used in court of a kid who, on being sentenced to death, said, 'I knew I'd never get to be twenty-one anyhow.'" In his practice, Algren has been faithful to his theory. He has written about the ugly, the sordid, the depraved, the fallen, and he has made them all morally significant — even, at moments, beautiful. It is thus especially unfortunate that Algren should have despaired of the success of his serious writing and abandoned it for journalism.

But Algren's ambitions as a social novelist notwithstanding, his ambition to write "influential" books, books that ameliorate unfair conditions, he has perhaps already accomplished something more important for literature: the scenes he has created have become part of our imaginative life, and his people are now among those we know. Algren's version of the whole truth in such works as *Never Come Morning* and *The Man with the Golden Arm* convinces us no more that his is the *whole* truth than does Dostoyevsky's vision of truth in *Notes from Underground*. Algren's truth, like Dostoyevsky's, attains its greatest conviction as a particular and imagined truth. Whatever validity it has to life, its larger validity is to art. I believe that Algren's truth attains this larger validity.

Bibliography

FURTHER READING

The 40s, perhaps because of distasteful memories of the period and the lack of any coherence in the literature it produced, has never been a favorite era with literary critics. No previous survey of the literature of the decade has been located, and already there has been much more writing about the more provocative 50s.

In 1951 the Henry Regnery Company of Chicago did release a series of books dealing with American literature of the first half of the twentieth century. Since these books were brief and were being composed during the 40s, they necessarily give only cursory treatment to the writings of the decade; yet they are significant because of the distinction of the authors: (all titles followed by *1900 - 1950*) :

Frederick J. Hoffman, *The Modern Novel in America*
Ray B. West, Jr., *The Short Story in America*
Louise Bogan, *Achievement in American Poetry*
Alan S. Downer, *Fifty Years of American Drama*
James Grey, May Brodbeck, and Walter Metzger, *American Non-Fiction* (not released until 1952).

The only literary genre to receive intense scrutiny is the novel. Chester E. Eisinger's *Fiction of the Forties* (1963) is an excellent summary of the important novels of the decade, discerningly grouped according to their intellectual content. There is no com-

311

parable study of the poetry or drama, but John Ciardi's *Mid-Century American Poetry* (1950), provides an excellent introduction to some of the major writers who developed during this period. The *Best Plays* of the year series, edited by Burns Mantle until his death in 1948 and thereafter by John Chapman, continues to be the best guide to theatrical works.

Many important comments on the literature of the period, however, are found in Ihab Hassan's *Radical Innocence* (1961) and Alfred Kazin's *Contemporaries*. One of the most highly praised works to deal with the decade is Isaac Rosenfeld's *An Age of Enormity: Life and Writing in Forties and Fifties* (1962), discerning comments from a group of liberal journals by a critic who died in 1956. The drama of the period is perceptively considered in Louis Broussard's *Contemporary Allegory from Eugene O'Neill to Tennesee Williams* (1962) and Winifred L. Dusenbury's *The Theme of Loneliness in the Modern American Drama* (1960).

THE LITERATURE OF WORLD WAR II

Again only the fiction has received intensive scrutiny. Chester Eisinger's *Fiction of the Forties* contains an excellent chapter on "The War Novel" (pp. 21-61). John W. Aldridge, a highly opinionated critic, also discusses the fiction of World War II in *After the Lost Generation* (1951). More valuable is the chapter in *The Mortal No* (1962), in which Frederick J. Hoffman discusses writings about the war, especially the novels, under the title, "Terror's Unique Enigma." *Contemporary American Novelists*, edited by Harry T. Moore for the "Crosscurrents" series (1964) contains two important essays on the fiction of World War II: "Some Children of the Goddess" by Norman Mailer, reprinted from *Esquire* (July, 1963) —a highly colored account by a leading novelist of his outstanding competitors, and "The War Writers Ten Years Later" by John W. Aldridge, originally published in the *New York Times Book Review* (July 29, 1962), under another title. Some of the most perceptive comments about the novels of World War II appear in the comparative discussions in Stanley Cooperman's *World War I and the American Novel* (1967).

Most critical histories of contemporary poetry and drama begin with accounts of works published about 1945 and mention works about the war incidentally.

INDIVIDUAL AUTHORS

There has been more attention to the individual writers of the 40s than to the literature of the period, but even they have been less exhaustively discussed than some of those who came to prominence during the 50s. Many of these discussions are found in the University of Minnesota Pamphlets on American Writers (abbreviated as UMPAW in the following entries) and the Twayne United States Authors Series (TUSAS). Beginning with 1963, excellent annual surveys of scholarly writing about the authors considered in this book may be found in *American Literary Scholarship,* edited by James Woodress. A semiannual listing of books and articles about modern novelists appears in *Modern Fiction Studies.* Quarterly bibliographies of articles on these authors may be found in *American Literature* and *Twentieth Century Literature.* Other journals of special interest are *Wisconsin Studies in Contemporary Literature,* which generally confines itself to works published since 1945, and *Modern Drama.*

NELSON ALGREN — No critical book has yet been devoted to this controversial figure, but some of his volatile remarks are preserved in *Conversations with Nelson Algren,* by H. E. F. Donohue (1964). His writings have not been collected, but many of them remain in print.

TRUMAN CAPOTE — No book about him has appeared, but many criticisms about his work appear in *Truman Capote's "In Cold Blood": A Critical Handbook* (1968), edited by Irving Malin. This handbook also carries Jackson R. Bryer's "Truman Capote: A Bibliography," a listing of works by and about the author. A book of *Selected Writings,* with an introduction by Mark Schorer, appeared in 1963.

JAMES GOULD COZZENS — *Critique: Studies in Modern Fiction* devoted its Winter, 1958 issue to Cozzens. For this issue James B. Meriwether prepared "A James Gould Cozzens Check List." Granville Hicks has written a pamphlet about the author (UMPAW, No. 58, 1966).

THEODORE DREISER — Much has been published about Dreiser, although relatively little about the novels of his last years. W. A. Swanberg's *Dreiser* (1965) is the most complete account of the novelist's life. Philip L. Gerber prepared *Theodore Dreiser* for the Twayne Series (TUSAS No. 52). Rob-

ert H. Elias has writtten a critical biography, *Theodore
Dreiser: Apostle of Nature* (1949) and has prepared a three-
volume edition of Dreiser's letters. No uniform edition of
the works exist, and some are out of print.

RANDALL JARRELL — Robert Lowell, Peter Taylor, and Robert Penn
Warren have edited *Randall Jarrell: 1914 - 1965* (1967), a
collection of reprinted essays and reviews with more than a
dozen original tributes by distinguished friends. The Spring,
1961 issue of *Analects* (University of North Carolina at
Greensboro) is also devoted to the poet.

ROBERT LOWELL — Lowell remains one of our most prolific poets
and playwrights. Several books about his work have appeared recently: Hugh B. Staples' *Robert Lowell: The First
Twenty Years* (1962) ; Jerome Mazzaro's *The Poetic Themes
of Robert Lowell* (1965) ; William J. Martz, *The Achievement of Robert Lowell* (1966), which contains many speci-
mens of his work.

NORMAN MAILER — No one else has yet written a book about
Mailer, but he has written several about himself, *Advertisements for Myself* (1959) and *Cannibals and Christians*
(1966). He has contributed a great deal of autobiographical
material to the *Village Voice,* a weekly newspaper that he
helped found, as well as to national magazines.

CARSON McCULLERS — Oliver Evans has combined many of his
earlier articles on Mrs. McCullers into *The Ballad of Carson
McCullers* (1966). Mark Schorer discusses her work in
"McCullers and Capote: Basic Patterns" in *The Creative
Present,* edited by Nona Balakian and Charles Simmons
(1963).

ARTHUR MILLER — Miller is the subject of books in two leading
series by Leonard Moss (TUSAS No. 44) and Robert Hogan
(UMPAW No. 40). Dennis Welland has also provided
Arthur Miller for an Anglo-American series of short critical
works (1961). Martha Turnquist Eissenstat has contributed
"Arthur Miller: A Bibliography" to *Modern Drama* (1962)
and Tetsumaro Hayashi's "Arthur Miller: The Dimension
of His Art and A Checklist of His Published Works" appears
in *Serif* (Kent State University, 1967). *Death of a Salesman*

and Tennessee Williams' *A Streetcar Named Desire* are reprinted with reviews and criticisms of both plays in *Two Modern American Tragedies,* edited by John D. Hurrell (1962). A volume of *Collected Plays* appeared in 1957.

MARIANNE MOORE — Miss Moore is the subject of a study by Bernard F. Engel (TUSAS No. 54).

EUGENE O'NEILL — has been the subject of many studies. Most highly regarded is Arthur and Barbara Gelb's *O'Neill* (1962). Other valuable critical studies are John Raleigh's *The Plays of Eugene O'Neill* ("Crosscurrents Series," 1964), Frederic I. Carpenter's *Eugene O'Neill* (TUSAS No. 66) and John Gassner's *Eugene O'Neill* (UMPAW No. 45). Jordan Y. Miller has prepared *Eugene O'Neill and the American Critic: A Summary and Bibliographical Checklist* (1962) and *Playwright's Progress: O'Neill and the Critics* (1965), the former listing and the latter sampling responses to the playwright's work. The first monograph to be devoted to *The Iceman Cometh* is Winifred D. Frazer's *Love and Death in "The Iceman Cometh": A Modern Treatment of an Ancient Theme* (University of Florida Monographs in the Humanities, 1967). O'Neill's *Complete Plays* were published in three volumes in "The Lifetime Library" in 1951, but some further works have since been posthumously published. John Henry Raleigh has collected criticisms of *The Iceman Cometh* for a book in the "Twentieth Century Interpretations Series" (1968).

EZRA POUND — Much has been written about Pound, but relatively few books deal with his troubles during the 40s. Two accounts of his difficulties with the American government are Julien Cornell's *The Trial of Ezra Pound* (1966) — (Cornell was Pound's lawyer) and Charles Norman's *The Case of Ezra Pound* (1968). Eustace Mullins' *This Difficult Individual, Ezra Pound* (1961) and Earle Davis's *Vision Fugitive: Ezra Pound and Economics* (1968) contain material about Pound's radio broadcasts. *The Cantos 1 - 95* were collected in 1963, and Pound has made a recording of readings from *The Cantos.*

RICHARD RODGERS AND OSCAR HAMMERSTEIN *II* — This musical comedy team has received more attention than many of the other writers of the period. Stanley Green concentrates on their work in *The Rodgers and Hammerstein Story* (1963) and David Ewen discusses them in *Complete Book of the American Musical Theatre* (Revised Edition, 1959). *Six Plays* (including the text and lyrics, but no music) was published in 1955 and added to the Modern Library in 1959.

WALLACE STEVENS — Stevens has recently become the subject of an enormous volume of critical writing. Early studies are listed in Jackson R. Bryer and Joseph N. Riddel's "A Checklist of Stevens Criticism," *Twentieth Century Literature* (1962). Since then there have appeared John Enck's *Wallace Stevens: Images and Judgments* ("Crosscurrents Series," 1964), Joseph N. Riddel's *The Clairvoyant Eye* (1965), and Frank Doggett's *Stevens' Poetry of Thought* (1966). Writings about Stevens are collected in *Wallace Stevens: A Collection of Critical Essays,* edited by Marie Borroff (1963) and *The Act of the Mind,* edited by Roy Harvey Pearce and J. Hillis Miller (1965). Stevens' poems are gathered in *Collected Poems* (1954) and *Opus Posthumous* (1957). His letters have been edited by his daughter, Holly Stevens.

ROBERT PENN WARREN — The earliest book-length study of Warren's art is Leonard Casper's *The Dark and Bloody Ground* (1960). Charles H. Bohner contributed *Robert Penn Warren* to the Twayne Series (TUSAS No. 69). Maurice Beebe and Leslie A. Field have prepared *"All the King's Men": A Critical Handbook* (1966), which presents selected criticisms of the novel. *Robert Penn Warren: A Bibliography* by Mary Nance Huff, appeared recently.

EUDORA WELTY — There are two book-length studies of Miss Welty's fiction: Ruth M. Vande Kieft's *Eudora Welty* (TUSAS No. 15) and Alfred Appel, Jr's *Season of Dreams* (1965). A standard edition of her work is needed.

THORTON WILDER — Several books concentrating on Wilder's plays have appeared in recent years: Rex Burbank's *Thornton Wilder* (TUSAS No. 5), Malcolm Goldstein's *The Art of Thornton Wilder* (1965), and Donald Haberman's *The Plays of Thornton Wilder* (1967). Two important statements by Wilder himself about his work are "Some Thoughts on Playwrighting" in *The Intent of the Artist,* edited by

Augusto Centeno (1941), and an interview with Richard H. Goldstone, first printed in the *Paris Review* and reprinted in *Writers at Work,* edited by Malcolm Cowley (1959). *The Skin of Our Teeth* was collected with *Our Town* and *The Matchmaker* in *Three Plays* (1957).

TENNESSEE WILLIAMS — The prominent playwright is studied in books for the Twayne Series by Signi Falk (TUSAS No. 10) and the Minnesota pamphlet series by Gerald Weales (UMPAW No. 53). A later study is Esther M. Jackson's *The Broken World of Tennessee Williams* (1965). Two important volumes of reminiscences are *Remember Me to Tom,* as told by Edwina D. Williams (his mother) to Lucy Freeman (1964) and Gilbert Maxwell's *Tennessee Williams and His Friends* (1965). Williams' publisher (New Directions) has kept his significant dramatic work in print in volumes with similar formats.

Despite enthusiastic criticism is scattered journals throughout the world there are no full-length studies of John Horne Burns, John Ciardi, Malcolm Lowry, or Lionel Trilling.

About the Contributors

C. W. E. BIGSBY (Tennessee Williams) is Lecturer in American Literature at the University College of Wales, Aberystwyth, where Prince Charles is to receive part of his education. Bigsby received his M.A. in American Studies at Sheffield University and his Ph.D. at Nottingham. He studied for a year in this country at Kansas State University on a Fulbright Student Exchange grant, and he did part of his doctoral work while a fellow at the Salzburg American Studies Seminar in Austria. In the spring of 1968, he was a visiting professor at the University of Missouri, Kansas City, and he has recently completed a book on his observations of the Kansas City riots in April, 1968. His earlier publications include besides many articles, *Confrontation and Commitment*: A *Study of Contemporary American Drama 1959 - 1966* (1967), sponsored jointly by British and American publishers, and *Edward Albee* (1968), for the Scottish Writers and Critics Series. He is readying an anthology of American Negro drama for British audiences.

JACKSON R. BRYER (Rodgers and Hammerstein) is Associate Professor of English at the University of Maryland. His major fields of interest are modern drama and modern American literature. He was managing editor of *Wisconsin Studies in Contemporary Literature,* and he has compiled many bibliographies of writings about contemporary authors, including that in *The Thirties.* He is the author of *The Critical Reputation of F. Scott Fitzgerald* (1967) and editor of the forthcoming *15 Modern American Authors.*

319

ROBERT A. CORRIGAN (Ezra Pound) is Assistant Professor of English and executive secretary of the American Civilization program at the University of Iowa. He has co-edited *The Poetry of Michael Wigglesworth* and published *The Diary of Samuel Sewall.* He has a biography of Sewall in progress. He has also edited *Uncle Tom's Cabin* and written several articles on contemporary literature. His most recent work is *Sixty Years of Ezra Pound Criticism,* and he has prepared a book-length study of the controversy over Pound's imprisonment. He was a Smith-Mundt and later Fulbright lecturer at the University of Gothenburg (Sweden) from 1959 to 1962. In 1968, he received a Standard Oil Foundation award for excellence in undergraduate teaching.

WILLIAM FREEDMAN — (Lionel Trilling) is back at Brooklyn College after a happy year in Israel at the University of Haifa. Although his University of Chicago dissertation is about *Tristram Shandy,* he has written about Whitman, Henry James, Dreiser, Faulkner, Steinbeck, and Shakespeare. He contributed an article on Henry Roth's *Call It Sleep* to *The Thirties.*

LOIS GORDON (Arthur Miller) recently returned to New York with her husband, a psychiatrist, after two pleasant years as a visiting professor at the University of Missouri/Kansas City. Her *Strategms to Uncover Nakedness,* a study of Harold Pinter's plays, has recently been published in the University of Missouri "Literary Frontiers" series, and she has prepared a bibliography of writings about Pinter for *Theatre Documentation.* She is revising for publication her dissertation offering a new interpretation of the plays of Samuel Beckett. She has also taught at the City College of New York.

SHELDON NORMAN GREBSTEIN (Nelson Algren) is spending his sabbatical year, 1968-69, as Fulbright lecturer at the University of Rouen. He is Professor of English and Director of Graduate English Studies at the State University of New York at Binghamton. His most recent book is *Perspectives in Contemporary Criticism* (1968), and he has also published two books in the Twayne United States Authors Series, *Sinclair Lewis* (1962) and *John O'Hara* (1966). If he can stop writing articles, he hopes to finish a book on Hemingway.

ROBERT J. GRIFFIN (Eudora Welty) is an Assistant Professor at Yale. Though his main teaching specialty has been eighteenth-century English literature, he has published criticism of Faulkner, James, Sinclair Lewis, Steinbeck, and Whitman, as well as Johnson, Sackville, Shakespeare, Sterne, and Thomson. His study of Lewis's *Arrowsmith* appeared in the Twentieth Century Interpretations series, and he contributed the essay on Clifford Odets to *The Thirties.*

DAN JAFFE (Poetry of World War II) is Associate Professor of English at the University of Missouri/Kansas City. His first book, *Dan Freeman* — a poetic history of the first homesteader — was published in conjunction with the Nebraska Centennial celebration in 1967, and his poems have appeared in many magazines. He has writen plays and the libretto for a jazz opera, *Without Memorial Banners.* He organized and directs the American Poets Series of readings at the Jewish Community Center in Kansas City.

KENNETH JOHNSON (Robert Lowell) is Associate Professor of English at Suffolk University in Boston. He has also taught at DePauw University and Loretto Heights College and has been a summer visitor at the University of Missouri/Kansas City. Many of his poems have appeared in national magazines, and he is now preparing a selection of them for publication.

JAMES JUSTUS (Robert Penn Warren) is Associate Professor of English at Indiana University. He contributed the article on William Saroyan to *The Thirties,* and he has written several essays on Robert Penn Warren's work. He is preparing "The Later Lectures of Ralph Waldo Emerson" for the MLA Center for Editions of American Authors.

SY KAHN (Eugene O'Neill) is Professor of English and Drama at the University of the Pacific and also Director of the Pacific Theatre. He is the author of five books of poems: *Our Separate Darkness, Triptych* (with Paul Ramsey and Jane Taylor), *The Fight is with Phantoms, A Later Sun* (with Don Gray), and *Another Time* (with Roger Mitchell). He has also published many articles on twentieth-century American literature (including those on Harry Crosby in *The Twenties* and Kenneth Fearing in *The Thirties*). He has been Fulbright Professor of American Literature at the University of Salonika (Greece) in 1958-59 and the University of Warsaw in 1966-67. His recent theatrical productions include *Marat/Sade* and *Six Characters in Search of an Author.*

A S. KNOWLES, JR., (Carson McCullers) teaches at North Carolina State University at Raleigh. He contributed an essay on "The Fiction of Henry Roth" to *Modern Fiction Studies.*

JORDAN Y. MILLER (Drama of World War II) is Professor of English at Kansas State University. A specialist in American drama, he has edited *American Dramatic Literature,* an anthology (1961), *Eugene O'Neill and the American Critic,* a bibliography (1962), and *Playwright's Progress: O'Neill and the Critics,* a casebook (1965). He also wrote the account of Eugene O'Neill in *American Winners of the Nobel Literary Prize* (1968). He was a Fulbright lecturer on drama in Bombay, 1964-65. During the summer of 1968, he led a tour of Greece.

DAVID G. PUGH (Popular Fiction) is Associate Professor of English at Western Michigan University, where he teaches primarily communications and linguistics courses. His essay — like the one on proletarian literature that he contributed to *The Thirties* — grows out of an undergraduate directed studies course. His writings are principally about student reactions to popular culture.

GERALD RABKIN (Thornton Wilder) is Director of graduate work at the Playhouse of the University of Kansas, currently on leave in London. He has also taught at the University of Indiana, and he is the author of *Drama and Commitment: Politics in the American Theatre of the 1930s.* He wrote the essay on the Federal Theatre for *The Thirties.*

GENE RUOFF (Truman Capote) is Assistant Professor of English at the University of Illinois at Chicago Circle. A Woodrow Wilson Fellow at Wisconsin, he has published essays on Wordsworth and John Dos Passos, and he contributed the study of the New Criticism to *The Thirties.*

DONALD SHEEHAN (Wallace Stevens) is Assistant Professor of English at the University of Chicago. He was managing editor of *Wisconsin Studies in Contemporary Literature,* and his

Wisconsin dissertation relates Dante to modern poetry. He has written about Stevens in *The Thirties* and other journals, and he promises a final essay in this sequence for *The Fifties*.

JONAS SPATZ (Theodore Dreiser) is Assistant Professor of English at the University of Missouri/Kansas City, in charge of the development of the undergraduate major. His book about the influence of Hollywood on American fiction will be published this year, and he contributed the article on Fitzgerald to *The Thirties*. He is now principally interested in the British Romantic movement.

ELEANOR WIDMER (Malcolm Lowry) is a novelist with a Ph.D. in English from the University of Washington. She has taught at several universities and worked as a researcher for an encyclopedia and the Great Books *Synopticon*. A long novella, *Mister Jack*, won a Random House award and was published in *Three: 1964*. Her first long novel, *Stillwater*, is slated for early publication.

KINGSLEY WIDMER (The Literature of the Bomb) is a combat infantry veteran of Europe in World War II, who was on his way to additional combat in the Pacific when the bomb was dropped. The revulsion which led to a pacificistic de-defiance of Selective Service when it was reinstituted in the Cold War resulted in a prison sentence (1948-49). Besides continuing as one of the first "resisters," he has taught at the Universities of Minnesota, Washington, California (Berkeley), Tel Aviv, and Simon Fraser, as well as Reed College. He is currently professor of English at San Diego State University. He has written many articles on literary and social issues besides the books: *The Art of Perversity: D. H. Lawrence* (1962), *Henry Miller* (1963), *The Literary Rebel* (1965), and *The Art of Perplexity: Herman Melville* (1969).

Appendix: Pulitzer Prizes For The Forties

The following works won the Pulitzer Prizes for fiction, poetry, and drama from 1941 to 1950 (awards, of course, are for works published during the preceding year). Some contrast between contemporary and later taste can be obtained by comparing the works listed with those discussed in this volume. Following in parentheses the names of the winners, are the names of the authors of any essays in this book in which the prize work is discussed.

WF

FICTION

1941—no award (Hemingway's *For Whom the Bell Tolls* was a contender.)
1942—Ellen Glasgow, *In This Our Life*
1943—Upton Sinclair, *Dragon's Teeth*
1944—Martin Flavin, *Journey in the Dark*
1945—John Hersey, *A Bell for Adano* (French)
1946—no award
1947—Robert Penn Warren, *All the King's Men* (Justus)
1948—James Michener, *Tales of the South Pacific* (French)
1949—James Gould Cozzens, *Guard of Honor* (French)
1950—A. B. Guthrie, Jr., *The Way West*

POETRY

1941—Leonard Bacon, *Sunderland Capture*
1942—William Rose Benet, *The Dust Which Is God*
1943—Robert Frost, *A Witness Tree*
1944—Stephen Vincent Benet, *Western Star*
1945—Karl Shapiro, *V-Letter and Other Poems* (Jaffe)
1946—no award
1947—Robert Lowell, *Lord Weary's Castle* (Johnson)
1948—W. H. Auden, *The Age of Anxiety*
1949—Peter Viereck, *Terror and Decorum*
1950—Gwendolyn Brooks, *Annie Allen*

DRAMA

1941—Robert Sherwood, *There Shall Be No Night* (Miller)
1942—no award
1943—Thornton Wilder, *The Skin of Our Teeth* (Rabkin)
1944—no award
1945—Mary Chase, *Harvey*
1946—Russel Crouse and Howard Lindsay, *State of the Union*
1947—no award
1948—Tennessee Williams, *A Streetcar Named Desire* (Bigsby)
1949—Arthur Miller, *Death of a Salesman* (Gordon)
1950—Richard Rodgers and Oscar Hammerstein II, *South Pacific* (Bryer)

Index

Adams, Franklin P., 164
Adams, Henry, 237
Albee, Edward, *The American Dream*, 213
Algren, Nelson, 156, 157, **297-309**; *The Man with a Golden Arm*, 297-302, 305-9; *Never Come Morning*, 302-5, 308-9; *Somebody in Boots*, 301
Alperovitz, Gar, *Atomic Diplomacy*, 147
"American Dream," 35, 276, 281
Anderson, Maxwell, *Candle in the Wind*, 71; *The Eve of St. Mark*, 72-74; *Knickerbocker Holiday*, 125; *Storm Operation*, 74-75; *What Price Glory?*, 65-66
Anderson, Sherwood, 242
Antoninus, Brother, 148
Aragon, Louis, 33
Arnold, Matthew, 43
Artaud, Antonin, 274
Atlantic Monthly, 290
Atomic Bomb, **139-151**, 163
Atwell, Lester, *Private*, 143
Auden, W. H., 148

Ballads, popular, 148
Balzac, 156
Bankhead, Tallulah, 111
Barzun, Jacques, 237
Basso, Hamilton, *Sun in Capricorn*, 189
Batchelder, R. C., *The Irreversible Decision*, 146-47
Beauvoir, Simon de, 300
Bellow, Saul, 8, 297
Bentley, Eric, 273
Berryman, John, 292
Bishop, Elizabeth, 230
Blake, William, 244
Blitzstein, Marc, 125
Bly, Robert, 35
Bollingen Foundation and Prize, 285-95
Boothe, Claire, *Margin for Error*, 66-67
Bourjaily, Vance, *The Hounds of Earth*, 145
Bowles, Paul, 3
Bowman, Peter, *Beach Red*, 20-21, 25, 28
Brown, Harry, *A Walk in the Sun*, 20

Bryant, Peter, *Red Alert*, **146-47**
Burns, John Horne, *The Gallery*, 27-32

Caldwell, Erskine, 40, 189
Camus, Albert, 223, 281
Campbell, Joseph, and Henry Morton Robinson's attack on *The Skin of Our Teeth*, 114-17
Capote, Truman, 97, 157, **259-69**; *In Cold Blood*, 259; *Other Voices, Other Rooms*, 259-69; *A Tree of Night*, 263
Carruth, Hayden, 291
Cerf, Bennett, 259
Cervantes, 252
Chamberlain, John, 262
Chamberlain, Neville, 43
"Christ Figures," 93, 208, 241
Ciardi, John, 54, 56-59; "An Island Galaxy," 59
Clark, Walter Van Tilburg, "The Portable Phonograph," 145
Coffin, Robert P. T., 164
Connally, Cyril, 263
Conrad, Joseph, 156, 194, 256
Conversations with Nelson Algren, by H. E. F. Donohue 300, 308
Cooperman, Stanley, *World War I and the American Novel*, 8
Cowley, Malcolm, 292
Cozzens, James Gould, 27; *Guard of Honor*, 9-15
Crane, Hart, 258
Crane, Stephen, *Maggie*, 302; *Red Badge of Courage*, 7, 9, 34, 65
Cummings, E. E., 8

Dante, 61
Deutsch, Babette, 44-45
Dickens, 156
Dr. Strangelove (film), 146
"Documentary-Novel," 142-43
Dos Passos, John, 8, 21, 189, 262
Dostoyevsky, 309
Dreiser, Theodore, **153-62**, 242, 302; *The Bulwark*, 153, 157-62; *The Stoic*, 153, 157
Dunlap, William, André, 64
Dylan, Bob, 148

Eberhart, Richard, 38-39
Eisenhower, President Dwight D., 20

Eisinger, Chester, *Fiction of the Forties*, 3, 22, 237, 241, 244, 297, 299
Eliot, T. S., 34, 42, 74, 275-76, 287, 288, 292; *The Waste Land*, 283
Evans, Luther (Librarian of Congress), 289-90
Existential guilt, 35
Expressionism (German), 118

Fail-Safe, by Eugene Burdick and Harvey Wheeler, 146-47
Faulkner, William, 3, 8, 99, 156, 189, 268
Fiedler, Leslie, 150, 255, 267
Field, Betty, 70
Fitzgerald, F. Scott, 8, 156, 262
Flintstones, The (comic strip), 118
Frank, Pat, *Alas, Babylon*, 149; *Seven Days to Never*, 146
Franken, Rose, *Soldier's Wife*, 76
Frost, Robert, 46, 295

"Genteel Tradition," 156
Gillette, William, *Secret Service*, 64-65
Gibbs, Wolcott, 115-16
Ginsberg, Allen, 35, 42, 148, 150, 230
Gordon, Caroline, 99
Gothicism, 97-99, 266-68
Green, Paul, 125

Haines, William Wister, *Command Decision*, 79-80
Hair!, 121
Hammerstein, Oscar, II, early works, 124
Hayes, Helen, 71
Heggen, Thomas, 262; *Mister Roberts* (novel), 25-27, 31, (play), 80-81
Heller, Joseph, *Catch-22*, 8
Hellman, Lillian, 164; *The Searching Wind*, 75; *Watch on the Rhine*, 69-71
Hemingway, Ernest, 8, 9, 27, 46, 156, 262; *Across the River and into the Trees*, 19-20; *For Whom the Bell Tolls*, 19; *The Old Man and the Sea*, 19
Herne, James A., *Shore Acres*, 118
Hersey, John, *A Bell for Adano* (novel), 15-16, (play version by Paul Osborn), 75-76; *Hiroshima*, 16, 142-43
Hicks, Granville, 11
Hillyer, Robert, 288-89, 292-94
Hollywood, 22
Howard, Bronson, *Shenandoah*, 64-65
Huie, William Bradford, 17-18

"Inner Sanctum, The" (radio program), 268
Integration problem, 13, 89-91

James, Henry, 107, 156, 240
Jarrell, Randall, 54, 60-61
Johnson, Josephine, 42-44
Johnson Samuel, 110
Jones, James, 8
Joyce, James, *Finnegans Wake*, 114-17
Jung, Carl, 285, 289, 294
Jungk, Robert, *Brighter than a Thousand Suns*, 144

Kahn, Herman, *Thinking about the Unthinkable*, 149
Kermode, Frank, *The Sense of an Ending*, 150
King Lear, 243, 281
Krasna, Norman, *The Man with Blond Hair*, 71
Kubrick, Stanley, 146
Kunitz, Stanley, 50-52
Lady in the Dark (musical comedy by Kurt Weill, Moss Hart, and Ira Gershwin), 125
Laurel, Stan, 120
Laurents, Arthur, *Home of the Brave*, 77-79
Lawrence, D. H., 206; *Lady Chatterley's Lover*, 254-55, 257
Lesser, Sol, 117
Lewis, R. W. B., 248
Library of Congress Fellows in American Literature, 285-95
Life, 261-63
Lively, Robert A., *Fiction Fights the Civil War*, 7-8
Lockridge, Ross, *Raintree County*, 265
Long, Huey, 189-93
Long, Richard A., 10-11
Longley, Adria Locke, *A Lion Is in the Streets*, 189
Lowell, Robert, 35, 47-48, 145, 150, **227-36**, 262; *Life Studies*, 230, 234-36; *Lord Weary's Castle*, 227-36; *The Mills of the Kavanaughs*, 235-36; *The Old Glory*, 231-233
Lowry, Malcolm, 156, **215-26**; *Dark As the Grave Wherein My Friend Is Laid*, 220; *Under the Volcano*, 215-26
Luce, Henry, 67
Lunt, Alfred, and Lynn Fontanne, 68
Lytle, Andrew, 99

MacDonald, Dwight, 120
MacLeish, Archibald, 45, 287, 293

Mailer, Norman, 10, 21-25, 27, 29, 156, 265; *The Naked and the Dead*, 21-25, 27
Malin, Irving, 266
March, Mr. and Mrs. Frederic, 111
Marshall, Margaret, 292
McCarthy, Mary, 118
McCullers, Carson, 85-98, 268, 285; *The Ballad of the Sad Cafe*, 97, *Clock without Hands*, 97; *The Heart is a Lonely Hunter*, 85, 86-94, 97; *The Member of the Wedding*, 85, 94-97; *Reflections in a Golden Eye*, 85-87, 94
Meredith, William, 293
Merton, Thomas, *Original Child Bomb*, 143
Michener, James, *Tales of the South Pacific*, 16-17, 25 (musical version by Rodgers and Hammerstein, 132-33)
Miller, Arthur, 252, 271-83; *After the Fall*, 258; *All My Sons*, 274; *Death of a Salesman*, 205-6, 271, 275-83
Mississippi, 99
"Modern Poetry," Myth of, 34
Molnar, Ferenç, *Lilliom*, 128
Moore, Marianne, "In Distrust of Merits," 36-37
"M u m m e r s," The, (theatrical group), 251-52

Nabokov, Vladimir, *Pale Fire*, 268
Nagai Tahashi, *We of Nagasaki*, 143-44
Nation, The, 264, 292
National Book Award, 299
National Institute of Arts and Letters, 163-64
"New Critics," 288, 295
"New Liberalism," 246-48
New Republic, 263, 292
New Yorker, 143, 264-65
New York Times, 179
Nims, John Frederick, 50, 52-53
Novel of Ideas, 22, 239-42

O'Connor, William Van, 293
Olsen and Johnson, *Hellzapoppin*, 115, 118
O'Neill, Eugene, **203-13**; *The Iceman Cometh*, 113, 203, 206-13; *Long Day's Journey into Night*, 203
Oppenheimer, Robert, 144
Osborn, Paul, *A Bell for Adano* (play), 75-76
Owen, Wilfred, 34, 35, 50, 61

Partisan Review, 237, 265, 288

Patrick, John, *The Hasty Heart*, 77
Perrine, Laurence, 232
Platonism, 169-76
Playboy, 280
Poetry, 291-92
Poetry Society of Texas, 294
Poets of the Pacific (LA Chapter), 294-95
Porter, Katherine Anne, 101, 110, 215
Pound, Ezra, 3-4, 49, 285-95; *The Pisan Cantos*, 285-95
Prose and poetry, distinction between, 107
Pulitzer Prizes, 15-17, 44, 114, 192, 227, 251, 254 (listed, 324-25)
Purdy, James, 263, 297
Puritanism, 232-33, 251-52

Rand, Ayn, *The Fountainhead*, 3, 179
Radziwill, Lee, 263
Rago, Henry, 265-66
Rice, Elmer, *Flight to the West*, 68-69
Riggs, Lynn, *Green Grow the Lilacs*, 129
Rodgers, Richard, and Lorenz Hart, 124-25
Rodgers, Richard, and Oscar Hammerstein, II, 121-37; *Allegro*, 130-32; *Carousel*, 128-30; *The King and I*, 133-36; *Oklahoma!*, 121, 125-28; *South Pacific*, 132-33
Roosevelt, President Franklin D., 26, 285
Rosenberg, Isaac, 35
Rosenfeld, Isaac, 109
Rotter, Fritz, *Letters to Lucerne*, 71
Rukeyser, Muriel, 40-42

Salinger, J. D., 297
Saroyan, William, 88
Sassoon, Siegfried, 34, 35
Saturday Review [once *of Literature*], 264, 288-91, 293-94
Science fiction, 149
Scott, Winfield Townley, 37-38
Shapiro, Karl, 47-48, 49, 54-56
Shaw, Irwin, *The Young Lions*, 9
Sherwood, Robert E., *There Shall Be No Night*, 67-68
Shute, Nevil, *On the Beach*, 148
Simpson, Lewis, 35
Skelton, Red, 120
Smith, Harrison, 290
Snodgrass, W. D., 230
"Soldier Shows" (World War II), 81

330

Sontag, Susan, 268
Southern, Terry, 146
Stallings, Laurence, *The Streets are Guarded*, 76; *What Price Glory?*, 65-66
Stafford, Jean, 202
Stafford, William, 35; *Down in My Heart*, 45-47
Staples, Hugh B., *Robert Lowell: The First Two Decades*, 234-35
Steinbeck, John, 3, 88, 156; *The Grapes of Wrath*, 19; *The Moon Is Down* (novel), 18-19 (play), 71-72
Steinberg, Rafael, *Postscript from Hiroshima*, 144
Stevens, Wallace, 99, **163-77**, 237; "Anecdote of a Jar," 163-64; "Notes Toward a Supreme Fiction," 164-77; "Sunday Morning," 163
Strunsky, Simon, 164
Stuckey, W. J., *The Pulitzer Prize Novels*, 10-11, 227

Thomas, Dylan, 34
Time, 263
Tolson, Melvin, 49-50
Tolstoy, Leo, 157
Tomorrow the World (play by James Gow and Arnaud d'Usseau), 74
Trilling, Diana, 264
Trilling, Lionel, 156, 157, **237-48**; *The Liberal Imagination*, 242; *The Middle of the Journey*, 237-48
Truman, President Harry, 20, 144
Trumbull, Robert, *Nine Who Survived Hiroshima and Nagasaki*, 143
Twain, Mark, 273

Updike, John, 182, 184, 262

Van Doren, Mark, 293
Vidal, Gore, 27, 31, 262, 265
Viereck, Peter, 288, 290
Viet Nam conflict, 7, 8, 22, 29, 35, 37, 48, 147, 183

Wakeman, Frederic, **179-87**; *The Hucksters*, 179-87
War novel (definition), 8
Warren, Robert Penn, 156, **189-201**; *All the King's Men*, 189-201, 227
Weill, Kurt, 125
Welty, Eudora, **99-110**, 156; *A Curtain of Green*, 101-110; "How I Write," 109; *The Wide Net*, 108, 109-10
Wilbur, Richard, 50, 53-54
Wilder, Thornton, **111-120**; *The Matchmaker*, 116; *Our Town*, 117-18; *The Skin of Our Teeth*, 111-120
Williams, Tennessee, 97, 113, **249-58**; *Battle of Angels*, 251; *Cat in a Hot Tin Roof*, 252; *The Glass Menagerie*, 205-6, 249, 253; *I Rise in Flame, Cried the Phoenix*, 255; "The Lady of Larkspur Lotion," 257; *A Streetcar Named Desire*, 249-58; *Summer and Smoke*, 254-55
Willingham, Calder, 262
Willkie, Wendell, 26
Wilson, Edmund, 116
Woolf, Virginia, 156
World War II — Drama, **63-82**; Fiction, **7-32**; Poetry, **33-61**
Wouk, Herman, *The Caine Mutiny*, 15
Wright, Richard, 85, 89

Yeats, W. B., 283
Young, Marguerite, 266

Zola, Emile, 156